Fall of an Icon

Polaroid after Edwin H. Land

An Insider's View
of the
Once Great Company

Fall of an Icon
Polaroid after Edwin H. Land

E.H. Land 1979 Polaroid Annual Meeting

An Insider's View of the Once Great Company

Milton P. Dentch

Riverhaven Books
www.RiverhavenBooks.com

Cover Credits

The front cover was created by Stephanie Zopatti using the 1972 *Life Magazine* cover highlighting Dr. Land's greatest invention, the SX-70 Instant Camera and Film.

The inside cover was drawn by the author's nephew, Michael McMenemy. It is based on a photograph taken of Land at the 1979 Polaroid Annual Meeting. Dr. Land was introducing the new "Time Zero" film, a faster developing version of the SX-70 film. It is one of the few public pictures of Land with a full smile.

Published in the United States by Riverhaven Books
www.RiverhavenBooks.com

ISBN: 978-1-937588-13-7

Printed in the United States of America
by Country Press, Lakeville, Massachusetts

Edited by Carol Chubb, Riverhaven Books
Formatted by Stephanie Lynn Blackman
Whitman, MA

With Thanks

In compiling this book over the last several years, I was assisted by many colleagues from Polaroid.

Al Hyland, Max Lawrence, Phil Ruddick, Sam Brown, Tom Tait, and Bob Ruckstuhl provided terrific anecdotes, histories and counsel. Paul Hegarty contributed some not-so-well-known tales of Polaroid's missteps into the electronic field and was a consistent collaborator and supporter. Polaroid manager from the Land to DiCamillo eras, Brian Milan assisted in the graphical representations and provided some supporting insight in the sales arena. Walter Byron provided a detailed history of the Camera Division. Colleagues Larry Kivimaki from the Film Division and Frank Ceppi, Battery Division, not only provided accurate accounts from their Polaroid days but also were my early editors, assisting with both composition and flow of my Polaroid story.

I'm very grateful to Stephanie Blackman of Riverhaven Books, my publisher, new friend, and advisor. Riverhaven editor Carol Chubb provided great assistance in turning my writing into a finished book. And to Bob Haskell, another Riverhaven editor, I also bestow my thanks for his polishing and input.

It is an interesting coincidence that Carol's former husband, Bill Chubb, his widow Rose, and father Lew Chubb all were Polaroid employees for many years. Bill's two inventor grandfathers long held the original polarization patents in the 1920s and 1930s, selling them to a then young "upstart", Edwin Land, in exchange for shares of Polaroid stock and a job in the headlight program for Lew Chubb.

Milt Dentch

Another Insider's View
-Ann Leibowitz

Virtually any description of Polaroid Corporation, even from the vantage point of an insider, calls to mind the famous Indian legend where several blind men touch an elephant to learn what it is like. Each one feels a different part, but only one part: a tusk, the trunk, a leg, a side. Each man, then, comes away with a different impression.

As a fellow-insider, I loved *Fall of an Icon*; it truly is an insider's perspective of how Polaroid operated after Dr. Land. Until just before the very end, strategic decisions were made by and large not by "business people," that is, finance, marketing, or sales executives, but by officers and executives whose background and expertise were engineering and manufacturing. This book captures the gestalt of that decision making. While much has been written about Polaroid's business strategies, the human factor that informed the company's post-Land decision-making is harder to capture, and probably impossible for anyone who wasn't there. Openness to unfamiliar and sometimes distasteful new ideas, willingness to take risk, confidence in and respect for fellow officers and executives — the book illustrates through its collection of anecdotes and observations how deficiencies at the top in these important leadership characteristics, together with perhaps an excess of hubris, led to Polaroid's demise. Milt accomplishes this without whining or finger-pointing. Rather, he manages in his book to evoke the sheer joy of working at this quirky but quite wonderful company even as we spent down Dr. Land's legacy.

I joined Polaroid in 1963 in the Patent Department, where as a patent attorney I spent my first eight years immersed in Dr. Land's photographic and chemical research organization; subsequently I became the company's labor and employment counsel, a position I occupied until I left in 1995 and then continued to perform on a consulting basis until shortly before the company's bankruptcy in 2001. So although I was never a "player," the people throughout the company belonged to me to counsel and defend. With a place at the table in a variety of corporate committees, I was privy to much of the decision-making that related to the management of employees (referred to as "members" of the company). My perspective, then, is undoubtedly colored by the issues, broad and narrow, that I encountered along the way. As with the blind men describing the elephant, none of us really saw it all.

The marketing world was of course Polaroid's glamorous persona to the outside; from the outset, the Polaroid brand was a reflection of Dr. Land's personal style and elegance. Much has been written about the intersection of science and art that developed and flourished under the auspices of the company's gifted marketing executives—Stan Calderwood, Ted Voss, Peter Wensberg and their talented staffs—and the many well-known photographic consultants who interacted with them and with Dr. Land and his acolytes. Here, as in Dr. Land's own research labs, it was not "corporate" behavior that mattered much (if at all), but intellect, talent and the willingness to dedicate themselves without reservation to Dr. Land's pursuit. Creativity, and of course the opportunity to demonstrate it, was the key to individual recognition; education and experience were almost irrelevant by comparison.

Coming from the highly structured and hierarchical workplace of W.R. Grace's research labs as I did, the culture of Polaroid's research group was as much of a shock to me as "getting polarized" in the manufacturing group as described by Milt Dentch in his book. Everybody was on a first-name basis—the entry level technicians, laboratory assistants, occasional tradesmen, secretaries and custodians chatted easily with "Howie (Rogers) and Meroë (Morse)," then the archons of color photography and black-and-white photography respectively-- with the exception of Dr. Land who was referred to with affection and awe as "the Boss." Aside from the very few people who had been with him at the outset who called him by his boyhood nickname "Din," he was addressed by most Polaroid people as "Dr. Land" and by those closest to him in research, simply as "Boss." He did not invite familiarity.

The environment was far more typical of an academic institution than an industrial setting. On arriving in the laboratories at 9:30 a.m., one would find most people scattered about, some sipping coffee over a newspaper, others chatting in small groups. By 10 or so the place was in gear. But at the end of the day, departing at 6 p.m., 7 p.m. or later was the norm. Leaving in the middle of an experiment was unthinkable. Although the ambience certainly wasn't glamorous, the tension and excitement of discovery were often palpable. However, to the dismay of some of the brilliant[1] PhD chemists who were regularly called upon to—and then DID—synthesize the impossible, to the extent recognition was given, it often went instead to innovative people who, uninhibited by the constraints of formal training, freely conjured up fanciful film layers, pH modifiers, stabilizers, viscosity enhancers or inhibitors, and the preposterous "dye developers" that ultimately became the basis of commercial Polacolor film.

As Director of Research, it was Dr. Land who set the agenda and the goals; it was he who determined the projects, the products, and the priorities. He was not totally unreceptive to ideas from others: occasionally someone would come along—not necessarily even a Polaroid employee—with an idea that

---

[1] Years later when he was an Executive Vice President, I asked Shelly Buckler, who joined the Research Division as a PhD chemist shortly after I joined Polaroid, whether the chemists were as brilliant as I recalled, or was I simply too young to differentiate. He assured me they were.

appealed to him (one such idea involved water desalinization!) that he would embrace and support to some degree. But he did not engage in "groupthink." Ideas and inventions, he asserted, came from a singular mind. In the Polaroid Research Division, that usually meant *his*.

In the Research Division (as indeed, occasionally in other reaches of the company), Dr. Land had an ability to inspire, not just as a showman as at Polaroid shareholder meetings, but at an individual level. If he became interested in the work a person was doing, or alternatively if there was something he wanted done that he thought a particular person could deliver, that individual would become a singular target of his attention and affection. Dazzling and irresistible, Dr. Land was able to induce effort and total dedication beyond what most people would think reasonable or even possible. Caught in the blinding penumbra of Dr. Land's light, people would commit time and effort to his requests seemingly without limit, and feel deeply flattered to have been so chosen. Unfortunately for them, when the project at hand was completed or when Dr. Land's interest shifted to another project, he abandoned them, not out of perverseness, but because he had, in essence, moved on. There was a small but discernible group of people who stayed with the company but never really recovered from having been, for a short time but only a short time, the center of Dr. Land's attention.

Apart from chemical research, there were engineering research and operations, first under the direction of Otto Wolf and Bill McCune and then under a succession of professional engineers, where designs were developed and refined for Polaroid cameras and for film assembly, and subsequently (after they were brought in-house from outside contractors) for negative and battery manufacture. Although no more an engineer than he was a chemist, Dr. Land's hand was often prominent in design and development, especially of the cameras, and he was typically the arbiter who made the final commercial decisions.

From a human perspective, however, manufacturing operations as described by Milt grew to become the beating heart of Polaroid, and they were a world away from marketing or research. Nevertheless, Dr. Land's imprimatur was as pronounced in manufacturing as in those relatively far-removed arenas. He asserted that people at any level are capable of extraordinary work under the right circumstances. Two tenets were paramount: people with degrees in "theoretical" industrial relations or worse, MBA's, were not to be trusted with supervision; and Polaroid's workforce would be non-union.

The pattern for industrial relations in Dr. Land's image was largely set by Richard Kriebel, a former advertising executive whom Dr. Land brought into the company in 1936 as Director of Public Relations, and who subsequently developed many of the innovative personnel policies and educational programs for which Polaroid became well-known. It was Dick Kriebel who put into writing and was instrumental in carrying out Dr. Land's ideas for open job postings up to management levels, for remedial and supplemental education for employees, for notice prior to termination for unsatisfactory attendance or performance, for discipline and discharge for cause, and other aspects of employment; the "First and Second Aim" so dearly embraced by people at Polaroid undoubtedly originated with his pen.

Dick created the Polaroid Employees' Committee[2] as a way of providing a voice to employees in the development of

---

[2] The federal National Labor Relations Act prohibits the establishment by an employer of any representative committee, even if the employees themselves, as they did at Polaroid, elect the representatives. At Polaroid, the Employees' Committee operated openly, and it was described admiringly in a number of papers and books authored by non-Polaroid professionals and academics at Harvard Business School and elsewhere. Dissolution of the committee by the National Labor Relations Board could only occur if someone filed an "unfair labor practice charge" against the company—which no one actually did until 1992. Even then, the charge

company personnel policy, and as a cadre of elected representatives to assist and speak on behalf of employees who had workplace grievances. He developed a formal grievance appeal process at which, in the early years, he himself presided, and which provided for outside binding arbitration if the dispute could not be resolved internally. Long after Dick had retired and the grievance procedure involved hearings before committees of Polaroid officers, from time to time I was asked whether company officers were really willing to overturn an employment decision which had been made, or at least affirmed, by one of their peers. In fact, perhaps as a result of Dr. Land's inclination to discourage collaboration among and between company officers—indeed, sometimes encouraging them by action if not by word to compete with one another—they seemed to take perverse satisfaction in doing exactly that.

As for manufacturing management, just as in the Research Division deference was given to bringing in supervisors and managers who demonstrated intelligence, curiosity, and an enthusiasm for embracing "the impossible." Accordingly, the most frequent profile of supervisors and managers in the Film Division, the first of the company's major manufacturing initiatives, was a liberal arts bachelor's degree plus some basic supervisory experience, often in a summer job.

The union avoidance strategy was very successful. Although an occasional murmur from an outside union organizer or from a sound truck parked outside a Polaroid facility was heard, what with progressive personnel policies where employees had

---

came from an employee whose intent was not to disband the Committee, but to "reform" it.

It seems astonishing that Polaroid's lawyers would not have urged that such a plan be abandoned when the Employees' Committee was first proposed in the late '40s. They may well have. How33ever, at around the same time, an amendment to the Act was pending in Congress which if enacted, would have allowed such a structure. Unfortunately, by the time the amendment was defeated, the Employees' Committee was off and running.

a say via their elected representatives in formulating and a formal appeal procedure to address grievances, not to mention profit-sharing through an annual bonus and a profit-sharing retirement plan, there was never any serious employee interest in unionizing. On one occasion, the United Rubber Workers acquired a mailing list of Polaroid employees and sent a letter seeking support, to which Dr. Land responded in an impassioned letter of his own urging Polaroid members to disregard the invitation and stay the course. At the time, the most frequent employee response was a demand to know how the URW managed to get his or her home address, a piece of data that was regarded as "private."

The success of the Land/Kriebel approach to management, however, can give rise to reasonable debate. It took a strong and self-confident supervisor or manager to stand up to Employees' Committee representatives, who behaved and strongly resembled union shop stewards. Concern about having a tough decision overturned in a grievance and worse, fear of appearing to be less than competent in a hearing involving one's boss, one's division manager, and several officers often created an imbalance when it came to judicious application of personnel policy. The Employees' Committee was thought to have the direct ear of Dr. Land, which though not generally the case (indeed, considerable effort was often made by a succession of Human Resources Officers and General Managers to make sure that didn't happen), the perception was enough to intimidate many a supervisor and manager. Manufacturing, unlike research, required structure, especially when running a multi-shift operation. But like research, with the exception of Dr. Land himself, everyone was on a first-name basis, and supervisors' and managers' doors were open to any employee at any level who had a concern, a complaint, or a suggestion.

So long as Polaroid was growing and profitable, a certain amount of slack and inefficiency in a relatively few number of employees was tolerated.[3] In general, though, people responded just as Dr. Land had predicted: they worked hard and willingly. With extensive company support, not just through personnel policies and generous compensation and benefits, but also in-house human resource department support, a staff of social workers who served as counselors for troubled employees, a sophisticated medical department, a company-subsidized cafeteria, and other employment amenities, a job at Polaroid was a prized privilege.

The culture and ambience of the Film Division were replicated in Polaroid's other manufacturing divisions (at least in the United States) as they were established and grew: camera manufacturing, battery manufacturing, and some of the smaller operations. To be sure, some parts of the corporation which, by their nature, were staffed primarily by professionals who gained their experience in other organizations reflected as much the culture of their profession as the one derived from Dr. Land. The sales division was staffed generally by people who had previously worked for large consumer product companies with internal sales training programs which Polaroid did not have (e.g., Nestle or Proctor and Gamble) and who brought with them the habits of people who spent much of their time on the road. Sales reps were paid partly on salary, partly on commission; little was tolerated in the way of slack. As is often the case with sales people who worked hard, they played hard too. Financial and treasury services including payroll, purchasing, and distribution were relatively no nonsense, although each had its own version of being "polarized." The same was true for the relatively small patent department, which had its own set of privileges because of its association with Dr. Land and the research groups.

---

[3] It is worth noting, that at the time of a major layoff (accomplished through voluntary severance) at a time when Polaroid was facing a hostile takeover in 1988, there was great concern that productivity would be compromised by the reduction in manpower. In fact, with the remaining employees facing a discernible "enemy" (Stanley Gold), despite a reduced manufacturing population, productivity soared.

When Dr. Land departed from Polaroid following the Polavision debacle, Bill McCune as President and Chief Executive Officer continued the same management philosophies developed by Dick Kriebel and embraced, endorsed, and proclaimed by Dr. Land. Having been with Dr. Land at the beginning, and having grown up in the organization, he believed in them. If anything, he strengthened them by virtue of being much more accessible to executives and managers—and to the Employees' Committee—than Dr. Land had been. Moreover, he genuinely liked most of the company officers and executives, and did not share Dr. Land's inclination to play one off against the other. Unlike Dr. Land, he enjoyed engaging with employees at all levels. He knew the company's strengths and quirks, and seemed at home in them.

At the same time, Bill was acutely aware of the fact that without Dr. Land, Polaroid would need to find new direction. Smart and perceptive, he recognized that Polaroid needed to make inroads into the new but burgeoning field of electronics, and to that end he set up a Microelectronics Laboratory devoted to doing exactly that. Perhaps had he remained as president for a longer period, he would have had the courage and confidence required to take a big piece of Polaroid's still significant but diminishing profit and invest it as venture capital to develop one or more of the promising innovations developed there. But Bill elected to retire at age 70, turning the reins over to the officer whom he had regarded almost as a son and protégé, Mac Booth.

It was hard not to like Mac. Earnest, direct, highly moral, honest to a fault (it was said of Mac that if he thought someone was ugly, he'd have to tell him: "You know, you're ugly!") and when he chose to be, charming. On the other hand, he could also be confrontational and highly combative, sometimes picking a dispute where there really wasn't any. He hated being told what to do, especially by lawyers (although he and I actually got along very well. Mac and my own mother were the only people who ever called me "Anna Banana," and it was with his blessing and support that I left employment at Polaroid and continued as its outside labor-and-employment lawyer.)

There were aspects of Mac, however, that were problematic. He was not a visionary, as had been Dr. Land, or even in his own way, Bill McCune. Moreover, with the exception of a very few officers and managers whom he had known throughout his Polaroid career, he fundamentally distrusted most people in Polaroid management; he was certain that they were trying somehow to manipulate him. His style of dealing with immediate subordinates was generally not to support or encourage them, but to challenge them: to announce to them and to anybody else in the vicinity that he doubted they could produce or deliver what they claimed. His response to anyone who brought news, reports, forecasts, or results that he didn't like or that failed to meet his expectation was that the statement made was "unacceptable" without regard to whether or not it was in fact accurate.

At the same time, Mac's reverence for the Employees' Committee exceeded that of his predecessors and for that matter, practically any other company officer or manager, a situation that only weakened managers who were otherwise uncertain.[4] When Mac wanted to know what was "really going on," he was likely to engage an Employees' Committee representative, and when the Employees Committee was disbanded, he devoted considerable effort, not to mention company resources, trying to create a replacement for it.

Mac desperately wanted to make the right decisions for the company—a difficult path certainly not made any easier by having to deal with a serious hostile takeover effort. Faced with diminishing profit, mounting debt, and a moribund technology (he often commented that we were in the "buggy

---

[4] Mac's father had been an executive in the automobile industry, and he claimed that his uncle was Harry Bennett, Henry Ford's infamous union buster. If so, perhaps he saw his affinity for the Employees' Committee as some sort of atonement.

whip business"), increasingly he turned to outside—and very expensive—consultants to help determine the company's future or to engage with senior management and meld it into a force for successful "strategic visioning." He closed the Microelectronics Laboratory, the one bright star that by hindsight might have offered some salvation, and abandoned or sold its output. New products were no longer defined, as they once had been, by the intersection of science and art, but rather, by what was thought to be the marketplace.

In all fairness to Mac, he was certainly not alone among chief executives who eschewed betting a company's profits on a new and different technology. With Wall Street clamoring for growth and earnings per share *this quarter*, it would be bold and risky indeed to bet the ranch, requiring confidence and nerve that weren't part of Mac's makeup. Other large and successful companies seem to have suffered their own versions of the same conundrum: Wang, Digital, and Kodak to name a few. When Dr. Land moved from polarizers to photography, there was little profit to lose and no concern for investors let alone Wall Street; when he later sought to invest the company's profit in Polavision, he was in essence ousted.

By the time Mac retired and was succeeded by Gary DiCamillo, an outsider from Black and Decker, much of what had been Polaroid had already disappeared. Its human capital depleted by repeated reductions-in-force or by departures of promising employees to other more promising employment (a once unthinkable phenomenon), its manufacturing supervisors and managers demoralized by slack employment practices no longer offset by high productivity and profitable product, its technology rapidly receding before the onslaught of the electronic age and digital imaging, the company would need a bold and brave genius to rescue it from its downward spiral. This, Gary DiCamillo, was not. A pleasant, willing, totally non-technical executive, he brought financial people in to help him sort out what to do. Several unremarkable products were introduced, based again on perceived customer receptivity. Small wonder the company went bankrupt.

For those of us who were fortunate enough to work at Polaroid during its heyday, it was a glorious ride. We were devoted to the company, and to each other. Drawn by the excitement of accomplishment, basking in the glory reflected by our technology, our community presence and our products, and the sheer fun of problem-solving among smart and engaged people, we couldn't wait to get to work in the morning. Even recognizing their drawbacks, we were proud of our employment practices; and we believed in the social contract of mutual respect, responsibility and loyalty between employer and employee. We were privileged to be part of it.

Fall of an Icon, as presented by Milt Dentch, with insightful inputs from several Polaroid employees and executives, captures much of the essence of the Polaroid Corporation. Milt describes many of the key events that allowed Polaroid to prosper under Dr. Land and Bill McCune- and then fail after they left.

Contents

Preface

For years, Polaroid Corporation staffers wondered when Founder Edwin Land, 65, would start giving up some of the titles that he had held for 38 years: Chairman, President, and Director of Research. In a surprise move, the inventor-autocrat last week handed one of his jobs, the presidency, to William McCune Jr., 59, Polaroid's executive vice president and, since the founding of the company in 1937, its senior engineer. The surprise was not merely that Land finally anointed a possible successor, but also that McCune's new job did not go to General Manager Thomas Wyman, 45. A sales and administrative whiz who came to Polaroid ten years ago from the Nestle Co., Wyman had been widely regarded as the heir apparent. But just before McCune's promotion was announced, Wyman quit, accepting the president's job at the Green Giant food company in Le Sueur, Minn. Wyman denied strenuously that he had had a falling out with Land, but he was clearly tired of waiting. The attraction of Green Giant, he explains, "really is a matter of running something myself." Unlike Wyman, McCune is not the sort to chafe at Land's tight grip. He has said in the past that he accepts Land's managerial motto: "You can do anything you want to – as long as you do what I want."

(Time Magazine: February 03, 1975)

Mr. Land did all the thinking; he was the only anointed generalist in the company," said Mr. Buckler, a veteran of 27 years at Polaroid. "He was a genius, a classic founder who had no great interest in organizational design," Mr. Buckler added. "He saw no reason to change." (New York Times, June 11, 1991)

Polaroid, founded by Edwin Land in 1937, had four leaders during its storied sixty-five-year history. Dr. Land led all aspects of the company from 1937 until his less than gracious exit in 1975 as President and Chief Executive Officer. Land continued as Chairman of the Board of Directors until 1982. William McCune was appointed President and CEO from 1975 until 1986 when Israel MacAllister (Mac) Booth took the reins. McCune chaired the BOD until 1992 when Booth assumed the chairmanship of the board along with the titles of President and CEO. Booth retired in late 1995 and the BOD selected Gary DiCamillo as CEO and chairman. DiCamillo ran the company, leaving after Polaroid's declaration of bankruptcy in 2001 and prior to it becoming a private company.

Although a company continues to operate under the name "Polaroid", it is mainly a marketing firm, employing fewer than 500 employees, a far cry from the former Wall Street darling with 20,000 employees. The "new" Polaroid ceased producing the Instant Film in the summer of 2008 and declared the second bankruptcy in January 2009.

When Polaroid declared bankruptcy in 2001, the central cause, in the opinion of Wall Street analysts and other Polaroid followers, was the emergence of digital photography and Polaroid management's failure to adapt to the new technology. After several years of research and reflecting on my own experiences during my Polaroid career, I concluded that there were many elements that co-joined to assist the demise, but the real cause was Polaroid's unique culture.

Certain concepts or principles were ingrained in Polaroid's way of running the company. These prevented changes from occurring which could have allowed Polaroid to continue as a viable enterprise in spite of the digital challenge: (1) The business model always centered on "give-away" cameras to sell film – the profits are in the media; (2) Employees' welfare is paramount –no layoffs; (3) Executives hired from outside Polaroid cannot succeed – they won't understand or embrace Concepts 1 or 2. While Dr. Land created this culture, his successors could have done a better job of leveraging the positive aspects of the Polaroid traditions into the next generation of technology.

In addition to the cultural mindset, the four CEOs, from Land to DiCamillo, had a common trait: they weren't very good listeners. One of Land's famous quotes, "We give people products they do not even know they want, so why should we invest in market research?" described his somewhat arrogant approach to customer focus. Each of Land's successor CEOs ignored advice or counsel from fellow executives, employees, financial advisors and shareholders that could have changed the eventual fate of the company. *Fall of an Icon* provides insight from those events, as witnessed by several Polaroid retirees and myself.

Many longtime employees and retirees suffered great financial loss leading up to and due to the 2001 bankruptcy. Some former officers of the company lost considerable retirement income, much of it from the government takeover of the pension system by the Pension Benefit Guaranty Corporation (PBGC), which caps maximum allowable payouts affecting former senior management and executives with a working lifetime of vesting. Executives, post-1996, profited better than deserved. Longtime faithful suppliers were hurt. Stockholders were heavily impacted.

As I tracked the rise and fall of the Polaroid Corporation over the last 75 years, it occurred to me the Polaroid history is very similar to the growth and decline in American industry during the same time frame. The U.S. industrial base bloomed in the 1930s after the Great Depression and was fueled by support for World War II. Land's Polaroid, likewise, came to be in 1937 and grew rapidly by supporting the war effort. Over the next several decades, Land formed the Polaroid Board of Directors, adding respected individuals from the finance and academic arenas. In 1982, Dr. Land was essentially removed from the board he chaired because of a difference of opinion on a failed product of his, Polavision. While I certainly believe that action was a terrible, insensitive decision by that board, the process to protect shareholder value was correct.

Twenty years later, in 2001, the last Board of Directors of Polaroid granted a retention payment to the CEO who had delivered not a failed product, but a failed company. The CEO received the payment prior to Polaroid's declaration of bankruptcy. That board had also extracted their deferred compensation funds just prior to the bankruptcy. All the actions of the board were within their rights – they had fulfilled their fiduciary responsibility to the letter of the law. Efforts to test the legality of the board's actions, led by Polaroid retirees and creditors, were ruled in favor of the board by the bankruptcy courts.

As an operating manager at Polaroid for 27 years from 1969-1996, I witnessed the decline of Polaroid from the "firing line." I saw the end of the Land era, observed the McCune and Booth years, and closely tracked the DiCamillo journey into bankruptcy. I kept notes and articles from the internet and newspapers. This is not a book about Dr. Edwin Land the inventor or a history of the early Polaroid. There have been several works on that subject, notably Peter Wensberg's *LAND'S POLAROID*. My story records lesser known examples of Land's vision on how companies should be managed, contrasting them with the way Polaroid was led after he left. Land's writings regarding pay structure, employee involvement and respect for people are common knowledge to most followers of Polaroid. He had strong opinions on race relations and development of scientists and engineers. Land served on scientific advisory panels for Presidents Truman through Nixon – not unsurprisingly resigning during Nixon's Watergate scandal.

Mr. McCune restored the short-term financial growth of the company by his leadership in expanding Land's overly-expensive SX-70 camera line to include the very successful, low-cost OneStep and Pronto! systems. He also put forth a vision, in 1981, of how Polaroid could merge with the electronic-imaging world. Unfortunately, the strategy got off to a shaky start and eventually collapsed. A younger McCune, insulated from Land's autocratic rule, might have led Polaroid into the next generation.

In chronicling Polaroid after Land, I've attempted to describe how a special company with a unique leader could shine so greatly in the first 50 years, struggle for several years and finally crash. *Fall of an Icon* captures the greatness of Edwin Land and his company, recording factors that led to its downfall.

Dr. Edwin Land was a troublemaker. He dropped out of Harvard and founded Polaroid. Not only was he one of the great inventors of our time but, more important, he saw the intersection of art and science and business and built an organization to reflect that. Polaroid did that for some years, but eventually Dr. Land, one of those brilliant troublemakers, was asked to leave his own company – which is one of the dumbest things I've ever heard of. So Land, at 75, went off to spend the remainder of his life doing pure science, trying to crack the code of color vision. The man is a national treasure. I don't understand why people like that can't be held up as models: This is the most incredible thing to be – not an astronaut, not a football player – but this.

(Steve Jobs - 1985 Playboy Magazine interview describing his hero.)

SECTION 1: Edwin Herbert Land

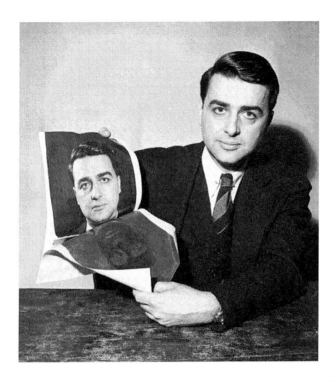

Edwin H. Land showing positive and negative print taken from a new camera that produces finished pictures.

(February 21, 1947. Bettmann)

.

The Five Thousand Steps to Success

If you dream of something worth doing and then simply go to work on it and don't think anything of personalities, or emotional conflicts, or of money, or of family distractions; if you just think of, detail by detail, what you have to do next, it is a wonderful dream even if the end is a long way off, for there are about five thousand steps to be taken before we realize it; and start making the first ten, making twenty after, it is amazing how quickly you get through those five thousand steps.

(Edwin Land to Polaroid employees, December 23, 1942)

Chapter 1:
Edwin H. Land

Edwin Herbert Land was born in Bridgeport, Connecticut, to Helen and Herbert Land on May 7, 1909. He attended the Norwich Free Academy at Norwich, Connecticut, a semi-private high school, graduating in 1927. He then studied physics at Harvard, leaving after his freshman year. Why he left Harvard is not certain, although a speech he delivered in later years suggested a disdain for the university curriculum:

> Nothing which I saw changed the latent conviction that I brought with me that the freshmen entering our American universities have a potential for greatness which we have not learned how to develop fully by the kind of education we have brought to this generation from the generations of the past.
> (Generation Of Greatness – Lecture at the Massachusetts Institute of Technology, May 22, 1957)

Additional clues as to why he left Harvard so soon derive from his childhood, during which he developed a fascination with polarized light and read books on the subject with the zeal of Bible study. Land entered Harvard College in 1927, in a hurry to do actual research on optics, particularly polarization. He left a few months later and went to New York, where he spent long hours at the New York Public Library continuing his research. He invented the first inexpensive filters capable of

2

polarizing light. After developing a polarizing film, Land returned to Harvard; however, he still did not finish his studies or receive a degree. Once Land could see the solution to a problem in his head, he lost all motivation to write it down or prove his vision to others.

Land's polarized film solved one of science's long-standing "unsolvable" problems – polarizing light without needing a large crystal of an esoteric mineral. His first patent for synthetic-sheet polarizer was filed in 1929. In 1933, the 24-year-old Land formed his own company in partnership with George Wheelwright III, a Harvard physics instructor whose family also provided the funding. Ironically, Kodak purchased polarizing material for camera filters, providing Land's company with its first major revenue. Sunglass material was developed for American Optical. In 1937, Polaroid Corporation was founded. The name "Polaroid" evolved as a truncation of polarized and celluloid. The company also used similar technology to develop stereoscopic (3D) motion pictures shown for the first time at the 1939 World's Fair. By 1941, sales reached $1 million.

But Land's major desire was to use the polarized material to reduce glare in automobiles – from both a strong sense of driver safety, as well as tremendous potential source for sales. A nighttime near-collision with a farmer's wagon had convinced Land that automobile headlights should be stronger, leading to the idea of blocking glare by use of polarization. The U.S. automobile industry in the 1930s was not too different from the industry that nearly collapsed in 2008. "Not invented here" blocked outsiders. Although the unit cost of Polaroid's anti-glare lenses was about $4 per car, this was the depression era and sales were not good. Ford Motor Company appeared to support the program but required Land to put up the development money and provide test material at no charge. The automobile marketing executives did not want to remind the consumers that their cars were unsafe without the anti-glare headlamps. The program died. I recall hearing from one of the Polaroid employees from that period that the auto industry claimed the anti-glare headlamps and windscreens could actually be a hazard. The premise was that if auto A had

3

polarized film on the headlamps and windscreen and oncoming auto B did not, the B driver might experience a blind spot. I never knew if this was conjecture or science.

World War II provided Polaroid with tremendous applications for military tasks, including developing dark-adaptation goggles; target finders, the first passively guided smart bombs; and a special stereoscopic viewing system called the Vectograph, which revealed camouflaged enemy positions in aerial photography. In 1941, Polaroid sales were $1 million; at war's close, in 1945, sales reached $16 million. With the war ended and sales shrinking, the challenge was what to do next. Even readers not aware of much about Polaroid's history have probably heard of Land's daughter asking her dad why she could not see the photograph as soon as it was taken:

> One day when we were vacationing in Santa Fe in 1943, my daughter, Jennifer, who was then three, asked me why she could not see the picture I had just taken of her. As I walked around that charming town, I undertook the task of solving the puzzle she had set for me. Within the hour, the film and the physical chemistry had become so clear that I hurried to the place where a friend was staying to describe to him in detail a dry camera which would give a picture immediately after exposure...four years later, we demonstrated the working system to the Optical Society of America.
>
> (E. H. Land, Life Magazine, 1972)

For me, Edwin Land's response in 1944 to his daughter's question summed up the man. His approach to invention was to pose a question and then set out relentlessly to find a solution or solutions. By 1948, Polaroid had its first camera, the Model 95, selling for $95. The camera was truly remarkable –built with the precision of a Swiss watch. The consumers' acceptance of the instant system was excellent. Polaroid went from a company on the brink of disaster after WWII to a $100 million going concern, poised for even greater growth as the instant process evolved to a color film format.

4

The next several chapters describe Land's efforts to build a great company, a company that would create products the consumer did not realize he needed or wanted. I believe many of Land's visions of the ideal company still have a place in today's world.

Chapter 2:
Land's Vision of Polaroid

We have two basic aims here at Polaroid. One is to make products which are genuinely new and useful to the public, products of the highest quality at reasonable cost. In this way we assure the financial success of the Company, and each of us has the satisfaction of helping to make a creative contribution to society.

The other is to give everyone working for Polaroid personal opportunity within the company for full exercise of his talents; to express his opinions, to share in the progress of the Company as far as his capacities permit, to earn enough money so that the need for earning more will not always be the first thing on his mind – opportunity, in short, to make his work here a fully rewarding, important part of his life.

These goals can make Polaroid a great company – not merely in size, but great in the esteem of all the people for whom it makes new, good things, and great in its fulfillment of the individual ideals of its employees.

Quoted from the Polaroid Handbook, mid-1960s, these words were Dr. Land's vision of how he wanted Polaroid to function. He backed them up with many initiatives, including generous, somewhat democratic sharing of profits. When I joined the company in 1969, Polaroid was coming off several years of outstanding profits based on the fantastic demand for the color-pack instant film, referred to as Type 108 and its industrial black and white version, Type 107. Using a simple, public formula, the company shared profits in excess of a percentage of total capital worth with all employees. Each employee would receive a percentage based on pay, ascending with pay level. It was not highly distorted towards senior management as seen in today's world. The "payout" would be translated into pennies per point, with one dollar being the goal.

I recall my fellow employees grousing about the poor payout in 1969, about 75 cents a point. I was not eligible for a bonus that year because I had less than a full year's seniority; but, for my future interest, I calculated what I might expect in future years. At an engineer's salary of $14,400 and pay-level contribution at 35%, I would have received $3,780 or 26% of my pay – outstanding in my opinion, but unacceptable to the longtime employees who had been receiving 30-40% of their pay in bonuses the last several years. As someone who had worked the first several years after college in a conservative, privately-owned New England factory whose owners arbitrarily decided which salary members were to receive a bonus, I thought I could really buy into this plan. I also got my first look at "entitled" employees, which represented one of the downsides of Land's first and second aim.

There were a few interesting sidebars to the bonus plan. The company paid the amount in two installments: one near the first of the year, the second after the books were closed. Since paychecks were not direct deposited in those days, many clever employees found a way to hide the second check from their spouses. It was their fun money for the year. The building manager in one plant bought a new Buick every third year, paying cash from that year's bonus. Other groups had two-day, all-night poker games with $500 minimums – a huge amount in 1969. In addition to the bonus, an equal amount was deposited in the employee's retirement account.

The bonus started its downward spiral about 1970, the year Polaroid started investing heavily in the next Instant Film product, SX-70. Because Land financed growth using retained earnings and the bonus plan was based on profits after capital spending allowances, the pennies per point dropped significantly in the '70s and, in fact, was never significant again until the Kodak patent settlement in 1991. Because the Kodak settlement ($925 million) was "extraordinary income", it was not expected to be included in the bonus plan. Mac Booth, the CEO in 1991, in thanks for the support of the employees during the hostile takeover in 1989 by Roy Disney of Shamrock Holdings, convinced the BOD to include a portion of the Kodak payout in the 1991 bonus calculation. I received a check for about $20,000 that year and a few thousand more the following year, my last payout. With the generous check, I purchased replacement windows for my 75-year-old home and a new computer for the family. In those days, when your personal computer booted up, it usually included a welcoming "name." I named our computer "Kodak." In retrospect, "Thanks, Mac" might have been more appropriate.

Land's bonus plan was visionary and would seem to be the right way to motivate employees. Unfortunately, Land's two product mistakes, the over investment in SX-70 and Polavision and his insistence on running all aspects of the company himself, never again allowed Polaroid to achieve consistently the profit levels of the 1960s. Compare the Polaroid bonus plan with other reward programs that evolved in the 1990s and beyond, where management-biased plans continued executive payouts even when the overall company's finances weren't so rosy. By using profits to support growth, Land shared profits with all members, but also secured the company's growth, avoiding debt. As pay and responsibilities rose, the percentage calculation for individual participation climbed proportionately; Land capped the top end at 100%, as well as keeping his pay at $100,000 per year. It was a very flat corporate pay structure and certainly more egalitarian than anything we see today. His vision for pay matched his second aim for employee rewards. I recall many employees chastising colleagues for shoddy work or waste. "Hey, you're screwing with my bonus," was the refrain.

The downside of his $100,000 salary was the fact that executive pay growth was limited by his compensation, possibly contributing to Polaroid's inability to attract and keep a suitable successor for Land.

Chapter 3:
Novel Employee Relations

Dr. Land had novel ideas on how his employees should be treated. In addition to the "First and Second Aim", he felt employees should be trusted and treated the same whether they were salaried or hourly. Land decided in the late 1960s to eliminate time clocks. Hourly and salary employees would be "guaranteed" a week's pay. He was bothered by the lines he observed waiting to punch out at 3 p.m. He thought it would be better to trust the employees – consistent with the second Aim – and allow the employees to complete their meaningful work, and then just walk out, without punching a 1940s-era time clock. Coming from a union shop background, I found the trust factor difficult to accept.

After managing a group for several years, I concluded Land was mostly correct. Possibly 90-95% of the employee base had sufficient self-pride or support for the company that they would give the company a full day's pay. Unfortunately, the 5-10% who did not put in a full day's work tended to cause "good" employees to resent management's failure to deal with the slackers. Over time, those good employees lost interest in maintaining productivity. In addition to "cheating" on the time sheet, a small group of employees liked the guaranteed weekly pay so much they decided maybe they didn't always have to show up on Mondays or Fridays. Around the company, various managers attempted to discipline the offending employees. The application of discipline was quite inconsistent.

The Polaroid Employees Committee (EC) was formed in the 1950s and was made up of elected representatives from across the company. Land described the Employees Committee as:

My invention. It was a very natural outgrowth of my relationship with Polaroid employees at the time. It meant that the employees' elected officials could meet with me and pass on employees' concerns to me.

Originally, the Employee Committee reps had full-time jobs as mechanics, machine operators or other rank-and-file positions. As the years went on and the company grew to over 15,000 employees, the majority of the committee reps had full time jobs representing employees. The chairman of the Employees Committee held a powerful position at Polaroid, having direct access to Land, initially, and then to McCune and Mac Booth. A major topic for the committee was representing employees relative to cost-of-living increases. It worked out for salaried employees as well, as we all received cost-of-living increases for many years.

The Employees Committee also represented employees who were engaged in the disciplinary process, similar to a union; however, there were no "dues" and there was no contractual arrangement or language. Instead, a Personnel Policy Manual applied to all employees, salaried and hourly alike. Over time, Polaroid developed a four-step disciplinary system. Step one was the verbal warning – eventually becoming the "written verbal warning", since the committee wanted the warning documented because of their concern that not all supervisors were universally diligent in describing the situation to the employee. One example was attendance. Since everyone was on a guaranteed weekly pay plan, the company did not set firm rules on how many sick days an employee was entitled to during the year. Healthy people were expected to show up for work (that was challenging and meaningful, according to Land's vision of work); but, if sick, they communicated their condition to the supervisor and were expected back when well again. Supervisors had some discretion on deciding when an employee was missing too much work. Patterns of absence got the added attention of the supervisor and perhaps the Personnel Department. There was a Personnel Policy statement to the effect that..." we can deal with the sick, but not the sickly."

I recall all five cases where I had to terminate, or attempt to terminate, an employee for poor performance or attendance. After the first verbal warning, if the employee was out again in a few weeks, he or she would receive the first written warning. Continued poor attendance would result in the second written warning. The next frequency of absence would generate a "warning in lieu of termination." One more frequency and a termination notice would be issued. The total process could easily take over one year or typically two. If the offending employee had a few months of perfect attendance, the EC would lobby to have the file stripped clean of all warnings. Not surprising, many poor-attendance employees would soon revert to form, and the warning cycle would start anew. Even after the successful documentation of the four steps, the Employees Committee would challenge the documentation or some other factor in the case, first to the manager; then, if the termination was upheld, to the senior manager or division manager. If all levels of management decided the employee should no longer work at Polaroid, the Employees Committee would bring the case to the Personal Policy Committee (PPC) made up of several vice presidents. Interestingly, the supervisor of the offending employee along with his manager was somewhat "on trial" during the hearing. Should the termination package include an error or the supervisor make a comment showing personal vendetta, the PPC was known to overturn the case and the supervisor or manager would have a bad career moment.

The case I remember most was an employee in my department who consistently missed work on Mondays; and, in the final case, disappeared for several weeks without notifying his supervisor. The department had a very solid case, having given the employee several opportunities to improve. The Personal Policy Committee (PPC) agreed with the case and his employment was terminated. The morning after the termination hearing, I received a phone call from one of the committee members, Al Hyland of the PPC. I was somewhat surprised at the call. I had at one time worked for Al and we had a good

12

relationship. After a few moments of chitchat, Hyland strongly suggested I help the fired member locate a job outside of Polaroid. This process, I discovered later, was fairly common, as this could help Polaroid's case should employees, especially minorities, women, or senior employees, take the company to outside arbitration.

As Polaroid's fortunes diminished and the pressure mounted on improving operations and reducing costs, the management-Employees Committee relationship soured somewhat. Similar to a union environment, the Employees Committee representatives felt they should represent every case, whether the employee's claim was legitimate or not. The Employees Committee, as originally constructed, ended in 1992 as described in the September 30, 1992, ruling by the National Labor Relations Board. The complaint had been filed by a Polaroid employee:

In May 1992, a complaint was filed with the U.S. Department of Labor, Office of the Labor-Management Standards (OLMS), alleging that the employees' committee violated certain provisions of the Labor-Management Reporting and Disclosure Act. Following an administrative investigation by the OLMS, Polaroid Chief Executive Officer Booth, by letter dated June 18, 1992, to all company employees, announced his decision "to dissolve the Employees Committee" and to "reassign its roles and functions elsewhere in the corporate structure, effective immediately." Booth further announced the creation of a team to design a new organization. Pursuant to this team's recommendations, Booth announced the formation of the EOIC by letter in January 1993 to all of the company's employees.

The finding was that Polaroid was in essence sponsoring its own form of bargaining unit. Because the company provided space and normal paychecks for the employees on the committee, it was ruled the committee was really a member of management. The company challenged the ruling all the way to

13

Washington, DC, but lost. The replacement for the Employees Committee, Employee-Owners Influence Council (EOIC) was similar to the original EC concept where reps had full-time jobs but became employee advocates known as "ombudsmen." This arrangement was also ruled illegal by the NLRB in 1999; the EOIC was dissolved in 1999 and not contested by Polaroid.

Harvey Greenberg, former director of Employee Relations at Polaroid, was quoted in the August 1996 Regional Review:

> It was expensive; Polaroid at one point paid the salaries of thirty-two representatives, and this was their full-time job. Dealings were often "difficult and painful," says Greenberg. He rarely received thanks as a line manager for anything done on labor's behalf. And each year, the Committee laid down wage demands in meetings that had the look and feel of a collective bargaining session.

From 1999 on, the employees were without the unique representation envisioned by Land. The employees had bigger issues on their minds – maintaining jobs and benefits. In the continuing irony of Polaroid life after Land, employees from 1950 to 1996 were very well protected from arbitrary actions by management – employees were only fired after extensive deliberations and counseling. Leading up to bankruptcy in 2001 and in its immediate aftermath, Polaroid downsized employees routinely and reduced benefits, without review.

> "The greatest difficulty has been what's happened to the reputation of a company we tried so hard to build up," says Paul Hegarty, 63, a retiree in Arlington, Mass., who lost his dental, health and life insurance. He's spending $7,200 annually to get coverage on the private market. "Polaroid was a true American icon, and now the name's being trashed about. Colleagues have had great difficulty in joining any action against the company," he says. In many ways, Hegarty personifies the classic Polaroid employee. He joined as a high-school graduate in 1956; packing cameras in

14

the Polaroid warehouse, and retired in 1996 as a purchasing manager overseeing a $135 million budget." (USA Today, Stephanie Armour, January 17, 2002)

I believe the Employees Committee as envisioned by Land was a much preferred option to conventional unions. Several of its leaders, notably Bill Graney and Nick Pasquarosa, worked to protect the employees while demonstrating strong support for Polaroid. Issues, when they occurred, were often due to management's inconsistent application of the policies. The EC's 1950 charter stated that its purpose was to "provide a medium of determining the will of employees concerning their welfare and the welfare of the company; to speak for employees on these matters in discussions with the management of the company."

In 1970, a group from the United Rubber Workers union made an attempt to form a union at Polaroid. Union representatives would meet with employees off-site, discussing the benefits of collective bargaining. Because of extensive start-up costs of the SX-70, cost-of-living raises had been reduced, so perhaps for the first time the employees were vulnerable. The union guys parked a pickup truck adjacent to the Polaroid property in Waltham for several weeks. As a manager, I attended several training sessions on the proper way to avoid saying things to employees that could be represented as opposing the union, resulting in a "forced vote." When Dr. Land heard of the attempt, he composed a handwritten note that was sent by mail to the homes of all 10,000 employees:

This is no ordinary company that we have built together. It is the proud pioneer that set out to teach the world how people should work together. Polaroid is on its way to lead the world – perhaps even to save it – by this interplay between science, technology, and real people. I have waited many years for this next great step in our growth toward the perfect scientific-

15

human company. I cannot imagine that many of you could turn away now. (E.H. Land)

The next day the union truck picked up and moved, never to be heard from again.

Chapter 4:
The Polaroid Way – Getting Polarized.

I was hired by Polaroid on October 1, 1969, because of my experience in film coating. I had worked during college at Worcester Polytechnic Institute (WPI) and for five years after for the machinery manufacturer Rice Barton of Worcester, Massachusetts. This family-owned company had been designing and building machinery for the paper industry since 1835. In addition to the huge machines that produced paper, Rice Barton was a pioneer in applying coatings to paper for magazines, brochures and other high-quality items. Rice Barton had supplied the machinery that coated paper for National Geographic Magazine – the benchmark of high-end coated paper. Additionally, Rice Barton had built the machines for Crane Paper in Dalton, Massachusetts, to produce U.S. currency for over 100 years.

My dad was a mechanic at the company for 30 years. As an employee's son, I had my tuition at WPI ($1,000 per year) paid by Rice Barton. The company also provided summer work for me as a draftsman. The last Mr. Barton, in an attempt to dramatically increase machinery sales, allowed several large projects to be quoted at the company's cost, resulting in several years of losses and, eventually, Chapter 11 voluntary bankruptcy. My brother-in-law used to tease me that it "took you five years to put the fine old company into bankruptcy. How long will it take you at Polaroid?" The answer was about twenty-seven years, but it was not all my fault.

I stayed with Rice Barton for a year after they declared bankruptcy. We were paid on the last Friday of the month. The salaried members, who remained with the company after layoffs, would get the paycheck at noon on Friday and scoot over to the local bank with the checks, only to be rejected because Rice Barton's account was insufficient. "Come back Monday," we were told. Additionally, since all the high-paid engineers had been let go, I had to travel excessively in support of paper mill start-ups all over the U.S. and Canada – not a good situation for a young, married guy with two children. Fortunately, in 1968-69 there were many engineering opportunities in the area. Several of the Rice-Barton engineers landed at Polaroid, as their coating experience was a good match for Polaroid's expanding use of coated webs and web-handling machinery. I followed them into Polaroid as an engineer in a new chemical plant.

My second week on the job in the chemical plant Waltham 8, I was called into the plant manager's office and duly dressed down. My offense was that I had paged a mechanic in the cafeteria during his lunch break. I was working as an engineer, assigned responsibility for improving the efficiency of the machines used to produce print coaters (those smelly pink cartridges that were used to coat the early black and white Polaroid film). The plant manager explained to me that at Polaroid "we do not page employees during their lunch hour." I told him I needed to improve the efficiency of the machines. There were three machine operators idly waiting for repairs to be done, and the mechanic had been gone for about an hour. "Nevertheless," he said, "you should have asked Butch to help." I decided not to tell him Butch had left the building to do an errand. This was all new to me; at Rice Barton, a mechanic would always be there to keep the machines running.

A month or so later, I saw the operators moving the finished print coaters from a container on machine Number 7 over to the box on machine Number 5. When I questioned what was going on, an operator told me the operator on Number 5 was due for a performance review, and he would do better if his output was higher. Since I was not the supervisor, I did not intervene. On another occasion, I witnessed an operator putting his hand in the

18

chemicals used to clean the machine. I got him some gloves. The quality technician informed me that this practice was common; if you developed a skin rash on your hand, you would be transferred to another job that could be more interesting, with higher pay.

I attended my first evening meeting with the Chemical Division (called Perkin) management team about three months after joining Polaroid. There was an old farmhouse in Waltham that had been restored several years earlier. The management from various company departments would attend meetings there after work hours to discuss new plans. It was really a great time. A retired cook from the Navy was working there several days a week. He would prepare an excellent dinner of roast beef with shrimp cocktail and two drinks per person. Unfortunately, some of the employees or managers would consume more than two drinks, and the business sessions would get rather rowdy. Remember, the year was 1969, and in those days companies had not yet realized that mixing alcohol with work was a bad idea. At this particular meeting, one of the first-line supervisors was giving the division manager a lot of heat. The chemical plant was expanding to provide new equipment to support the SX-70 film program. Unfortunately, the plant expansion was displacing the employee volleyball court. The supervisor insisted the division manager set finding a new location as a priority. Wow, I thought, this was crazy.

New supervisors like myself often had difficulty adapting to the special treatment given to employees. My prior work experience had been in a family-owned business where there were strict rules to be observed and subordinates didn't speak disrespectfully to the bosses. A whistle sounded at the start of a break and fifteen minutes later, signaling back to work. I was also surprised there were no time clocks and employees would leave the building during the workday for various reasons.

Over time, I backed off. After all, Polaroid was making money, I had a great job, challenges every day, so why make noise over the apparent lack of discipline? Early in my Polaroid career, colleagues told me you will eventually "get it"; you will be "polarized." Over time, Polaroid's altruistic approaches to work practices morphed into what was referred to as "unification," meaning all Polaroid employees, salaried and hourly, were equal; starting about 1969, there were no time clocks; promotions were from within; employees were fired only after many chances to improve.

While Land's aim was certainly admirable, the atmosphere of employee freedom was open to abuses and casual work habits. It wasn't only the hourly employees; the same culture allowed salaried members to have a lot of control over their hours of work and even travel expenses. In the 1980s, many Polaroid employees got caught up in the overtime syndrome, as some plants lacked machine capability to support the growing demand for film or components. It was not uncommon for machine operators and mechanics to earn up to $100,000 per year by working every weekend and some 12-hour days.

Polaroid had overtime policies more generous than those required by law. If a day-shift worker started his overtime at 3 a.m. for three days, his entire weekly paycheck would be increased by 15%, as that was the premium for workers on the 11:00 p.m.-to-7:00 a.m. graveyard shift. Some employees would conspire to take vacation days in concert with their colleagues, guarantying overtime. The overtime conundrum and open work-area rules were management problems that were never adequately addressed; managers and supervisors became polarized – why make waves? Polaroid was successful.

I soon became somewhat polarized; the few times I tried to tighten controls I failed or backed off. Additionally, I was privileged to work alongside some wonderful people at all levels. When Polaroid was building and booming in the 1960s-1970s, everybody in the company energetically made an all-out effort to make Polaroid successful. When the booming stopped in the mid-1980s, we should have found ways to start scaling back payroll costs by exercising controls. Instead, Polaroid invented early severance-early retirement plans. Unfortunately, some of the strongest employees took advantage of the programs. We lost skilled people, and the company was left with the bloated payroll costs that would help lead to eventual failure.

One of my collaborators on *Fall of an Icon*, Paul Hegarty, the retired purchasing manager quoted in the previous chapter, provided his slant on the Polaroid atmosphere:

> The thing that strikes me is the remarkable and sometimes painful struggle to develop SX-70, and the spectacular success that it became, fueled the ego that nothing can stop us or overtake us. SX-70, which was Land's crowning achievement, was so extraordinary those of us on the inside, who understood all of its warts in the early stages, were surprised when the demand was so great, so fast. That success bred into the leadership that we were going to be immunized from any competitive disadvantage. The icing on the cake was the patent victory over Kodak and the big payday that followed. That allowed all the leadership to feel even better about where we were and where we thought we could go: Spectra, Joshua, Helios, etc. So, when the '90s arrived and some evidence showed that our medical, ID and insurance business could be eroded by digital imaging, we looked the other way.

The next chapters will track how Land, his colleagues and Polaroid employees built the great company in spite of the open, undisciplined work environment. The programs referenced by Hegarty are also detailed.

Chapter 5:
1950s Manufacturing in Waltham-W1

Early manufacturing at Polaroid was dependent on outsourcing to vendors or shops. With the advent of instant film about 1950, Land decided to establish a manufacturing site to support his vision of the great demand for film, but also to maintain security for his prized inventions. He wanted to be near his labs in Cambridge, and thus located a plant in a former farm in Waltham, Massachusetts, about fifteen miles west. The building named W1, as it was Waltham's first, was constructed in 1953. It would house the receiving sheet for the roll film. Polaroid would continue to purchase the negative film from either Eastman Kodak or Dupont. Soon after W1 was operational, W2 was added to provide manufacturing space for roll-film assembly and, later, reagent (the developing chemicals that triggered the transfer of image from the negative to the positive sheet) manufacturing.

W1 was constructed without windows for security reasons. Additionally, Land had his top engineer, Otto Wolf, establish a group of engineers to design and build machinery to apply the complex chemicals to the positive sheet in continuous-web format. Originally, various shops built the equipment used in the Cambridge labs, but over the next decades, Polaroid established an elite engineering and machine-shop structure approaching one thousand employees. While it would have been possible to find more sophisticated machinery designers, Land's extreme need to protect his inventions precluded sharing concepts with outsiders.

22

Employees who worked in the mixing areas were not allowed access to the coating areas and vice versa. When I was hired as an engineer in W1, I was not allowed access to the secure X and Y labs that mixed the black-and-white chemicals. In fact, the guy who mixed the X chemicals was not allowed access to the locked, adjacent Y labs. For additional security, a new employee could not witness the application of the coating of these chemicals to the black-and-white coating area, called the Y&R, until he passed the probationary period. Finally, after serving one year in W1, my big moment occurred when I was tapped to head up the safety committee. My first visit into the X and Y labs allowed me to unmask a key secret: the chemicals were added by Harold using coded "X" chemicals in a five-gallon or so "lobster pot" and household mix-master. About 50 feet of plastic tubing carried the chemicals down to the "Y" area where part X combined with Y mixed by John. The coatings were sensitive to pumping so gravity was employed.

In the Y&R, I watched the unsophisticated roller equipment apply the coatings at low speeds. Some days the coatings ran perfectly; on other occasions, it would take folks like Bud Ostberg, one of Land's "lieutenants," several days to perfect the film. Sometimes, the time of year, winter or summer, would be an influence, thought to be water-quality issues from the nearby Quabbin reservoir. During the troubled days, the employees would resort to various techniques to get the process established. My favorite was resident character Bob Graf. He would wrap some sheets around his shoulders, add a crown and hand shaker to "bless" the Y&R machine. A procession would march into the room and Bob would chant and sprinkle the machine with "holy water." Graf for that moment was Popes-i-Cola, and even Bud would smile, although I'm sure Dr. Land never witnessed the scene. Other defects were uncovered when it was found the night shift employees were using the drying ovens to warm their pizza, thus contaminating the process.

The employees of W1 were special; they were employees of Polaroid's first large manufacturing plant, proud of their traditions, dedicated to Polaroid and Dr. Land. Sixty years after the opening of W1, a group of retirees from W1 continue to meet monthly for breakfast. They refer to themselves as "Cement Heads." Jim Kilroy, who spent most of his Polaroid career in W1, passed on this description of the group:

The company hired two female engineers for the coating areas in 1983. In the past, W-1 was an all male building with the exception of the building manager's secretary. After a while, we had a race-and-gender weekend workshop. There was a critique the following week and one of the female engineers spoke up. 'There is a lot of seniority in W-1, but they have cement between their ears.' The cement heads were born. To be a cement head you had to have 25 years seniority with at least one year in W-1. The first meeting was in 1983 at the K of C Hall in Watertown, where twelve members gathered. From this beginning, the group has met on a yearly basis with the largest group of 132 retirees in 1994. The initial goal of the group was to recognize an outstanding Building I Waltham employee. The selected individual would be crowned with a cement hat and given a wooden engraved clock made by John Dunn. Before receiving "THE AWARD," the selected person would be roasted by the Master of Ceremonies.

The following members were selected as "Cement Heads of the Year": Bob Graf, Nick Boccio, Bill O'Hara, Leo Boudreau, John Dunn, Tim Murphy, Hank Thormelen, Bill Poirier, Tony Mulone, Jerry Ristagno, Jim Kilroy, Dave O'Connell, Dick St. Lawrence, Dan Petinge, Bill Lewis, Marty Helsmortel, Bud Ostberg, Bill Herman, Larry Carroll, John Forbes, Bob McCune, Bill Watt, Peter Messina, Bill Cunningham, Joe Nangeroni, John Duffy, Jack Brady, Paul Manning, Hans Giesler and Roger Jalette.

We also meet for breakfast once a month on the third Thursday of the month at Bickford's on Main Street in Waltham near Banks Square. It was a great place to

24

work with super people. The product went out the door and we had some fun. Our motto was "FOR THE GOOD TIMES."

The group continues to meet in 2012. Sadly, many of the members are now deceased.

Chapter 6:
Polaroid's Explosive Growth - 1960-1980

With the move from Cambridge to Waltham, considerable investment in plants, people and equipment brought to fruition remarkable new instant film products: Type 108 Color and Type 107 Black & White film. This prototype in pack form differed from the roll version in that the negative-positive receiving sheet and the developing chemicals (pod) were assembled in a rectangular pack. The image was struck on the negative; the photographer would pull the leader material through the rollers of the camera, causing the negative and sheet to become aligned and the reagent in the pod to transfer the image to the positive receiving sheet. The photographer would then wait 6o seconds for the color product or 15 seconds for black-and-white for the picture to develop. "Shaking" the packet was unnecessary, but popular.

Pack Film was tremendously successful and vaulted Polaroid into a Fortune 500 company with fantastic profits. During the early sixties, Land had the ultimate Instant Film product in his sights, code named SX-70. The origin of this name, started in 1943, was the first photographic folder in Polaroid. The SX-70 project would be Land's ultimate technical achievement. He set the program goals, many of which would require revolutionary optics and electronic controls not yet invented. For example, the system would include:
- Folding, single lens reflex
- Integral film; combined positive/negative, develop in light

- Electronic shutter and exposures
- Small camera (pocket size, possibly)

In addition to his own perception of the perfect Instant System, Land was reacting to concerns with the Pack Film – too much trash. With the 107-108 products, the positive sheet would stay with the photographer; the leader, light masking sheet and reagent pods could be carelessly discarded and was, in fact, far too frequently. This "excess waste" contaminating national parks, recreation areas and all manner of public places was a major concern to the company, causing a reputation a consumer company did not want to have. One rumor had it that the new product would not have "excess" waste; therefore "no excess" would become "no XS," yielding the acronym "SX." The SX-70 film packet –positive, negative and empty pod –all became part of the finished photograph to be held, given away, or filed into an album.

Land also decided that 1960s battery technology and reliability were not worthy of the new product. Customer Service, during the roll- and pack-film sales life, had learned that a large percentage of film defects received back as complaints from customers were caused by dead batteries in the cameras. Polaroid had no control over this round cell life, but often had to placate customers with replacement film for flash or picture-taking defects caused by dead batteries. So, rather than count on a conventional carbon-zinc round cell, SX-70 would have a fresh battery in every film pack. A subsequent chapter will describe the trials and failures of the Polaroid battery. The plan was to outsource the battery manufacturing to one of the top battery companies, so a new Polaroid plant would not be needed.

Lastly, Land established a very aggressive timetable on the program. Eastman Kodak was planned as the source of the new, unique color negative (invented by Polaroid), as they had since 1957 for the pack film product. Early in the development of SX-70, Kodak and Polaroid had a disagreement, actually a major falling-out. Polaroid historians such as Peter Wensberg, in his book *LAND'S POLAROID*, indicated the situation gravitated to a "no-win" stand-off. Kodak did not want to continue to help

27

Polaroid gain market share in photography; Land was arrogant in his negotiations, overstating Polaroid's financial leverage with Kodak. Kodak eventually terminated the negative-supply agreement. So, a new plant was required to produce the SX-70 negative. The relationship and cause for termination of the supply agreement and everything that Kodak did in instant film later is described by Bill McCune, Polaroid's second CEO, in a later section.

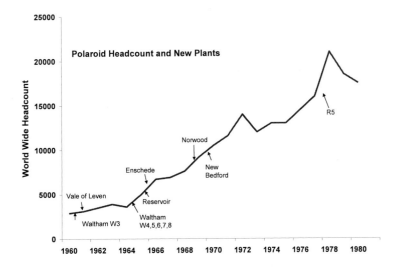

As the SX-70 film was being developed, a second coating plant in W5 was added, along with chemical manufacturing in W6 and W8. A research building, W4, was included to move some of the Cambridge scientists closer to manufacturing and provide R&D for the new negative plant in New Bedford, Massachusetts. Waltham 7 rounded out the building construction on the Waltham Main Street site; it provided utility and trades support. A camera factory was built in Norwood, about 20 miles from Waltham. To assemble the SX-70 film, a new three-building complex was added at the Waltham Reservoir site. When the battery supplier could not meet Polaroid requirements, a Battery Plant was added at the reservoir site (R5). By 1980, Polaroid had added an incredible number of plants, processes, equipment and suppliers. Employee head count grew from 3,000 in 1960 to over 20,000

28

in 1978. The totals also included the international manufacturing sites in Scotland and the Netherlands.

The next three chapters will describe Polaroid's European manufacturing sites, the development of the automated film assembly process to produce pack film and a history of camera manufacturing at Polaroid.

Chapter 7:
Polaroid Manufacturing in Europe

Having successfully launched the first mass-market camera in the U.S. through their domestic sales division and in Europe and other areas of the world through subsidiary marketing companies, Polaroid, it was decided, required a manufacturing presence in Europe to capitalize on this success and get behind the tariff barriers. Accordingly, in 1965, Polaroid Corporation established film manufacturing facilities in the Vale of Leven, Dumbarton, Scotland, and Enschede in the Netherlands for the manufacture of Type 20 roll film (used in the Swinger camera), with plans to expand these facilities to manufacture Type 107/108 pack film. The Vale factory was also to become the source of sunglass blanks for sunglass glazers in Europe.

Vale of Leven
The Polaroid site on the Strathleven Industrial Estate was established on the banks of the River Leven in West Dunbartonshire about twenty miles northwest of Glasgow, between Loch Lomond and the River Clyde. The attraction of this location to Polaroid was the availability of skilled labor in the area following the run down and eventual closure of the manufacturing facility of the legendary Burroughs Adding Machine, Ltd. on the estate, along with the closure of the Royal Naval torpedo factory in nearby Alexandria. This skilled labor pool, coupled with government incentives offered to companies prepared to invest in that area, made the Vale of Leven doubly desirable to Polaroid.

30

Polaroid was to be the last U.S. manufacturing company to locate at Strathleven and, indeed, the last major arrival in the Vale of Leven, although possibly the biggest and best. Polaroid had had a presence in the United Kingdom since 1962 when the marketing subsidiary was established in Welwyn Garden City, Hertfordshire. However, Polaroid's arrival in the Vale of Leven in 1965 was to have a long and lasting impact on the area. From the very beginning, it became an integral part of the community in a very positive, modern way, providing support and leadership on numerous projects and activities. The Polaroid approach was inspirational; they helped people to make things happen that, otherwise, would not have happened, rather than taking over and doing it for them. This was the approach that Polaroid management took in running its business. Employees were team-based and were involved in setting goals. They, therefore, felt ownership in achievement of the goals, and this led to a successful manufacturing operation virtually from the outset.

Polaroid was rightly regarded as a good place to work; people were, invariably, well treated and very well paid. For many years, it was a spectacular success as evidenced by the range of products which Polaroid introduced into the Vale: sunglasses, cameras and film. The standards and style were set from early on by the site directors. Harvey Thayer was the first, followed by John Kropper, and then by the first national site director, Rob MacLean. All of the directors, along with a dedicated management team and group of employees, managed, during the formative years at Strathleven when it had explosive growth, to establish the Polaroid way of doing things; and this stood the Vale in good stead for thirty years.

The work force grew throughout the late 1960s, the 1970s, and 1980s to a peak of over two thousand. Sister plants were opened in Enschede, Holland, and Newbridge, Ireland, to which Vale employees were periodically dispatched to assist in their start-ups. As the hectic period of growth leveled out and Strathleven became a more mature plant, Rob MacLaren went off in 1979 to facilitate Polaroid's entry into the potentially huge Chinese market.

31

The company continued to perform strongly under MacLean's successors, such as Tom Tait and Derek Taylor. Its pioneering work in employee relations continued. In particular, Polaroid was very strong on health and fitness. The company opened a gym and fitness room in part of the old Strathleven Estate canteen and promoted a number of programs in the community on that theme – the annual Ben Lomond Hill Race which became a Mecca for runners from throughout the U.K. and the Loch Lomond Boat Race which exemplified the competing-teams aspect pioneered by Polaroid and was subsequently adopted by many similar events. Polaroid manufacturing was, and Polaroid Eyewear still is, the sponsor for a series of 10K road races which take place each June over various courses in West Dunbartonshire. These road races were started by Derek Taylor, who was an avid marathon runner, and were continued under his successors, Mike Fitzpatrick and Jim Hall, who were also keen runners.

Production of Pack Film cameras began at the Vale in 1976 with half a million delivered in the first year. These cameras had previously been produced for Polaroid at Timex Corporation's facility in Dundee, Scotland, where production of the Type 20 Swinger for the European market had started in 1966. For the next twenty-five years, camera production at the Vale was an important contributor to Polaroid's manufacturing operations. As the company's fortunes declined in the late 1990s, employee head count dropped from a high of over two thousand to 750 by 2001. All told, approximately 3.5 million Pack Film cameras and 58 million Integral Film cameras were produced at the Vale.

In 2007, camera manufacture ceased, closely followed by the cessation of Pack Film production, leaving only the sunglass operation to uphold the name and traditions of Polaroid in the West Dunbartonshire area. Polaroid Eyewear International was born with Stylemark Corporation of the U.S.A. purchasing the Polaroid sunglass brand along with its manufacturing facility in the Vale. The business no longer simply produces lens blanks for glazers, but produces a complete range of sunglass products for sale and distribution to world markets; all researched, developed, managed and produced in a section of the original

Vale factory, staffed by a number of original Vale camera, film and sunglass lens employees. The Polaroid traditions and culture, therefore, live on in the Vale of Leven.

Tom Tait, a respected Polaroid manager for twenty-seven years, provided the Vale summary. When I asked Tom if he would contribute to my Polaroid history, he promptly responded and also added a nice comment: "I left Polaroid in April 1993. Being part of the Polaroid family was enlightening, enjoyable, and fun – never regretted one day since joining in 1966."

Enschede

To provide a similar accounting for the plant in the Netherlands, I requested assistance from another long-time Polaroid manager, Larry Kivimaki. Larry spent the majority of his Polaroid career in the Integral Film assembly plant R2 in Waltham, Massachusetts. I worked with Larry during my last four years at the company. He ranks at the top of my list of favorite Polaroid colleagues. While his major contribution to the company involved packaging technology for our film packs, Larry could and would delve into any assignment requiring engineering or business analysis.

While the Vale became Polaroid's major partner in camera manufacturing, the Dutch plant in Enschede formed a similar partnership with Polaroid in assembling instant film. Located about 75 miles east of Amsterdam, Enschede was once a large producer of textiles–cotton and linen fabrics. By the late 1960s, competition from cheaper Far Eastern countries wreaked havoc on the region and Enschede became one of the poorest municipalities in the Netherlands and was essentially bankrupt. Large areas of industrial wasteland came to mark the city. With the support of their national government, this property was acquired and rebuilt.

Polaroid was attracted to the area, as it was with the Vale, by the skilled work force as well as favorable incentives presented by the Enschede government. While the labor rates and benefits related to social programs in the Netherlands eventually approached the U.S. pay rates, the choice of Enschede was an excellent one. The Dutch engineers and machine operators were quite resourceful; their competitive nature provided a challenge to their counterparts in Polaroid, Waltham. Additionally, Enschede purchasing professionals developed excellent material suppliers in the Netherlands and Europe. The plant, early on, provided support to sunglass manufacturing and Pack Film, but the major contribution was the assembly of Integral Film – SX-70 and all later versions. Starting about 1990, Enschede produced about half of all Integral Film sold by Polaroid. In addition to the manufacturing operations, Polaroid's International Distribution and Service Center (ISDC) was established in Enschede to manage Polaroid product distribution outside the U.S.

I started to visit Enschede in 1986, first as a supplier, representing the Battery Division, then in my role as Worldwide Director for Integral Film, coordinating scheduling, planning and material sourcing for our Dutch counterparts. After a few visits and some initial uncertainty, I grew to respect the Enschede managers greatly; and I truly loved the visits to the Netherlands. Somehow, even though the Dutch were very strong partners with the U.S. team, there was the underlying sense that the Americans did not consider the Dutch to be their equals. While this may have been the case early on, by the time I started to work with Enschede, I believe most of the U.S. staff appreciated the contributions of the Enschede team. They contributed immensely to improvements in many areas, notably the complex manufacturing of developer chemicals and the pod foil packet that contained the chemicals.

Where the friction sometimes arose was the resistance to accepting some of the changes suggested by Enschede pod engineers. The U.S. Quality Assurance group was extremely cautious in accepting change after years of upsets in film manufacturing; the Dutch believed their engineering skill could allow changes to be implemented quickly, while the U.S. managers insisted on long shelf-life testing to avoid major failures. The mantra was "change is evil."

Overall, I think the partnership worked well. Polaroid stopped producing Instant film in 2008; several of the Enschede employees are still making a similar version of the Polaroid legacy Instant film in 2012, using the same machinery in the old Enschede plant. Called the "Impossible Project," this amazing accomplishment will be detailed in a later chapter. The Impossible Project did prove the point: the Dutch engineers and managers are quite resourceful and fearless.

Some of the Enschede people whom I had the pleasure to work with include Theo Gosen, purchasing, a skilled negotiator and great travelling companion; Rob van Tilburg, a tireless supplier quality engineer; Theo Kuipers, an excellent quality manager; Frans van den Broek, Materials Manager; Jan Geerdink, Plant Manager and, later, Director; and Andre Bosman, Engineering Manager and founder and leader of the Impossible Project.

Several U.S. employees were sent to Enschede on various assignments. Sam Brown, a manufacturing manager from Enschede's sister plant in R2, Waltham, provided his recollection of his family's time in the Netherlands:

In August of 1982, Polaroid offered me the opportunity to exchange roles with the Dutch production manager in the Enschede manufacturing operation. Jean Tomsin moved onto my role as Process Engineer Manager, and I assumed his role as Production Manager. Because of my background, I also absorbed the role of onsite Process Engineering Manager. It was an opportunity, typical of Polaroid, that allowed both of us to grow beyond our current responsibilities. After a one-week visit with my wife and two daughters, then ages 11 and 13, we agreed to take the two-year assignment.

There are many differences about that part of the "western world" versus our part of the western world. They are more to the left in their thinking politically and much more liberal socially. We were living in a duplex house that the company rented for us and were accepted into the social circle of the neighborhood immediately. I was included in the Friday evening activity which was made up of the men playing a card game called "Bonkin", and the women joining the men later in the evening for wine and chatter. Most people spoke some English and our Dutch came slowly since they would rather practice their English.

The work had some very different characteristics from the U.S. and, I must say, some of them were significant improvements. Meetings always began and ended on time. The purpose and the expected result were well known. As the end time approached, people knew it and would be upset if a conclusion was not reached and action planned. The whole idea was that nothing should be left hanging. There were no lunch meetings or dinner meetings. Work began at 8:00 and ended at 5:00. No one was late and, at 5:30, I was alone in the office. None of the above had any negative effect on operating efficiency.

The plant ran very well. When I first arrived (in Enschede), the Irish plant was still getting going. When the production cutbacks started due to the overbuild of capacity, the Dutch worked very hard to make sure they had maximum efficiency. The fear was that, if a European film plant was to be closed, they (the Dutch) were more vulnerable due to the common language between Ireland, Scotland, and the U.S. Although, at one meeting between the engineers from the two Pack Film plants, I brought two Dutch engineers who spoke very good English, when the Scottish electrical engineer started speaking with a very heavy brogue, the Dutchmen all turned to me and asked what he was saying; and I had no idea, since I could not understand his English either—so much for the common language.

The cooperation between the U.S. and the Dutch plant was excellent. There was an acknowledged dependence on the U.S. for materials and technical modifications. The U.S. depended on the Dutch plant to be more consistent, since most new materials and processes were proven before implementation in the Dutch plant.

One thing that stands out most in my mind is a government response to our need to cut back production in the Dutch plant and, subsequently, lay off some people. The province authorities proposed that we maintain the same number of people and operating shifts, but cut the work week back to three days or, in some cases, four days for a lot of the direct labor which were vulnerable to layoff. The government would make up the pay for the hours not worked, which probably amounted to less than the cost of unemployment and prevented any dislocation of people.

Polaroid maintained its highly-skilled work force; and, when the time came to get back up to full strength, it was a seamless operation. I believe this condition went on for about 6-8 months. In a country with a socialist bent, it was easy. I don't think that could happen here. I am not sure of the time span, but it was at the time we were discussing and closing the Irish plant, and that flexibility was probably part of the consideration that kept the Dutch plant viable.

After reviewing the recollections of Tom Tait of the Vale and Larry Kivimaki and Sam Brown regarding Enschede, as well as my own experiences, I realized how well these two sites functioned. In the Vale and Enschede, both the management team and workers demonstrated a strong focus on producing products equal to or better than their American counterparts. They were grateful for good-paying, interesting jobs in areas bereft of any jobs before Polaroid's arrival in the 1960s; and they worked hard to prove their worth.

In a sense, the Vale and Enschede managers and employees maintained the spirit of a healthy competition, while their U.S. counterparts operated in a manner that might be expected of employees who felt they had guaranteed jobs based on Polaroid's monopoly on instant film.

The next chapter, "The P60 Experiment," will describe the onset of this unfortunate culture that helped fuel the eventual downfall of Dr. Land's great company.

Chapter 8:
The Project 60 Experiment

By 1963, over 5 million Polaroid instant cameras were sold using the black-and-white roll-film process. That year, the first color Polaroid film and the Automatic 100 pack film camera, along with Type 107 black-and-white and Type 108 color-pack film, were introduced. The pack film introduction would expand Polaroid sales by a factor of five times, reaching $500 million by 1970. The manufacturing plant in Waltham, W3, was constructed during that time. The new equipment to assemble the pack film was highly automated compared to the previous roll-film machinery, so there was concern that the workers might not be allowed to exercise their brainpower sufficiently. Consistent with Dr. Land's second aim, "to make his work here a fully rewarding, important part of his life," the operators of the pack-film machinery would be accorded special arrangements so they would not have to work a mindless daily routine setting up rolls of materials and then watching the assembly line transform them into a finished pack.

Project 60 was the first new product activity Dr. Land did not personally supervise. It was also the first to have someone from manufacturing working on the early development phase. Caleb Roehrig from W2 was given this job. As he ran his small pilot operation in a General Radio building on Windsor Street, Cambridge, few employees were aware of his presence. His project, P60, was one of Polaroid's best kept secrets. Working beneath this cloak of anonymity, he began laying the groundwork for a new manufacturing facility and for a new work organization that would provide meaningful jobs for its hourly employees. By background, Caleb was a manufacturing man. Before joining Polaroid he had managed a plant of his own. Caleb was a humanist. He had seen first-hand the effects of modern engineering and technology on manufacturing jobs. He had seen productivity suffer as more and more of the challenge and responsibility had been taken from production jobs. Caleb was also an optimist. He believed that technology and challenge could go hand in hand if someone made the effort to design jobs properly. He had heard Dr. Land many times outline Polaroid's two great aims. Now, given the chance to develop Pack Film's manufacturing process and organization from scratch, he planned to make these two aims a reality.

Rather than design the new work plan, Land commissioned a group of managers and employees with the charter to find a way of operating the automated assembly equipment while still allowing the employees time to contribute to the total process. It was called the Project 60 (P60 for short) experiment, and would set the stage for the Polaroid work culture over the next 40 years. (Portions extracted from "P60 Express", Phelps K. Tracy, November, 1977)

This was pretty radical thinking in the 1960s. During this time period, there were different views, from Frederic Taylor's "scientific management" approach to running a factory as man as extension of machine. While many of Taylor's ideas included de-skilling of the worker and dehumanization of the workplace, Taylor's methods began from his observation that, in general, workers forced to perform repetitive tasks work at the slowest rate that goes unpunished. So, how do you work on an automated assembly machine and not become bored with the repetitive tasks? After many meetings with employees and managers, the concept evolved that P60 operators would spend half their workday tending the machine and the other half improving their product knowledge or other more interesting challenges. Early on, this concept worked fairly well, as there was much to learn about the new product, meetings to attend and such. While many longtime P60 employees put in a good workday, others discovered a part of Taylorism they could really adapt to: "in-for-four-and-out-the-door."

Since there were twice as many operators to attend the machine over an eight-hour shift, a clever team could decide to work either the first or second half of the day or night and then slide out to the nearest bar or other entertainment. This was particularly easy to accomplish on the evening shifts. Land had eliminated use of time clocks years earlier, so the honor system was the only record of attendance. The abusers would start the shift by being visible in the plant, leave for four hours, and then return to finish the shift; their counterparts would cover the first half and leave for the second half. In Tracy's study on P60, he interviewed several technicians. A senior technician on the second floor recalled:

There were many times when I had absolutely nothing to do ... I might as well have stayed home for all I did. That's as close as I have ever come to developing a drinking problem. I don't know whether that's because of the free time I had or because I had nothing to do and I was nothing here.

Some parts of P60 operated similar to a union shop, where employees could not work outside their assigned job title or area. Each assembly machine would have a crew of three assigned. Assembly operators refused to cross departmental lines; they were not the only ones. Mechanics refused to work on another floor level. Those assigned to the second floor would not work on the third. Neither group would help their counterparts in Press and Mold or Pods. The feeling surfaced around Polaroid that there was fat to be trimmed in P60 if someone had the nerve to go after it. This abbreviated workday was most certainly known to members of management. I had some firsthand involvement while I was managing the mechanics in another division. I received a call from Bob Jacobs, my supervisor. Bob said he had an experienced mechanic who could start work immediately for me in the battery plant. Protesting, I told Bob I had sufficient mechanics.

"Not negotiable," said Bob. "If you don't take John, we fear the P60 folks will initiate a serious accident for him. You see, John transferred from camera division into P60 recently. He's threatened to blow the lid on "the in-for four and out-the-door crowd." John started in my shop the next day.

When I relate this story, I feel a bit like an enabler to the "time cheaters." Should I have told Bob to go to somebody in higher management and force the issue to be addressed? It was not even considered, as I was convinced that P60 management had known of the practice for years. As long as P60 makes money, don't rock the boat. Additionally, the workers really had little else to do during their "off-time." Management could have provided other tasks in quality or maintenance, but they didn't.

While the P60 experiment was a noble experiment, consistent with Land's second aim, it was in some ways a failure, as the relaxed workday established a culture of entitlements for the next generation Polaroid worker. The pack-film plant was the genesis of the culture described in a previous chapter – the Polaroid way – getting polarized. There were continual employee challenges over pay vs. job tasks, even though many employees did not have a full workday. The management team was caught in a perfect storm of steadily increasing film demand, concerns with employee slowdown and even a union organizing attempt. The aforementioned Phelps Tracey, in the "P60 Express," described the situation in P60 in the early 1970s. Joe Oldfield was the plant manager at that time. He and his staff wanted to tighten controls on worker productivity. They felt the best path to that end was to reduce the crew size on each assembly machine, called "one on one." The country was in recession and Polaroid sales were down; a layoff was being considered. Joe explained to Tracey:

It came during talks of the possible layoff. The company was in trouble, McCune was asking us all to find new ways of doing things. I presented (the "one on one") proposal as an alternative. I had received counsel both from Bruce and Max, not to do it. But, where I was coming from, the timing was right. If we were ever going to do it, now was the time and my motivation was to do it, get it behind us, and start ahead with the job of making this a better place to work. I laid it out and Fernald went crazy. Then I explained to him what we had in mind, and he said it might be appropriate if I laid it out for the staff. He said okay. So he knew what was coming. He let me do it. But, he then read me the riot act in front of everybody.

Bill McCune was company CEO then, and George Fernald was the Film Division Manager, Oldfield's boss. Bruce Henry and Max Lawrence preceded Joe as P60 Manager. Bruce, Max and Joe all went on to high positions in subsequent years; they will appear in later chapters. In addition to having responsibility for pack film, Fernald was in charge of the W4 research building and the New Bedford negative plant under construction. His background was mostly in R&D, not having much experience with film assembly or hourly workers. Fernald and his staff did not support Oldfield's plan to reduce manning, which would have forced the assembly operators to spend more time at their machines. Instead, Fernald instructed Joe to focus on productivity improvements and meet his budget. For several years, P60 had used a productivity index to measure output, "X" number of packs of film for each man-hour worked. Expectations were a 6% improvement should be budgeted each year and met. In the past, since reduction of crew size was not acceptable, the gains came by way of machine efficiency as well as improved materials.

Fernald's reluctance to support the crew reduction was most likely due to not wanting to get into a major battle with the employees committee or, worse, have the P60 employees walk off the job. There had been an undercurrent of possible work stoppages a few years earlier. Recall that in 1970, a union had attempted unsuccessfully to organize Polaroid workers. Additionally, I can't imagine any division manager wanting to tell Dr. Land his treasured employees had walked off the job; he would have not understood how you let that happen.

I worked in a W1 adjacent coating area during that time. There was a strong work ethic in W1. Because of flammable chemicals, you had to leave the building to smoke, and breaks and lunch hours were strictly controlled. The operators worked as a team, where each individual's effort was needed. Perhaps the process-type coating equipment was easier to adapt to productive work teams than assembly machines. But I'd also suggest no-nonsense W1 managers and supervisors such as Hal Page, John Dunn, Joe Nangeroni, Dave O'Connell, Leo Boudreau and Tony Rymsha probably had something to do with the needed control. The W1 workers used to joke about the P60 employees, "Look out, management, P60s going out on the hill!" The hill was the small mound of grass at the entrance of W3. When W1 employees heard P60 was getting another free lunch or dinner, W1 management had to follow suit.

While the P60 experiment helped establish a lax work environment that would plague the company for the next three decades, it should be noted that the majority of the workers were conscientious employees; a minority caused all the problems. The managers and supervisors did their best, considering the reluctance of top management to support the plant management's efforts to rectify the situation. Pack film sales allowed Polaroid to grow to a $1-billion business with profits sufficient to fund the new SX-70 film lines, resulting eventually in a $2 billion-plus company.

Pack Film was the "engine" that funded the future successes of Polaroid.

Chapter 9:
Polaroid Camera History

Walter Byron joined Polaroid in 1968. He spent most of the next 33 years as a manager in the camera division, including several years in camera development. Walter kept notes during his time in the Camera Division, including a tally of all the various cameras produced over those years. Excerpts from Walter's history of Polaroid's camera operations follow:

(Full Text, Appendix D)

****

Polaroid cameras were first introduced in 1948 with the Model 95, which took its name from its $95 starting price. For the next twenty years, Polaroid managed the manufacturing of many models of roll film and pack film cameras, primarily through contract manufacturing, using Bell and Howell in Chicago and U.S. Time (Timex) in Hot Springs, Arkansas, and Dundee, Scotland, as suppliers. During this time, the contract manufacturing management group evolved into the Camera Division, which was located at 640 Memorial Drive, Cambridge. From 1948 to 1971, some 34 million cameras were produced by those two contractors for Polaroid.

In the mid-60s after Polaroid decided to manufacture the future SX-70 cameras in house, the manufacturing

44

of some of the pack camera sub-assemblies (non-rotating spread system, folding boot assembly, shutter, etc.) were brought into Polaroid in order to grow the internal manufacturing expertise necessary for the future SX-70 camera factory. Additionally, an evaluation of which of the four parts of the camera – optics, electronics, mechanical parts and packaging / literature–Polaroid should also produce, resulted in a decision to establish an Optics Manufacturing unit, while continuing to purchase other components. The nascent Optics unit was housed at 640 Memorial Drive in Cambridge.

The Camera Division during this time was led by Mark Sewall, a veteran Polaroid manager, who oversaw both the contract and internal manufacturing parts of the division. When Sewall retired in 1969, a new leader was appointed, Christopher C. Ingraham, also a Polaroid veteran from the film manufacturing side of the business, where he had successfully helped lead the start-up of pack-film manufacturing at W3. Chris led the division for the decade of the 70s, through the startup of SX-70 camera manufacturing in Norwood and beyond, into hard-body integral camera manufacturing both in Norwood and at the Vale of Leven factory near Glasgow, Scotland.

Other key leaders of the division in the decade of the 70s included: Hugh MacKenzie – Engineering, Gerry Sudbey – Quality Assurance, Vince Gatto – Materials Management, Bob Wood – Optics Manufacturing, George Trumbour – SX-70 Factory Manager, Bill Lally – SX-70 Final Assembly Manager, Bob Eastman – SX-70 Shutter Manufacturing, and Marshall Snider – Industrial Hardware Manufacturing.

The SX-70 camera, Polaroid's first integral film-using device, was to be produced in a new building in Norwood, Massachusetts. The task of delivering a new revolutionary product with all its technical complexity, while simultaneously building a new assembly factory with all its administrative and manufacturing processes, proved to be a daunting task which was accomplished, but with difficulty, at considerable cost, and after many process and material inventions. The team was led by Milt Dietz and John Pasieka, augmented by people from the Norwood factory with camera manufacturing experience, produced a follow-on, non-folding hard body camera design (the Pronto!) that, in its many variations, was eminently cost effective, much easier to manufacture ,and lasted more than thirty years in its various design variations.

For the SX-70 camera, a continuous-flow production system, similar to automobile assembly, was chosen as the camera production methodology. Employee training was important and was emphasized by the many production line supervisors, assisted by a training department, and complemented by an industrial engineering effort at individual job design and production-line flow analysis. "People are our machines" was often the explanation given to company members as to how the camera assembly factory worked. During the SX-70 startup, many teams of Polaroid manufacturing engineering personnel lived at suppliers' factories for months, assisting in the development of the supplier parts-manufacturing processes.

In 1976, production of pack cameras began at the Polaroid facility at the Vale of Leven. As the SX-70 camera sales and manufacturing matured over a short few years, it was followed up by the first hard-body, integral film camera, the Pronto!, also that same year. In 1977, Kodak introduced their version of an integral film system. This challenge was met by Polaroid with an intense six week period of redesign and factory reconfiguration to adapt the Pronto! camera design into the OneStep, which became the best selling Polaroid camera ever. 1978 saw a worldwide production of more than nine million cameras from the N1 and Vale factories and a half million from contract manufacturing, for a total of nine-and-one-half million.

The N1 facility was running around the clock on three shifts and the Vale factory was on two shifts at this time. Camera Division population peaked that year at over 4,000 in the Norwood factories. In 1980, Chris Ingraham moved to a new position and Gerry Sudbey assumed the leadership as Vice President of Camera Division. Camera manufacturing peaked in 1978 and in the first half of the 80s, then steadily declined to a worldwide low of two million, eight hundred thousand in 1984. Polaroid developed a larger format integral film/ camera system named Spectra in 1985. The Spectra introduction gave a boost to Polaroid camera sales that year and the factories delivered five million cameras in total in 1986.

The Joshua system –a smaller integral film and folding, single lens reflex camera with a chamber on the back into which the picture was moved as it exited the spread rolls –was launched in 1993, under the name Captiva, in the U.S., Vision in Europe and JoyCam in Japan. This design allowed the user to shoot multiple shots, without the worry of where to put the pictures coming out of the camera, as was the case with earlier designs of Polaroid integral film cameras.

In 1993, a new Polaroid camera production factory was opened in Shanghai and operated for the next seven years. From 1993 through 2000, the Shanghai factory produced nine million, six hundred thousand cameras. Also in that year, a small Polaroid camera plant was opened in Moscow, where the final assembly of cameras was done using subassemblies made at the Vale. The Moscow operation was open for five years and produced about six hundred thousand cameras over that period.

The epitaph for the camera Division really reflects that of Polaroid in general. The story of the Division was one of increasing manufacturing competence, product quality and reliability, scale-up ability, organizational growth and use of technology that was on a par with the best in the U.S. The philosophy the

47

company and the Division adopted was "make the cameras where you sell them." Unfortunately toward the end Polaroid had to use outsourced vendors in China or other low-cost labor countries, "they make the cameras and Polaroid will sell them." As with all parts of the company that achieved excellence in performance over the years, the Camera Division ceased to exist when the company failed. (Walter Byron)

****

I had always felt the decision to bring camera manufacturing in-house was a key mistake in Polaroid's history. If Polaroid had continued to use outsourced camera vendors in the 1970s and on, the company could have responded better to seasonal adjustments and cost concerns. Most of the instant camera models were sold at below manufacturing cost. For the low-end models selling below $40, the loss was made up with the sale of three-to-four packs of film; for the high-end SX-70 and Captiva cameras, several more packs needed to be sold to break even.

After reading Walter's Camera-Division history, my bias softened quite a bit. From 1972 to 2000, Polaroid built and sold over 200 million cameras, of over a dozen different models. As described by Walter, the complexity and logistical challenges faced and conquered by Camera Division managers and employees at all levels was remarkable. Without their contribution, Polaroid would have never become a $2.5 billion company. It is hard to imagine how Polaroid could have used outside vendors to produce the SX-70 and later cameras.

Chapter 10:
Polaroid's Engineers and Manufacturing Specialists -The Implementers of Land's Inventions

After working in the W8 chemical plant for about a year, I was transferred to the Waltham 1 coating plant. When I was allowed to see the coating machines in Waltham 1, I was struck by how rudimentary they appeared compared to the commercial machines I had experienced previously. They were about one generation back in technology, in my opinion. When I suggested looking at professional machinery manufacturers for newer equipment, my colleagues in W1 explained that the processes were so proprietary, Dr. Land would never allow an outside firm anywhere near the coating areas. In fact, Bud Ostberg was the only one allowed to approve Polaroid visitors to enter W1.

When I needed a new Polaroid plumber, Bud asked, "Why do you need a second guy? Where's Ed, our regular plumber?" Over time, I grew to understand why building our own machines made sense. In addition to the product security, the fast-paced programs, with often-changing specifications, would not have been possible using outside builders. In later years, Polaroid did start to outsource machinery manufactures with less than good results (Helios Chapter later).

By 1970, Polaroid's engineering department and machine shops had grown to 700 employees. As a reference point, my

49

former firm, Rice Barton, had 500 employees with annual sales of $18 million in 1965 dollars. There was a large machine shop at 750 Main Street in Cambridge, complete with the latest machine tools, welding and sheet-metal shops. The engineering groups, Engineering, Facilities and Equipment Division (EFED), were located at Wyman Street in Waltham. One group designed and oversaw construction of the plants; another provided the designs for the Cambridge shops to fabricate.

The coating design group was headed by Tim Murphy. He was formerly the W1 building engineer, a role I eventually inherited. Tim was quite protective of the machinery in W1, as he had managed the creation of Polaroid's full-size coaters. I made the mistake of modifying them without his permission. I soon learned that was not the Polaroid way. Tim had several key engineers working with him: Dick Martin was an expert in designing the equipment that dried or cured the unique coatings; Gerry Kheboian, a colleague of mine from Rice Barton, provided the designs for the drive and control mechanisms; Spencer Beckwith, Charlie Mach, Fred Sleeper, Bob Bagley were notable among the coating systems designers.

The chemical design group was also innovative. Claude Valle and Bob Wohler built a strong team, using several chemical engineers from Northeastern University of Boston, many by way of Northeastern's co-op program. This group took on the complex challenge of designing reactors and chemical processing equipment for the unique chemicals developed by Land's labs, chemicals often nearly impossible or dangerous to make.

The assembly group, headed by Max Lawrence and John Sturgis provided the machines that assembled the negative-positive pods and related materials employing novel pick-and-place devices. The Polaroid engineers that designed the cameras for instant film were skilled. Conventional cameras for 35 mm or similar film products have to manage light, control the shutter, strike the image on the negative and store the film for later removal, enlargement and development. The Polaroid instant process does all of that, but also strikes the image on a full-size negative and initiates the development reactions. The instant camera includes a pick-and-drive mechanism to advance

50

the positive-negative package to rollers that squeeze the developing chemicals between the positive and negative. In a few minutes the finished picture is visible. Many photographers who have tracked the Polaroid camera and film system from the beginning in 1950 consider Land's SX-70 as not only instant film system's best version, but also a major breakthrough for all photography because of its elegant design, unique lens and state of the art electronics.

Walter Byron, the Camera Division historian from the previous chapter, provided the following story from the introduction of the SX-70 camera at the stockholders' annual meeting in 1972. I was at the event, along with several hundred employees and stockholders. Most Polaroid executives involved in the program felt we were about a year away from having a working SX-70 system, but Land had teased the stockholders and Wall Street the last few years; sales were not moving and the stock was in trouble, so Land decided not only to make the announcement, but have a full-blown demonstration. It was a wonderful experience and one of my proudest moments as a Polaroid employee. Dr. Land and the SX-70 pictures wowed the crowd. As Walter related:

The SX-70 system was Dr. Land's culmination of his 1940s dream of developing instant photography. From the original sepia tone, on to black-and-white roll film, then color roll, through several generations of black-and-white and color pack film, Dr. Land pursued that ultimate goal of a self-contained color film format. After many years of effort, in the spring of 1972, the SX-70 film and camera development were far enough along for Dr. Land to decide that he wanted to make them the center of his "show" at the upcoming annual shareholders meeting. The previous year, at the annual meeting, he had teased shareholders with a glimpse of the camera as he withdrew it from his suit coat pocket and briefly held it aloft before returning it to its hiding place. Now it was time for the real thing to be put on display.

51

At the time, I was working for Gerry Sudbey, who had the responsibility for Quality in the SX-70 camera program. I had been working on various tasks for Gerry, including running tests of shutter-blade materials to overcome a shutter exposure problem, when Gerry turned to a group of us, led by Gary Hamann, and said, "Okay, we're going to build and qualify 50 cameras for the annual meeting." That was an enormous challenge at the time, because there had been few cameras built to date in the several years it took to develop the product. The camera factories were just getting established and were building low volume runs of non-saleable cameras to wring out both the product and assembly and testing processes. But, the group went to work and, in cooperation with the factory personnel at 38 Henry Street, where the shutters were made, and the gang in N-1 where the rest of the camera was made, the 50 cameras were assembled and tested.

Recalling the setup for that 1972 annual meeting, there were about two dozen octagonal raised platforms, each about ten feet across, set on the floor of the warehouse at 140 Kendrick Street in Needham. On each of the platforms, a different group of Polaroid employees was engaged in a performance of one kind or another, and the SX-70 cameras were used to take pictures of the action. I can't recall all of the scenes, but I do remember Shelly (Dr. Sheldon Buckler) and a few others on one platform playing poker and, on another, Steve Benton was conducting a birthday party for his two children.

Not all the 50 cameras survived the testing over the subsequent days and when we began the annual meeting that afternoon, we had only 24 cameras to support the 12 or so platforms. One camera for each platform was in use and a person was assigned to stand nearby with a spare camera to swap in case there was a problem. I was assigned to Steve Benton's platform with a spare camera. When we reached the part of the meeting where the platform performances began, Steve and his kids went into their party mode and really enjoyed themselves. Steve was helping the children; opening presents, eating cake and ice cream and taking pictures. Now, if you remember the SX-70 camera, the lens focus wheel was also a gear that turned the lens and other gears inside the shutter. Birthday cake has frosting, and, in the heat of the moment, the cake cutter is likely to get frosting on his fingers. Sure enough, as Steve took a picture, his right index finger, covered in frosting, got frosting all over the focus wheel gear teeth. As he focused the lens, the frosting was transferred right inside the shutter which promptly ceased to work. A quick camera swap was arranged, and I raced off behind the scenes to a camera repair station we had established. There, among others, Art Cianci, a model maker, waited to repair the cameras that exhibited problems during the meeting. Art and his colleagues were plenty busy, but he took my camera and removed the shutter housing only to find the frosting. After he calmed down, he just shook his head in exasperation, and we assigned that one to the pile to be fixed later. The other people assigned to those platforms with spare cameras were shuttling in and out with cameras with problems also.

At the end of the day, we had just 12 cameras left functioning, and most of those had been through Art's shop once or twice. But, we made it, and as far as the shareholders and the attendant media were concerned, there were no problems. It was another Polaroid success and, for me, another story to tell my grandkids. We couldn't let Dr. Land down, and we didn't! The pictures taken that day were spectacular. They were displayed to the public at just about eye level by punching a hole in the pod, then slipping them into a slot in the railing around the edge of the platform, followed by about a 3/16-inch diameter pin being inserted through one side of the rail, through the pod hole and then through the other side of the rail. That left the picture area displayed above the top edge of the railing. The idea was not to lose any pictures since the product was not yet ready for release to the public. And, I think of the several hundred taken; only one picture was unaccounted for at the end of the day.

Another quality and photographic professional during this time frame was John Wolbarst. John had worked as editor at *Modern Photography*, covering all camera types, and had developed a keen interest in and knowledge of instant photography. His book *Pictures in a Minute* became a primer to help educate Polaroid photographers. Polaroid hired him as a senior manager in Customer Service in 1965.

One of Land's immutable design features for the SX-70 camera was full-frame focusing. In simple terms, a thumbwheel was used to bring the subject into focus, similar to a set of binoculars. As used in the SX-70 camera, it was a disaster –an expensive disaster. I recall clearly having difficulty using the system without producing blurry pictures; so did thousands of customers who returned the cameras to Wolbarst's shop for repair. Land steadfastly insisted the problem was education, not design. Wolbarst requested an audience with Land to present the need to change the focusing system. While the evidence was overwhelming, in both customer complaints and statistics, that Polaroid could not continue with the current design, Land resisted for several more months to authorize a viewfinder, a split-image range finder with cross hairs to assist the photographer. That new view-finder was an excellent solution; thousands of cameras were retrofitted after Land acquiesced and SX-70 started to build an enthusiastic user base.

According to Polaroid lore, while John Wolbarst continued a successful career at Polaroid, retiring at age 65 as a divisional vice president, Land never spoke to him again. Later in a chapter on Polavision, another strong individual will suffer the fate of disagreeing with Land. I suppose those born with genius traits probably aren't prone to lose graciously.

Chapter 11:
Land's Third Aim

The Type 108 and 107 pack films were hugely successful. Polaroid sales grew to $465 million by 1969; employee headcount rose to 9,000. Polaroid was the darling of Wall Street, a member of the elite "Nifty Fifty," with stock price to earnings per share (P/E) at greater than 50, reaching 91 in 1972. In today's investment community, companies with P/E ratios of greater than 15 are considered poor investments. While Land had the First and Second Aim related to making unique, useful products while ensuring employees' well-being, he also had a very firm commitment to build his company using profits as opposed to borrowing. Perhaps it was more the traditional business model of the 1960s, or maybe it was easy not to borrow when Polaroid's sales were growing and margins were strong. Polaroid had zero long-term debt during the 1960s and 1970s. I like to think of this concept as Land's Third Aim:

Polaroid is anything but a conventional corporate giant. It has no long-term debt, because Land is convinced that he should be "financially conservative and technologically audacious." (Time Magazine, June 26, 1972; Full Article, Appendix B)

55

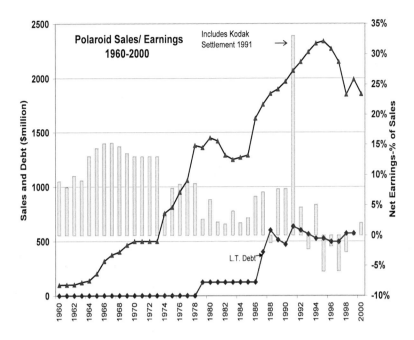

The decline of Polaroid started in 1980 when the company incurred its first debt. Over the next twenty years, the debt rose to nearly one billion dollars (combined short and long term) with bankruptcy on the horizon in 2001. The interest payment to service the loans was approximately $100 million per year, greatly reducing earnings. The chart above tracks Polaroid's sales and net earnings after taxes and adjustments (Source: Polaroid Annual Reports). The lower line is the debt in millions of dollars. The peak in earnings in 1991 was due to settlement of the Kodak patent suit. While the settlement was $925 million, the earnings included the portion ($872 million) not shared with the employees as the 1991 bonus. A later chapter will detail both the Kodak patent suit and the Shamrock hostile take-over attempt.

The chart defines the financial stewardship of Edwin Land. His leadership up to 1975 built a $1-billion company, providing capital for growth with profits. While financial analysts felt he overspent to develop the SX-70 program during the late 1960s and early '70s, he did it with Polaroid money. When Land stepped aside and Bill McCune became CEO, McCune leveraged the plants and machinery built for the SX-70 by developing lower cost cameras, the very successful 600 and Spectra camera and film lines. Starting in 1981, the 600 and Spectra film product and residual pack film sales provided approximately 70% of Polaroid's sales revenue and 100% of earnings. In trying to build a $2.5 billion company, and continually reacting to pressure from Wall Street, starting in 1979, Polaroid management began its journey into bankruptcy by breaking Land's Third Aim: Polaroid should be "financially conservative and technologically audacious."

Chapter 12:
Land's Princesses and Lieutenants

There are over five hundred patents in Edwin Land's name, second in the U.S. to Thomas Edison. Land certainly was a visionary, as evidenced by the way he created polarized sunglasses, instant imaging and other concepts. His leadership style was, however, completely autocratic. He surrounded himself with devoted followers who would do his bidding. While Land was building the company, he used trusted colleagues to run the day-to-day administrative side of Polaroid. When it came to product-related research and management, Land conceived concepts or inventions and his assistants in the laboratories carried out the experiments that either proved or disproved the theory. As related by Peter Wensberg in his book *LAND'S POLAROID*, Land had adopted a research style as a young man, where he would present himself with a "problem" or challenge, and then lock himself in the lab to work out experiments that would prove or disprove his theory:
.

> During his time at Polaroid, Land was notorious for his marathon research sessions. When Land conceived of an idea, he would experiment and brainstorm until the problem was solved, with no breaks of any kind. He needed to have food brought to him and to be reminded to eat. He once wore the same clothes for eighteen days straight while solving problems with the commercial production of polarizing film. As the Polaroid Company grew,

Land had teams of assistants working in shifts at his side. As one team wore out, the next team was brought in to continue the work. (LAND'S POLAROID, Peter Wensberg)

To carry out his research, Land recruited bright young people, many were women, often fresh out of college. The term "princesses" derived from an early group of liberal arts graduates from Smith College, namely Doxie Muller and Meroe Morse, who became students of Land after WWII, in the late 1940s when Land was fully engaged in developing the first instant product. In addition to being bright, the two women were also strikingly attractive; hence the unfortunate choice of the expression "princess." In the 1940s, perhaps the term was not considered offensive; however, as Land continued with this style of research, the women assigned to his personal laboratory were referred to as Land's "princesses." I'm not sure if Land was aware of the moniker.

Although I did not know either Doxie or Meroe, I did get to meet one of the later day laboratory assistants, Vivian Walworth. Vivian worked closely with Land for many years and joined him after he left Polaroid to establish the Rowland Foundation in Cambridge, dedicated to research on the perception of light and the vision-impaired. Ms. Walworth came to visit me around 1998, when I worked for a custom coating company in Worcester, Massachusetts She was seeking a company to provide unique coatings for 3-D type printing material. Although my company could not assist her research, we had a wonderful discussion and a delightful lunch of fried oysters at a nearby Irish pub. If there is an acceptable use today for "princess," Vivian would certainly fill the bill.

Marian Stanley, a 30-year employee who rose from Customer Service "letter writer" to vice president, captured the essence of Dr. Land's unique ability to get the best out of uncredentialed people in her May 16, 1996, Concord Oral History Program interview. (Full Text, Appendix F)

His corporate philosophy was that the company existed for two reasons. One, to create useful and exciting products, and, secondly, to bring the best out in people and give them useful, exciting work. This was called the dual aim or the two aims of the company. The first aim was exciting enough, but the second aim was very, very unusual in those times. We were constantly experimenting with different ways for people to contribute to the company, and it was important to create exciting jobs, but to also create exciting products. As a result he was able to do both.

For example, the man that invented color instant photography, since the first instant cameras were black and white, was a man named Howard Rogers. Howard Rogers was an automobile mechanic that Dr. Land thought was particularly skilled. He gave Howard a lab and money and told him to go away and develop color photography. Dr. Rogers went away. (Later, he was granted an honorary doctorate because he'd never even finished college). He came back some years later with not much heard from him in between-time, and said, "I think I've done it." And he had done it. Similarly, the people that worked in the laboratories were not credentialed. I ran a film program seven or eight years ago and the best scientists, if you consider empirical scientists, were his old lab techs who came to him out of the Navy or other such places and never had college educations. When I worked on the film program with them, it was so interesting. A couple still had tattoos up and down their arms. They understood the chemistry after working with him and so they understood empirically how the chemistry would react. It is really quite amazing. He believed that every person had enormous potential. Because he treated everyone that way, people responded.

The male counterparts to Land's lab assistants were "technical specialists" or "Land's lieutenants" in manufacturing. I worked with a few of them at Polaroid. They illustrate Land's need for control without teamwork or group input. Three high seniority employees, Frank Martin, Tom McCole and the previously mentioned Bud Ostberg had each proven to Dr. Land they were faithful to him and Polaroid. He used them to get straight to the manufacturing issues, by-passing the management chain. They had several things in common: each had a long history with Land; they were extremely loyal; they were not necessarily advanced schooled in science or engineering; and they were tough to deal with if you were reluctant to carry out their bidding. Insulated from management reporting structures, they could pick up the phone to Land if ever challenged by managers above their level; they never lost. If one of the three were to say "Let's call Din," you knew you were in trouble. (Din came from Land's sister's inability to pronounce Edwin). Only the inner circle dared the familiarity.

Ostberg was in charge of the black-and-white coating process in W1, the receiving sheet or positive film. Even 25 years after the first sale, it was a mystery to produce. Bertil "Bud" Ostberg was a tall, handsome individual, a delight to know; however, he was clearly in charge of the black-and-white coating process with absolute power.

My favorite Bud story is about an occurrence at a weekly quality review meeting during which suspect film was identified and released. The quality engineer from the adjacent test area in W2 would take samples of the black-and-white receiving sheet produced in W1 and match it with negative and developer in order to create mock-up black spreads. These spreads would highlight possible defects in the receiving sheet to allow culling out the bad sections.

Bud would take the defect spread, hold it at various angles to catch light reflection, and inform the group what the defect was and whether it was a W1 problem. He looked at this particular spread for several minutes, paused and handed it to his assistant, Bill O'Hara. "Hey, Bill," said Bud, "looks like a QC tech's fingerprint to me. What do you think?" Bill agreed, and the QC engineer returned to W2 shaking his head, while the W1 entourage strained to control their laughter. Of course it wasn't a finger print, but the engineer knew better than to challenge Bud.

I also worked with Tom Mccole in the Battery Division and Frank Martin in Developer Manufacturing. While they were similar to Bud in sometimes overusing their power, actually it was the potential to use this power that made them so effective in producing results. This was consistent with one of Land's interesting expressions: "The most important thing about power is to make sure you don't have to use it." Ostberg, McCole and Martin, in a unique way, helped bring Land's laboratory concepts into manufacturing in a role similar to the princesses.

The use of "Princesses" and "Lieutenants" to carry out his bidding and disdain for corporate structure is best illustrated in a speech he gave at MIT in 1957, "Generations of Greatness." Land said college education was destroying the dream each student had of "greatness," that is, an original contribution. Group research and "community progress" must not take over. In a democracy, one must cooperate, but democracy's "peculiar gift is to develop each individual into everything he might be. If the dream of personal greatness died," he said, "democracy loses the real source of its future strength." He wanted arriving students to be assigned an "usher," an experienced researcher, and to be launched at once on research. Drawing from his life, Land said that "education must produce people who, no matter how tightly they conformed to the innumerable commands of society, would find one domain where they would make a revolution. Students should go as rapidly as possible through all the intellectual accumulations."

To work in his inner circle, you were expected to be available during all hours of the workweek and weekend. Often times, the concepts were based on Land's intuition with some loosely held scientific foundation. Almost all the major product introductions under Land were sent to market unready for commercialization. Possibly another example of Land's unique brilliance was his ability to keep customer excitement and anticipation for Polaroid products for over 25 years, since the first instant product in 1950. Polaroid prospered under the classic "pull" market during these years. The manufacturing and development costs to correct or recall the poor quality early releases were dwarfed by the wonderful profit margins of instant film. When Polaroid became a "push" market in the mid-80s with teddy bears and airplane ticket promotions more exciting to the customers than the instant film, the death knell to Polaroid resonated clearly – all long before the digital age.

Chapter 13:
Land's Big Product Failure – Polavision

The Tiger-Rover project was the first of two projects of Land that were failures. "Rover" was an exciting idea of Land's, a vision where every office worker could have an inexpensive copy machine on his or her desk. Polaroid would build the copier, and of course make huge profits on the sale of Polaroid exclusive copy paper. The "Tiger" machine would produce the paper. Land reluctantly agreed with his close-in advisors that the cost of the early prototypes was too far off the planned less-than-$100 selling price to ever be commercial. Technical issues plagued the copy paper as well. I was originally hired to work on the project based on my prior experience in coating. The program was cancelled the week before I was hired, so I was assigned to the chemical plant and then later W1. My supervisor in W1 was plant manager Bob Malster, one of the most intelligent, enthusiastic managers I have encountered. Bob had been program leader on the failed Rover project and was respected by Land, having worked closely with Land early in his career at Polaroid.

A few years after the closedown of Rover, Land contacted Malster. As Bob related the story, Dr. Land picked him up in a limousine one day in the early 1970s. Land, with full enthusiasm, described his latest "vision": instant movies or "Polavision." He offered Bob the program leadership position. As bright as Bob was, he was equally forthright. He made a career-changing decision – he graciously declined. Bob was a keen observer of technical developments and informed Land

64

that black-and-white video systems were very near commercialization and would soon evolve into color versions, negating the potential market for Polavision. Bob never confided in me Land's counter arguments; Land was not one to debate with underlings. Bob spent the last few years of his Polaroid career in an internal consulting role, never again in the limelight. Quite a waste in my opinion, as I believe Malster probably understood the instant film chemical reactions as well as anyone, including Land.

Polavision was an expensive flop, the first really major loss in Land's portfolio. The film was incredibly complicated to produce – more so than the very magical Polaroid instant negative. The film speed was under 25, similar to the quality of 1930s movies. I recall visiting a warehouse in the mid-'70s, observing all these boxes with German printing on them. They were the Polavision players, built by our Austrian partner. I also recall the write-down of $65 million one year, small by comparison to the later product boondoggles; but, in contrast to those failures, Polavision was funded out of current earnings, so it did not burden the company's future, as the SX-70 program was starting to contribute excellent profits.

Ironically, the instant movie fiasco was the first occasion where digital imaging helped lead to the eventual demise of Polaroid. From the 1970s digital camcorders to the 1990s still prints, digital development helped put the nail in the growth of instant film. While Polavision did not excessively tax financial resources, its failure did indeed remove the only visionary leader Polaroid had at the executive level. Where Land had managed to give up Rover of his own accord, the board of directors fought him heavily on Polavision. Land stubbornly resisted the board's counsel to shut down the instant movies venture. Instead, he relinquished the CEO position to William McCune, staying on as project leader of Polavision.

As Polaroid lore goes, when the subject of Polavision was being debated during one of Land's last board meetings, Land left the room for a break. Board member, Ken Olsen, founder of Digital Equipment and one of the outspoken opponents of Polavision, locked Land out of his own boardroom. The remaining members voted to stop work on Polavision. Not long after, Dr. Land announced his retirement and plans to start a new independent venture, the Rowland foundation, not surprisingly devoted to the concept of researching novel techniques for the vision-impaired. Polaroid certainly lost its vision with his leaving.

A former Polaroid marketing consultant, Paul Giambarba, who had initiated Polaroid's corporate-image development and product identity in 1958, remarked about the new Polavision system: "I tried using the product, but it was obviously a turkey compared to anything I was using that Kodak offered. Instant movie film was an engineering achievement, but it's precisely what separated Polaroid techies from Polaroid pragmatists. There just weren't enough customers out there on whom to work the magic."

Many insiders at Polaroid believed the strong difference of opinion on Polavision between McCune and Land created a rift between the longtime associates that would never heal. A later chapter will describe McCune's disappointment in Polavision.

Chapter 14:
The Polaroid Flat Battery – Land's Pet Project

While there are over 500 patents held by Edwin Land, three product groupings contain the vast majority: polarized films and devices, instant film products, and – surprise – batteries. When the development of the SX-70 integral film product was well under way, Dr. Land decided to incorporate a battery in the film pack. Land was project leader in the development of this innovative power source and was granted many patents relating to the battery. The Polaroid flat battery was a prime example of Dr. Land's fearless approach to challenging existing science with his own set of rules. Commercial batteries in the 1960s were typically round. Polaroid's had to be flat to match the landscape and geometry of the film pack. The flatness requirement ultimately provided a tremendous benefit to the performance of the battery, as having the anode and cathode electrodes facing each other allowed much higher energy discharge than conventional round cells.

Several battery manufacturers were asked to bid on producing a 6-volt flat battery, using Leclanché cell (carbon-zinc) chemistry, which was the technology of the standard dry-cell battery used in flashlights, etc. In addition to having six volts, the battery would have low internal resistance, high reliability, and a cost of six cents each. Ray-O-Vac of Appleton, Wisconsin, was the successful bidder; and, by 1970, had installed equipment at their factory and developed a process to produce the first-generation battery. Polaroid and Ray-O-Vac formed a partnership that resulted in many Polaroid employees relocating to Appleton to bring the new product on line. The intensity and importance of the entire SX-70 program resulted in Max Lawrence of Polaroid taking up residence in Appleton to manage the combined R.O.V.-Polaroid effort. Dr. Sheldon Buckler was Polaroid's senior officer on the program reporting to Dr. Land. Dr. Buckler would lead the company through several generations of batteries.

SX-70 went to market in 1972 using the R.O.V. battery. The battery performed as advertised relative to energy; however manufacturing yields were poor and the six-cents-cost goal did not materialize. Customer failures were also at an unacceptable level. In retrospect, the R.O.V. machine attempted to combine too many steps in one. A design flaw that eventually caused the machine to be replaced was the slitting step that separated the finished batteries with rotary metallic blades. If cutting was not done perfectly, the blade would short between cells and destroy the battery or, on occasion, cause a fire.

The R.O.V. battery machine supplied batteries during the first few years of SX-70 production. When the yield problem and slitting concerns were not showing the required improvement, it was decided to redesign the process into a more manageable operation. The battery failures were near catastrophic at the customer level. While many of the failures would occur before insertion in the film pack, others would happen after the film had been sold to the customer. As a short-term solution to the problem, batteries were stored in the warehouse for three months to allow the bad batteries to die and be culled before assembly in the film pack. Even then, about 5-10% would fail in the customers' cameras. Experienced Polaroid photographers developed techniques whereby, if the camera didn't operate because of a dead battery, they would go into a dark closet and slide a new battery into the pack without exposing the film to light.

This major problem led to the creation of the Automatic Battery Assembly Machine, or ABAM, which was built and put online in Polaroid's own facilities. The ABAM used the same webs from R.O.V., but the slitting was done before assembly, thus avoiding the shorting problem. A total of seven ABAMs were built, each capable of making one battery at a time at the rate of 140 batteries per minute. By the mid-1970s, each ABAM was producing approximately 30 million batteries per year. The first three machines were installed at 45 Fourth Avenue in Waltham. Although many people were involved in this program, Louis Bruneau and Bob Keene, from Polaroid's Engineering Division, were considered by most to be the designers and guiding spirit of the ABAMs.

The ABAMs increased the production yield and lowered the cost significantly; however, reliability at the time of use by the customer continued as a concern because of difficulty in sealing the edges of the flat battery to contain the battery chemicals. So, the aging of the batteries continued in the warehouse for the three months before assembly in the film pack. To improve the battery seals, Dr. Land and his team invented a unique vent for the battery assembly which allowed hydrogen gas to escape, relieving pressure on the seals. While the vent alleviated the seal problem, there was now evidence the vented gasses were contaminating the photographic film. Again, Land developed another addition to the battery, a "getter" that absorbed the gasses and eliminated the contamination. At about this point, many Polaroid executives developed a strong distaste for anything (and anybody) related to the Polaroid battery. Later chapters will expand on the challenges the Polaroid flat battery placed on the company.

As SX-70 sales increased, the additional machines required more space. W45F contained ABAMs 1, 2, and 3. To provide space for electrical testing, 186 Third Avenue in Waltham was rented. R5 was constructed a mile from W45 Fourth Avenue on Winter Street in 1977-78 and became the home of ABAMs 4, 5, 6, and 7. By 1980, the three buildings contained about 700 people. On a good day, about 700,000 batteries were produced by the seven machines. A number 8 ABAM was planned but was never installed.

The first SX-70 cameras had a flash bar triggered by a low energy electrical impulse; hence, the battery mainly had to power the motor drive and electronics. When the 600 Star cameras incorporated a strobe, the battery was required to charge a capacitor at high amperage to minimize recharge time, about four seconds. Polaroid loved customers who rapid fired film every four seconds. The 600 strobe system required approximately four times more energy than the original SX-70 camera. Although the P70 battery could power the 600 system, there was little margin for someone using a two-year-old pack of film in cold weather. If the battery had high internal resistance, the recharge time was increased. Studies had shown then that customers did not want to wait much more than 10 seconds to take the next picture.

The need to pack more energy into the battery (and reduce internal resistance) led to the development of the third-generation battery – the P80 and its assembly equipment, notably the RBAM (Rotary Battery Assembly Machine). While the P80 was being developed, the 600 Camera was introduced along with a modified P70 battery called Bigfoot. This battery had the same external dimensions as P70 but packed more chemicals into the electrodes. This provided sufficient energy for the strobe. However, it was difficult to contain the additional chemicals, and high failure rates resulted during manufacturing and customer use. Bigfoot was a product for about three years.

By early 1985, the P80 process was performing well enough to cease ABAM production. There was much discussion on this, considering that the P70 could power the SX-70 (TZ) cameras, which accounted for approximately 15% of the battery requirements at the time. The decision finally to phase out P70 was based on quality. The first few years of P80 had a failure rate at least four times lower than P70. The adhesive in P70 would be difficult to improve on the existing ABAMs, and thus poor seals would continue to be a problem. Additionally, there was considerable dependence on non-Polaroid suppliers with P70, while P80 placed more manufacturing within Polaroid.

The P80 battery development was another example of Polaroid scientists, engineers, tradesmen and manufacturing groups combining to create a unique process unlike anything existing in the battery industry at the time. The previous ABAMs employed what was referred to as "pick and place", intermittent motion machinery stamping out one battery at time; the RBAM produced four batteries side by side, as a continuous web. The capacity of the machine, when initial start-up issues were resolved, would be 500,000 batteries a day, compared to the 100,000 per day produced by each ABAM. The program leader, working under direction of Dr. Buckler, was Vince Merry. Knowing and working with Vince made up a special time in my Polaroid life. Scientifically trained and organizationally gifted, Vince worked with the zeal and passion of Land. He lacked the ego issues of the company founder and worked to build a team environment. He died from heart failure, brought on by kidney failure, working at his desk late one evening, laying out the plans for Polaroid's new battery prototype. He was 37 years old.

Bob Keene was the key engineering designer of the state-of-the-art, one-of-a-kind RBAM. Many on his team made contributions: Ron Fawcett, Jim Stevens, and John Kennedy come to mind. The manufacturing efforts, including the building of plants and infrastructure to support the battery operations were led by Division Manager Al Hyland with his staff: Bob Jacobs, Plant Manager; Bill Wilson as R5 Program Manager and Manufacturing Manager; Doug Holmes, Technical Director; Bob Wolf, Purchasing Manager; Dave Clifford as Quality Manager. I was Engineering Manager. An unsung hero in the Battery Division's history was Frank Ceppi, Quality Manager for more than a decade from 1985-96. Frank, with his diligent oversight of the battery quality department, developed a tight discipline on change control, preventing the mistakes in process or material substitutions which plagued the division from its inception.

Paul Plasse developed an excellent team, the Battery Development Laboratory (BDL), to support the division by designing and testing the webs and chemicals used in the P80 battery. Paul was a Polaroid treasure, having many of the characteristics of Dr. Land – a hard-driving combination of a scientific-empirical inventor. Paul developed several excellent scientists: Kasey Norvaisa, Alfredo Kniazzeh, Dennis Mailloux and David Kennedy, who went on to fine careers at Polaroid after BDL was dissolved.

Over time, all of the Battery staff moved on to other assignments in the company. The moves were not always voluntary, as continued upsets with the battery caused Film Division management to search for new folks to run the battery operations. Instead of "relocating" the managers, the company might have been better served if it had relocated the battery from the film pack into the camera. By the early 1980s, the commercial battery industry had solved all the original concerns that caused Land to make his own flat battery. Additionally, newer alkaline and lithium batteries (including rechargeable NiCad,) were now available that could have efficiently managed the power requirements of the camera. A later chapter will explain my futile attempt to bring about this change.

I was the last of Hyland's staff to leave, actually be "relocated" from the Battery Division. I had cycled through each of the staff positions; after Engineering Manager, I was the Manufacturing Manager during start-up of the RBAM, finally Technical Manager, after a multi-million-dollar battery disaster. Gary Levy replaced Bob Jacobs as plant manager and did a fine job guiding us through the phase-in of the RBAM as the sole source for batteries, ABAMs removed. When Gary was promoted to Polaroid's Corporate Director of Materials, I served as acting Plant Manager for several months. I was told by my boss, Ed Coughlan, Film Division Director, that his supervisor, Joe Oldfield, felt I was too set in my ways and too politically insensitive to be manager of the battery plant. Janet Cramer, an up-and coming-manager, got the job. I was promoted to Worldwide Director of Materials for Film Assembly – a disappointment for me, as my preferred job was the Plant Manger assignment.

The choice of Janet was a good one. She brought a refreshing, much-needed change to the plant. The RBAM had been struggling with run-time issues that the engineers, mechanics and I could not solve without assistance from the machine operators. Many of the machine operators were women. They, along with their male counterparts, rallied behind Janet's leadership. Within a few months into Janet's assignment, the RBAM was setting records for productivity. Janet went on to manage the larger film-assembly plant and eventually was promoted to divisional vice president in the DiCamillo Polaroid.

My new assignment, as materials director, allowed me to see much more of Polaroid, providing me with numerous insights used in this book. Oldfield was certainly correct in my lack of political sensitivity at Polaroid, as will be demonstrated in subsequent chapters.

Chapter 15:
Edwin H. Land – Philosopher-Patriot

Polaroid started out as Land-Wheelwright Laboratories in 1933, based on Land's invention of the first synthetic sheet polarizer in 1929. Polaroid Corporation was founded in 1937, producing polarizing material for Kodak camera filters and polarized sun glasses. Combined with minimal sales of Polaroid stereoscopic (3D) motion pictures used at the 1939 New York World's Fair, Polaroid sales reached $1 million in 1941. When Polaroid glasses found acceptance in the desert battles of World War II, Land and Polaroid started a long-term relationship with the U.S. government, as both supplier to the war effort and as a "think tank" invited to bid on several highly-challenging projects. In 1941, Land and his team outbid several groups to produce a working model of an optical instrument to measure the elevation of an airplane above the horizon. This led to unique field goggles, airplane windshields and the first heat-sensing attachment to bombs. By the end of WW II, Polaroid sales grew to $16 million. A detailed chronology of the early Polaroid appears in Appendix A.

My goal in this chapter is to capture some of the characteristics of Land that drove him to be both a great inventor as well as a philosopher. The following examples highlight some of the unique concepts Land harbored on various subjects. His quotations and viewpoints on education, marketing and finance are unique and, often, visionary, having application in the current world.

Edwin H. Land died on March 1, 1991, at the age of 82.

74

Philosophy and Quotes of Land:

The University and the Student

He is given courses, he is instantly given tests, and he is given examinations. Now I ask you, if this is preparation for life, tell me where, where in the world, where in the relationship with our colleagues, where in the industrial domain, wherever again, anywhere in life, is a person given this curious sequence of prepared talks and prepared questions, questions to which the answers are known? Where again is he ever marked in this way? Where again is a structure of authoritarianism masked by the genuine friendliness of the democratic people who are his leaders? Wherever again is a person brought to the Day of Judgment every single week?

The above excerpt is from a speech Land gave at MIT in 1957. He built a case that conventional universities did not serve students very well in preparing them for work in the scientific or engineering fields. At MIT, the speech was a prime motivator for the development of UROP (Undergraduate Research Opportunities Program), although UROP addressed only a fraction of Land's vision and there was a 12-year gap between the lecture and the launch of the UROP program. Worcester Polytechnic Institute, my alma mater, also adopted a plan in the 1980s to move away from conventional course work and grading, focusing on project work with a faculty sponsor similar to Land's vision in 1957.

The Scientific World

-We work by exorcising incessant superstition that there are mysterious tribal gods against you. Nature has neither rewards nor punishments, only consequences. You can use science to make it work for you.

-An essential aspect of creativity is not being afraid to fail. Any problem can be solved using the materials in the room.

-Creativity is the sudden cessation of stupidity.

-Don't do anything that someone else can do. Don't undertake a project unless it is manifestly important and nearly impossible.

-Science is a method to keep yourself from kidding yourself.

-What we don't know, that's what we'll teach ourselves.

View of the Educational System

There's a rule they don't teach you at Harvard Business School. It is: if anything is worth doing, it's worth doing to excess.

Disdain for Teams

-Politeness is the poison of collaboration.

-The most important thing about power is to make sure you don't have to use it."

Disdain for Marketing:

- It's not that we need new ideas, but we need to stop having old ideas. Marketing is what you do when your product is no good.

- We give people products they do not even know they want, so why should we invest in market research?

- All of our confidence has to come from making things. Let us not make more of something there is too much of. Let us find out what is desperately needed, although people may not know it. Let us find out what will beautify the world, although people may not know it. Then let's learn and learn and teach ourselves, and support each other in doing that until we lose ourselves in those tasks. (February 1960 Polaroid Annual Report)

Some Polaroid followers describe this anti-marketing, anti-customer stance as somewhat arrogant and the reason Land's success at Polaroid ended with the SX-70 program. Land did not want to degrade his superb SX-70 camera with low-cost models. Fortunately, Bill McCune understood the market for the very successful 600 and OneStep camera lines that generated the major sales during the late '70s.

Disdain for Financial Analysts
The only thing that matters is the bottom line? What a presumptuous thing to say. The bottom line's in heaven. The real business of business is building things.

Land was responding to an analyst's question at the 1977 annual stockholders meeting.

Land's Vision of the SX-70 Camera Becoming as Common as the Telephone

Dear Shareholder:

This annual report, like those of all dynamic companies, must have a Bergsonian flavor: the present is the past biting into the future. The "present" for Polaroid is the time of transition from the whole ten-year period of conceptualization and embodiment of SX-70, to the "future" in which millions of people will be learning to achieve with SX-70 new kinds of insights, photographic competences and rewards. It is as if the telephone company, having learned to build instruments, transmission lines and switching stations, suddenly stood ready to encourage people to try talking over the system in order to find new ways in which people's lives could be enriched by the use of the telephone.
It is one thing to imagine the future in order to design an instrument for the future; it is quite another thing, having built the instrument, to undertake the new and satisfying task of teaching people the hundreds of ways in which the instrument has individual meaning for every individual. Thus, standing in the present, we must take a 180-degree turn from the past in which we built SX-70, toward the future in which

77

we initiate the new adventure of worldwide enjoyment of the SX-70 experience. Just as the "product" of the telephone company is conversations (not instruments) so our "product" is neither mechanism nor film –our product is visual conversation between the photographer and the total scene of objects and people with which he is involved – the picture itself becoming the reiterative reminder of the pleasure of taking it.

Now that we have the competence to meet promptly any demand for the SX-70 system, we look forward enthusiastically to making it an integral part of daily life. (E.H. Land, Polaroid Annual Report for 1973)

Land's exciting vision was of his SX-70 becoming so popular that every household in America would have one, just as most homes had a telephone. Ironically, Land's vision was correct, but somewhat in the inverse: most households have a phone –a cell phone that takes photographs – digital, that can be seen instantly! Bergsonian refers to 19th-century French philosopher Henri Bergson, whose philosophy asserts that the flow of time personally experienced is free and unrestricted, rather than measured on a clock and contends that all living forms arise from a persisting natural force – the "élan vital." Land embraced this concept when setting about on a project. He didn't need project plans or teams to manage his inventions – take the 5,000 steps and the invention would occur almost magically

Love of Photography
Every good picture we take – one that is taken with care – should make our lives that much bigger. Photography is an illustration of the use of technology not to estrange, but to reveal and unite people.

Land in 1972 Time Magazine Article before His SX-70 Was Released

I think the new camera can have an impact on the way people live. I hope it can become a natural part of people. It can make a person pause in his rush through life. It will help him to focus himself on some aspect of life and, in the process, enrich his life at that moment. This happens as you focus through the view finder. It's not merely the camera you are focusing; you are focusing yourself. That's an integration of your personality, right that second. Then, when you touch the button, what's inside you comes out. It's the most basic form of creativity. Part of you is now permanent.

Intersection of Science and Art – Land's 1980 "Letter to Shareholders"

There seem to be two modes of integration. The first is anchored in the concept of a field which is wonderful, new, useful, technically exciting and socially delightful. The second mode of integration is in terms of quasi-moral maxims: Do not undertake the program unless the goal is manifestly important and its achievement nearly impossible; do not do anything that anyone else can do readily; industry should be the intersection of science and art; the second great product of industry should be the fully rewarding working life for every person; the most intelligent use of a science requires understanding that comes only from increasing the knowledge in that science; it is relatively easy to organize a company with a homogeneous set of good minds, but the ultimate greatness of a company depends on the variety of kinds of good minds within it.

Land's altruistic view of company employees, described previously, was often contradicted by his actions. While he may have wanted a challenging workplace for the hourly workers, Land's managerial motto was, as Bill McCune stated, "You can do anything you want to – as long as you do what I want."

Chapter 16:
Land's Legacy

There are two portraits in my office. One of Jack and Bobby Kennedy hangs next to a panorama of Edwin Herbert Land, Celebration of His Life, September 2, 1991. I receive inspiration from both: the Kennedy brothers, in 1962, who would attempt to lead the United States to a better place, with a fearless vision built on equality and prosperity for all Americans; the genius Land, who built a fantastic company with a strong sense of equality for all who worked at Polaroid. One evening in April 1968, Dr. Land visited the night shift in the large cafeteria in the Route 128 Waltham plant. It was 11:00 p.m., and the supervisors in the W2-3 buildings were instructed to have the employees meet with Land. This was not unusual, as Land often visited the work sites to explain some new pay plans or similar topics. As Peter Wensberg describes in his book:

As Land stood up, the noise in the room died, with a curious ripple of surprise. He was not like his pictures. He was short. He wore a topcoat against the chilly room. He was not going to talk about pay. He looked at them, and silence pulled tightly across the room. "Martin Luther King is dead," he told them. They were surprised to hear this, not because they had not heard the news – it had been the biggest story in Boston for the past thirty hours. The surprise was this meeting, Land telling this predominantly white audience of workers something they knew already. Land telling

80

them. What was it all about? The black members of the shift were the most surprised.

Land talked without a microphone to the silent crowd. He told them that the events of the past day marked a crisis point in American society. He told them that Polaroid was a leader and a model of American industry. He asked for their help in bringing more black workers into Polaroid and, as the astonishment of his audience deepened, he asked them if the company's goal should not be to train and promote black workers to achieve parity with the other Polaroid workers, equivalent to their percentage of the Boston population, about 10 percent – Land paused – at all levels of the company. He said that, since Polaroid was growing so rapidly, he believed this would not impose a hardship on anyone, and that Polaroid was the ideal company to take the lead since there was more than enough opportunity for everyone. When he stopped talking the silence stretched tighter than before. Then applause scattered across the room as Land got slowly down from the table. The meeting was over. The C shift walked out without saying much, heading for their cars in the parking lot under bare maple trees. They hadn't said yes to Land's question. But they hadn't said no.

Land's sense of equality for all his employees was sincere, as he backed up the 10% black commitment with a novel employee training center in Roxbury, a predominately black community in the greater Boston area. Called "Inner City," the operation provided opportunities for minority members of all ages to learn manufacturing skills while also establishing a consistent work record. The various divisions would provide real work opportunities such as packaging or re-packaging film or cameras. Initially, the site was managed by a white member of Polaroid; after a few years, black members of Polaroid would take on leadership positions, providing a training opportunity for black managers. As Inner City's reputation spread, other companies in the area would hire some of the graduates. Since 1968, more than 1,500 Inner City graduates have been placed in permanent jobs. Data gathered from employer and graduate surveys found that approximately 60% of the Inner City graduates were still employed with their original companies at the time of the survey. The Inner City operation was highly successful for over 30 years, disbanding in early 2001 as Polaroid approached bankruptcy. I questioned several Polaroid retirees on their recollections of Inner City. Elaine Savage summed up the consensus opinion nicely:

I had worked for Jim Myers at 620 Memorial Drive, Cambridge. In 1974 when a secretarial position became available, I went to work for Jim Myers at Inner City, Inc., on Columbus Ave. I also worked for managers Jim Hayes followed by, I believe his name was, George O'Neil. When I left in 1977, I think they had around 100 trainees. At the time, it was truly a remarkable place with a very dedicated, small staff. The three years I worked at Inner City was one of the best experiences I had at Polaroid.

According to Time Magazine, June 27, 1972:

A more controversial segment of Polaroid's race relations involved use of Polaroid film in South Africa to control movement of blacks – apartheid. In October 1970, a dozen black-militant employees tacked up posters on Polaroid bulletin boards accusing the company of supporting apartheid in South Africa by allowing its cameras and film to be used in internal passports and by paying much lower wages there to blacks than whites. The charges turned out to be embarrassingly accurate. Even though the Polaroid operation in South Africa was owned by an independent distributor, rather than by the parent corporation, Land was deeply hurt by the employee protest. He decided on a novel solution: he asked a small group of four employees, including blacks, to visit South Africa and study the case. "Your decision will be implemented, whatever it is," he promised. The group eventually agreed unanimously to stop selling to the government but to continue other operations in South Africa, while ordering Polaroid's distributor to upgrade black wages.

Chapter 17:
Land's 1981 Message to Shareholders

Edwin H. Land built Polaroid very close to his own self-image of dedicated scientist and humanitarian philosopher. Land's Message to Shareholders in the 1981 Annual Report, his last as CEO of Polaroid, provides an excellent insight into the complex genius of Edwin H. Land. He reveals his philosophy on a number of issues: the prolonged Iran hostage crisis, the high inflation and interest rates, and the emergence of Japan as a viable competitor. He was also challenging America in 1981 to learn from the Japanese, get off our butts and take charge again. While Land's focus was on the photographic world, his vision also applied to the automotive industry. The lousy, rusty 1981 Hondas and Toyotas emerged in the next decades as the very successful Accord and Camry, while General Motors and Chrysler spiraled into bankruptcy.

Somewhat hidden in the eloquent prose is his concept of the organizers of ideas-inventors vs. organizers of people – managers. He was reminding Bill McCune and the board of directors that the inventors were more important than the managers or concluders.

Land never recovered from the shoddy treatment he received from the BOD over the failure of Polavision. Unfortunately for the future of Polaroid, Land was never replaced. His 1981 Message to Shareholders was describing how Polaroid would fail without him or other inventors. For the next 20 years, Polaroid would be managed, not led. Land was essentially predicting the failure of the great company he founded and led for 50 years. Land's address follows:

As I write to you this year, Cambridge is immersed in a wonderful augury: the barometric pressure is at a record high, the air is cleaner, the stars brighter, and a sense of inspiration and hope that is the chemical consequence of such an atmosphere drives away our hard won sense of national doom. Here at Polaroid, our loyal New England effort to join the country in seeing things at their worst is being frustrated by the fact that both technically and financially we have had a pretty good year. All these irresistible harbingers of spring lead me to review and examine our early dreams of an ideal industry to see how they should be restated to serve us best for the next decade.

There seem to be two modes of integration. The first is anchored in the concept of a field which is wonderful, new, useful, technically exciting and socially delightful. The second mode of integration is in terms of quasi-moral maxims: Do not undertake the program unless the goal is manifestly important and its achievement nearly impossible; Do not do anything that anyone else can do readily; Industry should be the intersection of science and art; The second great product of industry should be the fully rewarding working life for every person; The most intelligent use of a science requires understanding that comes only from increasing the knowledge in that science. It is relatively easy to organize a company with a homogeneous set of good minds but the ultimate greatness of a company depends on the variety of kinds of good minds within it. Subject to all these criteria, and after budgeting generously and precisely for a non-profit and charitable domain, projects should be so managed as to make a generous profit, but no project should be selected merely on the basis of making a profit. There are men who organize ideas and men who organize people. It is the duty of the latter to protect the power of the former.

While exquisite precaution is required in the control of the massive sums spent in the final stages of manufacturing, distributing and advertising, as well as talent and inspiration, these later stages of corporate life are completely dependent on the profundity and validity of the initiating ideas. The significance of the initiator must not be hidden by the grandeur in scale of the concluders.

Needless to say, these are not preachments for others nor ideals which we achieve ourselves, but they are the guides and goals which hold us together and give us our strength and confidence. A distinguished Japanese executive pointed out recently that every Japanese product has started with what Japan learned from our industry. To that learning, she added her own special genius, while we stood still. Everything we know about the democracy we all live for would seem to teach that peoples are enough alike that mimetic learning on a national scale can exist.

Now it is our turn to transfer from the Japanese to our own activity the sense of perfection in detail as a source of beauty and strength. Is it not exciting to discover that without special training, without art history, without tutoring in technological or aesthetic detail, people in the mass recognize and value those excellences which the Japanese have added to many western products? Presently, we shall stand on their shoulders for our kind of accomplishments, just as they have stood on our shoulders for their kind of accomplishments. And the world will be a better world.

As a shareholder, you will remember that our own contributions to photography, to cameras, to film and to processes are pioneering and unique. For example, we were the first to design and manufacture the kind of electronic shutters most widely used today in cameras of all kinds. We designed the first folding reflex camera and the first acoustic rangefinder for automatically focusing lenses. All instant color pictures use pods, viscous reagents, fully formed dyes transferred from the negative to the positive, stratified control of the alkalinity of the interacting layers, pods which are moved with the negative and positive through the rollers to break the pod and spread the reagent between containing sheets with dry outside surfaces, and so on. All these and many, many more are our contributions.

In gathering our strength for a vigorous drive into the future, it is important for all of us to remember that it was we who generated the great revolution in photography, in concept, in detail and in implementation, and that the attitudes and kind of people responsible for our past can be relied on to create a future that is open-ended.   (E.H. Land, 1982
"Message to Shareholders")

Land's eloquent address to stockholders described not only the position Polaroid found itself in as the he left the company he founded, but also provided a vision for American industry. Land lamented the way the U.S. had allowed the Japanese to overtake us in improving products of the Western World. He was prodding Americans to learn from the Japanese and re-take our leadership position. Land believed the companies who provided simple, "me-too" products, always looking to profits, would not prosper in the future – inventors and scientists would be needed, not managers.

Steve Jobs, the founder of Apple Computer, had a mindset similar to Land. Jobs started building his successful company about the same time Land was pushed out of his.

Chapter 18:
Steve Jobs and Edwin Land

Steven Jobs of Apple, a fan of Dr. Land, went to Polaroid in 1985 to meet Land and tour Polaroid's automated camera assembly plant. In October 2011, after Jobs' death, I corresponded with Steven Syre, a Boston Globe columnist, who had reported on Polaroid for many years. He has allowed me to include his excellent article, describing the relationship of the two geniuses:

Steve Jobs' greatest gift was an extraordinary ability to imagine new products that would completely capture the public's heart. Jobs proved himself many times on that score; as a young man, with the creation of the Macintosh computer, and, later, with products like the iPhone and the iPad. Talent like that is extraordinarily rare. But Jobs clearly saw similar qualities in another kind of innovator from another generation: Edwin Land, the late founder of Polaroid Corp. As it happened, both men met at Land's office in Cambridge in the mid-1980s and talked at length about that creative process at the intersection of art and technology.

There were remarkable parallels in the careers of Jobs and Land, a pair of college dropouts with big ideas. Both were driven, demanding, and stubborn – qualities that led them to great things, but also got both into trouble at the companies they created. They

88

envisioned products that were technically sophisticated, but also sparked a sense of excitement among the millions who had to have them. Steve Jobs and Edwin Land shared a connection as iconoclasts who understood consumers. Jobs, in his 20s at the time, was selling the new Macintosh computer. He had recruited John Sculley, the former PepsiCo chief, to Apple with the famous line about choosing between selling sugar water and an opportunity to change the world. Land was in his 70s. The glory days of Polaroid's original instant photography camera – a true sensation in its time – were behind him. He had been pushed out of the company he'd founded, but continued to work at a lab in Cambridge.

The meeting between Jobs and Land went on for hours. It had been arranged by Tom Hughes, the art director for Macintosh who once worked for the Polaroid founder. Sculley came along to meet Land. "I think they agreed that what each of them did was to turn technology into magic," Sculley recalled yesterday. "It was magical when you could create an instant photo. It was magical when Steve created the Macintosh. So these were two geniuses who totally understood each other from the vantage point that they knew how to take technology and transform it into magic." Land described a sense of not inventing something so much as discovering it. The camera and the concept of instant photography had existed all along, and he was simply the one who was able to see that. Jobs felt the same way about Macintosh.

"On an emotional level, I did see a side of Steve with Dr. Land I had not seen before," Hughes told me yesterday. "It was sort of a father and son reunion. Steve was so clearly in admiration of Dr. Land and taken with every word he had to share. It was a very touching moment in time."

Jobs himself spoke about Land in a 1985 magazine interview with Playboy. "Eventually Dr. Land, one of those brilliant troublemakers, was asked to leave his own company – which is one of the dumbest things I've ever heard of," he said. Jobs – a brilliant troublemaker in his own right, was pushed out of Apple months later. Polaroid drifted after Land's departure, and eventually filed for bankruptcy. Apple also fell on hard times after the Jobs exit, but the company revived when its founder returned to lead it again. Jobs and Land shared a creative gift that gave the world products it had to have. Call it genius or call it magic. You can't replace that. (Steven Syre, the Boston Globe, October 7, 2011)

Upon researching Steven Jobs further, I concluded that while he and Land had several common traits, they had one major difference: Jobs sought to work with only "A" players –high energy, forceful people; Land trusted only "B" players that would carry out his bidding. Recall, in earlier chapters, his use of the princesses and lieutenants to conduct his experiments, his stubbornness over Polavision, and his disdain for teams and marketing.

While I'll always be a great admirer of Dr. Land and be grateful for the great, rewarding work life he created for me and thousands of Polaroid colleagues, I do wonder whether Polaroid would have continued to be a great company if Land allowed other strong leaders, or "A" players, to manage Polaroid's business while he created Polaroid inventions.

SECTION 2: William McCune

One of the interesting things about Land was that his great achievements really were around solving problems. He didn't invent something by having some extraneous idea and then trying to find a use for it. He set about to solve a problem. (Bill McCune, Concord Oral History Program, July 11, 1996)

Bill McCune in 1958 in his Porsche with Edwin Land
(Photo Credit: Nancy Lane, Polaroid Chemist and Model, 1958; Ms. Lane was a Smith College Graduate, typical of many of Land's laboratory assistants)

We do not expect non-photographic products to make significant contributions to our sales in the near term. However, we are convinced that there may be substantial future opportunities for us in areas of business new to Polaroid, but which fit well with our competencies and culture.
(Bill McCune, 1981 Polaroid Annual Report)

Chapter 1:
Bill Mccune – Land's #1 Aide

To many Polaroid employees, Bill McCune was sort of a "Tonto" to Land's "Lone Ranger." He was a skilled engineer, the one who put in place many of Land's inventions. As I continued my research and discussions with Polaroid people, I discovered McCune was much more than the individual who implemented Land's ideas.

A 1937 graduate of the Massachusetts Institute of Technology, McCune joined Polaroid in 1939, two years after the company was founded by Dr. Land. McCune's first job was to establish the company's quality-control program. During World War II, McCune worked with Land on Polaroid's guided-missile project. After the war, McCune worked on the development of the original Polaroid Land camera and film. He established the R&D building in Waltham (W4) that developed the new Polaroid negative eventually produced in New Bedford. In the late 1970s, Land had put everything into the development of the SX-70 camera and film system. While the sophisticated, $135 camera was an instant hit with photographers, the cameras were sold at a loss – film burn was not covering costs. Wall Street demanded more; the stock plummeted. McCune led a program to provide a lower-cost version of the SX-70, possibly saving Polaroid from financial ruin.

In 1977, Polaroid introduced the OneStep Land camera, an inexpensive fixed-focus camera. Many will recall the television advertising campaign featuring the actors Mariette Hartley and

James Garner. The OneStep reigned for four years as the best-selling camera, instant or conventional, in the United States. It was largely believed Land dismissed the OneStep as a poor offspring of his elegant SX-70. Fortunately, McCune was correct and Polaroid sales increased over 50% the next few years. The next generation film system and camera system Type 600 continued to be the top selling items for Polaroid, allowing company sales to reach $2 billion by 1991.

Without McCune's leadership in rescuing the SX-70 program with lower cost cameras, it is hard to imagine how Polaroid could have survived the 1980s. Where Land was mostly consumed by his inventiveness, William McCune was much better rounded. He was an excellent skier, played the oboe in a community orchestra and drove a Porsche. In 1976, there was an attempt to kidnap McCune on a street a few blocks from his Waltham-4 office. McCune foiled the abduction by fighting off an armed attacker, taking away his shotgun and chasing the assailant away.

McCune put forth the following strategy for Polaroid related to electronic technology in his President's Address to Stockholders in the 1981 Annual Report:

It is in the TechPhoto area that electronics with its rapidly growing capability for recording, storing and viewing of images is initially interfacing with Polaroid instant photography. Of course, electronic imaging has substantial, but perhaps longer term implications, for amateur photography as well. We recognize that the rapid development of this electronic technology presents both a threat to and an opportunity for photography. We are devoting increasing effort and resources to this field. While we are generally not known as an electronics company, electronics has for many years been a fundamental part of our technical base in both manufacturing technology and product design. In fact, we have been leaders in the application of electronics to photographic products. We continue to add to our capabilities in this discipline.

The Diversified Products group is in the embryonic stage of its development. We do not expect non-photographic products to make significant contributions to our sales in the near term. However, we are convinced that there may be substantial future opportunities for us in areas of business new to Polaroid, but which fit well with our competences and culture.

This was McCune's electronic vision. Over the next several years, Polaroid began to invest in electronic imaging. While there were some successes, Polaroid never found the path that would merge its wonderful knowledge of chemistry and light management to the electronic world. A future chapter will describe the fits and starts of Polaroid's electronic transition. In a way, as Bill McCune had been Ed Land's faithful implementer, it is a shame another Polaroid executive did not emerge to, similarly, carry out McCune's electronic vision. Later, we'll discuss a few that tried but were pushed aside.

****

Bill McCune delivered the following history of Polaroid to the Concord Oral History Program on July 11, 1996; Renee Garrelick, Interviewer. It describes his fifty or so years of Polaroid quite efficiently, describing Polaroid technology in layman's terms:

The thing that is unique about instant photography is that it is a system in which both camera and film make it possible to obtain a photograph, we say instantly, but it is within a minute or so of the time you expose it. This is in contrast to having to take the film out of the camera when it is completed, take it to some photo finishing station to have it developed and prints made, get it back and see what you've got. Whereas with the instant system, it's possible to see on the spot the results of your photograph and to make corrections and

94

make additional photographs or share the photographs you've taken with your friends or even to give them away, which is one of the things that happens when you're traveling. People often would like to have a picture which was taken on the spot.

How does the actual process work? It's very complicated, and it is particularly complicated if you get into the question as to how the color works. The basic concept is of a transfer system in which the normal photosynthesis element of the system, commonly referred to as the negative, is combined with another element that becomes what one would call the positive or is a viewing image. When the negative is exposed and then processed, in our case running it through a pair of rollers which spreads a viscous liquid between or over it in one way or another, the exposed elements of the negative are developed and that causes reaction which results in the transfer from the negative of either colors or, in the case of black and white, silver, which is then deposited in the deposit substrate and becomes the viewing image. Now that is a thumbnail sketch!

I first knew Dr. Edwin Land when he was 28 and I was about 22. He evolved and changed a great deal over the period of time I knew him, but he was an extraordinary person and a delightful person to know, although he could be difficult, too, as we all can. He is difficult to summarize in a way. He was an extraordinarily creative person and a very intense person. He was a person who devoted enormous amounts of his time and energy to accomplish the things he set out to do. He was, of course, a genius, and lots of people think that a genius is a person who accomplishes what he does simply because he's very bright. My observation is that geniuses accomplish what they do because they are not only very bright but because they work very, very hard with great

95

concentration. He was of course that kind of person. He would spend endless hours, nights and days and on weekends, in his laboratory working on whatever was foremost in his mind to accomplish at the time. One of the interesting things about Land was that his great achievements really were around solving problems. He didn't invent something by having some extraneous idea and then trying to find a use for it. He set about to solve a problem.

One of his first-rate inventions was the thing that was the basis for The Polaroid Corporation which was the creation of the inexpensive sheet polarizer. It is the first product that Polaroid made and commercialized and was sort of the genesis of the word Polaroid. The reason for that accomplishment was that he became obsessed with the problems of night driving in the late '20s, and the accidents that were occurring because of narrow roads and bright headlights from oncoming cars that were blinding other drivers, and so he set about to solve the problem. His notion of the way to do that was to have polarized headlights and polarized viewers so that the headlights of oncoming cars would be dimmed or illumination reduced but it would not reduce the illumination from your own headlights. At that time the only polarizers available came from natural crystals and were very small in size and extraordinarily expensive. So, he conceived of the idea of making an inexpensive sheet polarizer which could be used in large areas, and he set about to do that.

In the case of the camera, instant photography, it actually came about because his wife was in the West with the two children and he went out to visit them and took some pictures of the young daughter who was seven or eight years old at that time and she said, "Why can't I see the picture?" So he said well, why can't you, and set about to solve that problem. During the war he was a consultant to the Office of the Chief of Naval Operations, and there again his contributions were about making quite unique solutions to problems. He was also the creator or the originator of the U2 spy plane and that came about again because he was a member of the President's Advisory Committee and at the time in the late '50s, Eisenhower and everyone else was worried about what was going on behind the Iron Curtain and Land said, "Well, why don't we take a look and find out." So he had this notion of building a plane that flew so high that nobody else could catch him and developing very powerful photography that could make photographs from those heights and still have very high resolution. So he set about to get that done. That's really the kind of person he was in that regard.

Originally, Land wasn't sure what he wanted to do for a career. He was torn between science and a literary career, and eventually ended up in science, I guess because he really wanted to solve problems. He always had a great interest in the arts of all forms, music, visual arts and literature. He had a great many academic friends, and he brought into the company in various ways, mostly as consultants, people from the academic world and others including such people as Ansel Adams, who was a very early consultant and a very close friend of many of us in the company. But Land naturally attracted people of various talents and of various interests. He leavened the company with them. Because of this environment, it attracted to the company as employees people with a whole variety of talents and interests and people who made enormous contributions to the company, not only in science, but in a lot of other ways. I think that is one of the things that made Polaroid an extraordinary and unusual company. He was interested in people who were creative. Lots of people think, without really knowing, that Land invented everything at Polaroid, which of course, simply wasn't true. He just attracted and made an environment which attracted creative people, and the things that the company accomplished really depended on a lot of other creative people, the cumulative effect of creative people and an environment in which they were encouraged to do their best.

He was quite a showman. He was better than P.T. Barnum. He really was a very good showman. Our company annual meetings would sometimes have as many as a couple thousand people, which is extraordinary. Mostly they just came to see Land and hear what he had to say. It was because of his personality and his showmanship and unusual topics. He always had something unusual to talk about and he got everyone interested and excited.

The company was formed in 1937. Land and a fellow named George Wheelwright set out much earlier than that to try to develop the sheet polarizer. George Wheelwright was a fellow who was a physics instructor at Harvard, and when Land left to work on this which he did in his sophomore year, George joined up with him and they had this laboratory. After they were successful in developing the sheet polarizer, Land had a friend who had been a camp counselor whose name was Julius Silver. He was a lawyer in New York at the time, so Land went to him to get some help on what to do about a company. Julie was an extraordinary person also, very astute, very well connected, so he helped Land. Really, Julie was the one who set about to get the company organized and raise the finances which he did from a small number of people in New York including Averill Harriman. So the company was formed on the basis of commercializing the polarizer, and of course the objective at that time was to sell the automotive companies on having polarizing headlights, which never came about because they never wanted to do it.

The company was formed in 1937 as The Polaroid Corporation and I joined it in late 1939. I had gone to work for General Motors overseas operations and I was supposed to go work in Germany. Hitler went on the rampage in August of 1939 and I decided I didn't want to stick around General Motors at that point. The appeal of going to work in Germany was very great to me because I had never been out of the country. I talked to some people at MIT and they suggested that I talk to Polaroid. It was very difficult to find anything out about the company at that point. It had no reputation. There had been one Fortune article about the polarizing sheet. The company at that time was located in a small second floor loft on Columbus Avenue. I went over there and had an interview. The fellow that was interested in hiring me was Jack Latham, an old time friend of Land and also an MIT man, as I was. He took me to the building that they were renting in Cambridge. It was an old candy factory on the corner of Main Street and Osborn Street. I ended up joining Polaroid. Nat Sage at the time was advising alumni in job opportunities and I had been in touch with him. He's the one who had sent me to Polaroid, and I went over to see him on my way back from the interview and told him that I thought it was very interesting and there were a lot of fascinating things about it, but it was also difficult to learn anything about what was going on. So we sort of left on that note and I was living in New York at the time and took the train back to New York and when I got there, there was a telegram from Nat that said, "Think twice before you turn down Polaroid." Well, I didn't have any intention of turning it down, so right then and there I accepted the job.

I was hired to set up quality assurance operations at the company. The automotive companies hadn't bought into Polaroid's headlights, and the main commercial product was lenses for polarizing sunglasses. The final sunglasses were assembled by American Optical Company. They had a license to do this and sell them under the trademark Polaroid and they bought the lenses from Polaroid. It was a somewhat complicated process to take a polarizing sheet and to slit it and coat it with an adhesive and then blank it out and sandwich it between two pieces of precut glass that were cut to a specific shape. The sandwich and the glass all had to be properly oriented and laminated and there were all kinds of opportunities for problems and defects to arise. American Optical being an optical company had rather high standards for its products and Polaroid was having a very difficult time getting a product satisfactory to their requirements. So I was hired to try to help solve these problems.

As I said, the main products of the company were flat sunglass lenses and some specialty scientific polarizing filters of one kind or another, but of course there was a lot of work going on in research areas and in other kinds of filter media and in new kinds of polarizers. I remember that Land had a company meeting which consisted of all 75 people or so in one of the rooms in the building on 730 Main Street at Christmastime, and he gave a little talk. One of the things he said was that he was convinced that the war that was going in Europe was of much greater significance to the United States than most people felt, and he had decided that from then on the company was going to devote its main efforts as far as research for new products and new things to do with military work and not more commercial work. Land had become associated with some people from ordnance and had gotten involved in consulting to solve some of their problems, and the result of that was the awesome problems were brought back to Polaroid and work was done there to derive solutions for them. Frequently this led to products that we made and frequently it didn't, but the result was that it wasn't very long before practically the whole company business was devoted to military activities. At the beginning of the war the total business was less than a million dollars, and by the time the war ended, it was $14 million or $15 million and the number of employees had grown to 1200-1300.

One of the major projects that we ended up with was developing a heat homing missile for the Navy. The specific problem was how to hit a maneuvering Japanese war ship in the middle of the Pacific Ocean from an airplane at 15,000-20,000 feet. That was the problem and our solution was a heat homing missile which was the very first heat homing missile ever made. It was developed when the problems about air-to-air missiles surfaced; a big argument came up as to how to do it. The Air Force wanted to use radar, but the Royal Ordnance people involved knew of our work and had seen our success with heat homing, and engines of an aircraft were pretty darn hot targets, so they insisted on developing their own system which turned into the Sidewinder missile. It is based on the techniques we developed on the heat homing missile, but the technology, the hardware, and the electronics and all that were entirely new.

We developed rubber goggles for General Patton's tanks. They had a variety of filters in them and they were also used in the Navy with a special filter which was called the dark adaptation filter. They could darken very quickly at dusk to see enemy aircraft and submarines and so forth. There were a great many things. There was a whole infrared system developed for the military to use infrared headlight and infrared viewers so they could see at night without being seen by the enemy.

It was during the war period, about 1944, that Land got interested in this question of an instant camera. With a couple of young ladies that had been working in one of his laboratories, he set aside a little room and got them working on some ideas he had about this transfer process that I mentioned. By the time the war ended we were making reasonably decent images in the laboratory not with any cameras of any sort. We simply decided we didn't want to continue in the war business and we were going to put everything we had in trying to develop an instant system. So we started from scratch when the war ended to develop this camera and film system. The result was that we dropped the military contracts. We got Kodak to take the heat homing missile project because it hadn't run out yet. So we didn't have any products to sell. There was very little income and lots of outgo because we were going on and trying to develop the film camera. So the company shrank a great deal.

Fortunately, we introduced the first cameras at Thanksgiving in 1948. As I recall we had about 240 people at that time. The first official announcement was at a talk that Land made in 1947. The objective of the announcement was first the technical announcement of the process and some demonstrations, and part of the purpose of the demonstrations was to show that it was feasible to make a hand-held camera that would deliver such a photograph. First of all, we had to give a paper. My wife Elizabeth did a lot of work on the paper. She was a chemist. We built a big camera that gave an 8x10-inch photograph and that was on a tripod. We had to make the film for that by hand practically. Then we made two or three different kinds of hand-held cameras with the idea that some of us engineers and developing people would be around to take photographs of the press and others to show them that we could actually make photographs. It was a very active period. The meeting was to be held at the Pennsylvania Hotel in New York City. We packed all the stuff in a truck here in Boston and got everything all organized and took off for New York. The truck driver started out and got into one of the biggest blizzards we'd ever had. We woke up the next morning and New York was shut down. There was no traffic, no nothing. We were wondering about the truck, but he got through. We had the meeting and all went well – fascinating meeting. Of course, it astonished everybody. The wonderful thing was Land, being the showman that he was, got the then president of the optical society to come up and had him stand and took his photograph. Out it came and he hands it to him and of course, everyone went wild.

We had practically no profit before the war, and we were doing quite a lot of business and made quite a lot of profits during the war, and one of the features of the contracts was that you had an excess profits tax and that excess profit was based on what profits you made before the war, so a great deal of any profits we made were taken in taxes. But there was a provision that you could draw back on the excess profits tax for costs involved in conversion back to civilian work. So the thing that kept us alive from 1946 through 1948 was the ability to draw back these excess profits. We were going to run out of any excess profits and we had very small commercial revenues in that period, so one way or another we had to have a product on the market in 1948. That's how we got it out in November of that year. The first commercial sale for the camera was to Jordan Marsh.

We were so interested to find out how our cameras reacted. It was expensive at that time to buy the camera. I've often said that one of the elements of success of a camera was the fact that we couldn't make very many. At that time there was a tax on amateur cameras of 25% or something like that, and our camera was not small and it was fairly heavy, but the amateur camera was classed as a camera that weighed less than 4 pounds. Ours was close enough to that that we decided we would make it heavy enough so we wouldn't have to pay the taxes. So we had this rather heavy camera that was quite large, and it was a fairly complicated device for us to make at that time. We only made 50 cameras in 1948. The selling price was $95. Well, $95 was a lot of money for a camera in 1948. There were just enough people who had $95 that they wanted to spend on something like that and who were adventuresome so we sold all we could make. That was the best thing you could do was to sell all you could make rather than have a lot of inventory.

We wanted to get started and 50 cameras were all we could make. We were just getting going and we were also making and assembling the film pretty much by hand. We didn't have our final film assembly equipment. We ended up designing and building much of our specialized manufacturing equipment which was also one of my jobs. We had to work in air conditioning in order to keep the material we were working with, which were paper-based materials. Dimensions would change a great deal in changes in humidity, so in order for all of them to come together properly, we worked in buildings with temperature and humidity control. The factory was air conditioned but none of the offices were. This was all automatic machinery that did this; you couldn't do this by hand. I remember at one point we were spending quite a lot of money and proposing to spend a lot of money on this automatic machinery and the board was kind of skeptical about this so they asked one of the board members, Jack Latham who hired me, to run an investigation to see what he thought about it. He came and worked with us, and he readily saw that automatic machinery was the right thing but we had a very early automatic factory and part of it was because a good deal of it had to be done in the dark. It needed very high accuracy working in the dark.

The company decided not to market the product through distributors but to market the product directly to dealers. There was a lot of discussion about that. It was very interesting because initially photographic dealers weren't interested in the product. I don't know quite why. We had a great deal of trouble in getting them interested. We decided to go through department stores and other commodity dealers. That was one reason we went to Jordan Marsh, and they were very much interested. The big department stores at that time became some of our best dealers. It was only after several years, three or four years, that the photographic guys began to realize that selling Polaroid film was a very lucrative business. Of course, we actually got into the drugstores too. We felt positioning the product and marketing it could be much better handled by our own people.

The reason that I mentioned about the film is that the repeat film sales is something that is very important to the dealers, and the dealers, because of the price cutting in the long run, began to find it difficult to make very much on cameras, but they could make quite a bit of money on the repeat business of film.

Kodak was extraordinarily helpful to us. We first showed the idea of the instant process to the then head of research at Kodak. We had a good relationship with Kodak for many years. Land had known some people there and then we had done some work with them and had done some things during the war. When we got into this field, it was clear that we didn't have either the know-how or the facility to make the light-sensitive product. That is the part that is generally called the negative. We very much needed to have someone who would make negatives for us. We also felt that for a variety of reasons we wanted a negative that had some special characteristics. We just couldn't go and buy one off the shelf. Since we'd had some good relations with Kodak before that, we talked to some of their people there and invited down the head of research and two or three others. He came and looked over what we were doing and I think was quite impressed by the whole thing. The Kodak management was a very enlightened group at that time. I always think of them as being good statesmen. In any event, they saw this as very interesting and early on decided they didn't want to try to get into doing it but would help us with it, and so developed this relationship between the people in research. It started out with people in what was then known as the Paper Division which is the division that made all their coated paper products. The reason for

105

that is that we wanted the negative to be on a paper base not on a film base. They develop a special negative for us on paper base and that was what we used in the initial product. Then as we went along we kept working with them all the time to develop better bases and improved negatives which are all black and white.

Then in about 1948 Land told one of his associates, a young fellow named Howie Rogers that he wanted him to stop working on polarizers and concentrate totally on how to make color. So Howie started out and went through a whole lot of things. There was also a bright young man trained as an engineer but a very good scientist named Otto Wolf who worked with me a great deal, and he and I would go talk to Howie about his processes. He was very creative and he would have a lot of ideas and some of them we thought would never be something you could make very well. He kept working on it. In order for Howie to do his experiments he needed a source of the light sensitive emulsions that are coated onto negatives in order to make the sensitized film. Again we didn't have any facilities for making such things and so Land asked Sy Staud at Kodak, who was then director of research if they would be willing to supply us with the emulsions. They agreed to do that but on the basis that when we had a product or something we thought would be a product that they would have first opportunity to bid on making it for us. So that went on, and as we got to the point where we thought we had a good product, we showed to them and they were enthusiastic and we set up a very unusual cooperative development program. They had their own kinds of manufacturing facilities and processes. To develop the negative further around our inventions and our special chemicals, they wanted to have a development that would go readily into their manufacturing without a lot of changes. So we had a team from their research and our research and Land and me and we used to have a meeting a month, one month in Rochester and one month in Boston, until we got to the point where we had a product that looked as if they were going to make it. They made all the color negatives for us initially. It was a very fine relationship in my opinion. They were very helpful and I don't think we would have gotten where we were without them.

The relationship continued until the early '70s. They very much wanted to get a license from us to make instant products. Land and I used to have meetings with a man named Wren Gable who was one of their executive vice presidents. I'd known him for years there and he had always been involved with the other development work that went back to the '40s. We kept saying we'd love to give them a license but we just didn't know how to give them a license that would make sure that they just didn't swallow us up. They were a great big company and we were a little company, and if we gave them a license, they could make products like ours, and how are we going to survive? We'd go over it and over it with him and try to find some way to do it. In any event there was another man who was an executive vice president at Kodak and when the time came to appoint a new president, he was appointed president and Gable resigned from the company. I always thought that was a great mistake. In any event, the new fellow decided that his tactics were to beat us into it. Since they were the only people making negatives for us, he used every whip he could get to try to make us agree to a license. We finally agreed to a license that we knew wasn't going to be any good to them because at that time we were also working on the SX-70 development. The license didn't include anything in that field.

*****

Back in 1958 or 1959 I had also got to worrying about the fact that we had only one source of color negatives, and if anything ever happened we would be in trouble. So I decided to sort of, over Land's dead body, that wasn't quite true, he supported it, but Land didn't want to make anything. He always thought we should just buy it. That wasn't entirely true, but that's basically it. But I felt we should have some facilities so I started a small group working on trying to learn how to make color negatives. We eventually built up a group in Waltham in a special building, Building 4. They developed all kinds of techniques for making emulsions and negatives and so on. At that time we were just beginning to develop the SX-70 system. It required a new negative entirely different from the one we'd been making. Land had this dream that he was going to sell enormous numbers of negatives and he thought that maybe we could appease Kodak by having them make the negative and there would be so much negative that the business would be great for them. Well, that turned out not to work. We had some meetings there and I remember I came back from a meeting in Rochester and I and another fellow who at that time was the head of research at Polaroid, Dick Young, had been there. It hadn't been a very satisfactory meeting because Land had as usual pretty high demands and they said they couldn't meet them. So we came back and I talked to Land and I said they say they can't do it. He was angry and he looked at me and said "Can you do it?" Well we didn't have any building or anything, but I said "Yes, we can do it. I won't guarantee we will make all you said you wanted from them, but we'll make enough so you'll never be short of it." I think this was in late 1968 and we started the building design in New Bedford in 1969. So we started to design that building and we had it built and running in 1972, and I think at the time it was finished it was the most advanced negative factory in the world. Mac Booth was working for me out in Building 4, so I asked him to take charge of the program and run the building. So that's how we got into the negative business.

A fellow named Walter Fallon who we had known very well from the old color negative days in Stanley Kodak Park became president of Kodak. He came down to see us one day with a couple of their lawyers and said they were going to make some instant products and they were quite sure that they weren't

108

going to infringe our patents. In any event, they hadn't actually seen the SX-70 yet but they started out to make the product. Then at one of the annual meetings the first SX-70 cameras were shown. They had people there and they went home and said, "Look, all the things we're doing are no good any more. We've got to start over again." We know this came up from the records of the trials and so on. So they scrapped everything they were doing and started all over again. Then they found that it was very difficult to make a camera that would compete with the SX-70 without somehow coming close to infringing our patents. Well, they always felt that they came close to not infringing them or infringing valid claims as they put it, but when the trial came, the judge didn't think so. I think their first camera came out in about 1975, and that's when the lawsuit started.

One of the things I've said a number of times is that we were the only company that I know of that had a unique very important commercial field of that kind all to itself. The reason was exactly what I just said, that the company was so creative and Land was so creative and he kept driving these ideas into systems so that by the time one set of patents had run out and might have been possible for someone to compete with more systems, we had new patents and new systems that they just couldn't compete with. That just went on and on. That was perhaps the final nail in the coffin, you might say, when this SX-70 thing came out.

All of our cameras before then had used what we always called the peel-apart process, and that is when the picture develops, after a certain length of time, you had to remove the positive from the negative, then you could see it. The difference was that the SX-70 photograph came out and it was dry, as far as handling is concerned, and you could watch it develop in the light. That was a whole new thing. It interestingly was a culmination you might say of what Land had described to me when he first described his idea for an instant camera. What he said was, I remember very well we were standing there and he had shown me this little transfer thing back in 1944, and he said, "You know I can imagine a camera that is simple and easy to

109

use. You simply look through the viewfinder and compose your picture and push the shutter release and out comes the finished dry photograph in full color." Well, that was the SX-70, but that was about thirty years later. It actually came out in 1972. First color was introduced in 1962 and the new packed cameras with color were in 1963.

In 1975 I became president and chief operating officer. That was a very important transition for the company. Land still dominated in a way. He was still CEO and chairman and director of research. He stayed in that position until 1980. We always had our arguments and our disagreements. We did still but we worked pretty well together for the most part. We had some serious troubles, but he was an extraordinary person and a very wonderful guy to work for. I guess you had to be sort of tough.

The new SX-70 system was just really coming into fruition, but we had a lot of troubles with the first system. Land always had great vision. He was a great optimist. He had all the characteristics that made it possible for him to devote his life to doing what he did. Without those characteristics he might not have put in what he did. So things never came out quite the way he dreamed and they always took longer and they always cost more and always were a little more difficult to make work. That was certainly true of the SX-70 system initially. He and I had had some serious disagreements about that in the early stages, such that he really didn't want me involved for a while and then finally as things began to get in trouble, he asked me to kind of take over. That was really kind of coming to fruition in '75.

Polavision was just beginning to take form. It was another issue on which he and I didn't agree. He wanted to go ahead and make this system and build the building for making the film. He got a contractor in Austria to make the hardware better, but at that time it wasn't such a big deal. But that became a big issue about 1978 or 1979. Again, he always wanted to do things in a big way and he really insisted on commitments for quantities on the Polavision system and the investment and resources for making it. Of course, it turned out to not ever be useful. But, you know, he didn't have many failures. Most things he planned on we pulled out of the fire in some way or another. That one, there was no way to do it.

As to Polavision, I'm going to speak of my own prejudices in this case, but I thought that it was not a very good system. It was a great technical achievement and you looked at the problems that had been solved and the technology involved in it, there was a lot of very, very clever solutions and technical work. But I thought the system wasn't very good, to be frank about it. It was based on an additive color system, and the problem with the additive color is that it uses up a lot of light for viewing slides. You get wonderful color rendition and excellent resolution but the slides are dull. In order to make them bright you have to have an enormous amount of lighting unprotected. The process was quite slow photographically. One of the solutions that was made was to have a backlit projector that you could set up, you didn't have a screen or anything, and viewed it on its screen. That gave you a fairly small image. The other thing is that you had a system in which you got about five or six minutes of viewing for, I've forgotten the exact price, but for about $8 or $9 which is fairly expensive.

If there had never been any video, it might have been able to do something, but here was video coming along. One of the interesting things to me was that Land would never recognize it. He would get angry and wouldn't recognize it. It was so different because he was usually the first one to pick up on some new technical thing and see the potential of it for the future. Of course, when the video systems were first starting there weren't any nice, little compact ones for home use, but you could see they were there soon. All you had to do is just look at the way the systems were going, and he knew that because he had done the same thing in all our own cameras. We'd started out with electronics and had electronics in some of our early cameras and then made the first really integrated camera that was ever made. That's what the Japanese copied for all their systems. But somehow he didn't want to see it. Polavision just never had a chance.

We've talked about the personal use of our cameras, but we also did about half our business with industrial uses. Now there are markets in China and Russia. We started in Europe in the 1950s and gradually built mostly marketing companies there, and then we built a manufacturing company in Scotland, and we built a manufacturing company in the Netherlands. We had a company in Japan, and I guess we've had that company for 35 years. We started in the Soviet Union and China about ten years ago, and those are both moving very well now. I think the company has now grown to over 16,000 employees. I was an employee of the company until 1990 when I retired and stayed on as chairman for another year. I left in 1991.

We had so much product evolution and design, but there is also the marketing component. They don't go in tandem. Many people would argue whether you should have market research and so on, and my opinion is that when you are creating things that people don't even know exist and people don't know about it and can't really understand until they see it, market research is no damn good. The interesting thing to me is that more recently the company has gotten into a lot of market research and focus groups and things of that sort. The products that have had the most of that and had the highest success and the highest enthusiasm in this area have usually been the biggest flops for the company. It doesn't mean that that sort of thing isn't of use, but I think to try to get consumers to tell you something about a new product that they really don't know about is a mistake. The same thing is true concerning Walkman. That is an interesting story. Marita, who was one of the founders of Sony, was telling me the story about his partner, Ibuka, who was sort of retired but did a lot of creative work on the side. Ibuka came into his office one day with the forerunner of the Walkman walking around with it in his ear. Marita got very excited. He took it to the market group, and they said there is no market for that. So Marita said if we don't make that product, I'm going to resign. That's a great story!

SECTION 3: Israel MacAllister Booth

The above photograph, from the Polaroid Corporation 1982 Annual Report to Shareholders, captures the three men who would be the top executives at Polaroid for the next 13 years, replacing Dr. Land. At the time of the photo, their titles were: left, I.M. Booth, Executive Vice President and Chief Operating Officer; seated, William J. McCune, Chief Executive Officer; rear, Dr. Sheldon A. Buckler, Executive Vice President.

Land left a tremendous void. Booth seems an unlikely choice for the role of a corporate Knute Rockne. He describes himself as "dull and colorless," punctuates his conversation with "gosh" and "heavens to Betsy," and commutes to his Cambridge, Massachusetts, office in a Jeep. Yet he is a driven leader who made his mark by building a pioneering color-film factory and bringing the three-year project in on time and within budget. Morale is on the upswing, Booth's subordinates say, because he is so willing to listen to new ideas. He wanders the halls and asks questions.

A quiet, private man, Booth confesses that changing his management style was a tough personal challenge. "In retrospect,"' he says, "I have to give myself some bad marks for not going out and explaining our troubles to people. Talking is better than hiding in the closet. I hid in the closet but I wouldn't do that again." Booth rocked the technocrats at Polaroid by insisting that marketing had to become more important – and get more sophisticated. (Fortune Magazine, February 16, 1987)

Chapter 1:
Mac Booth's Rise to CEO

Israel MacAllister Booth was born in Atlanta, Georgia, and reared in Michigan. He received a mechanical engineering degree from Cornell University in 1955 and a master's in business from Cornell in 1958. That same year, he joined Polaroid as a supervisor in the Film Division. He retired from Polaroid in 1996. In 1966, he was the Manager of Packaging in P60 (W3); and, along with Whitney Robinson and Max Lawrence, formed the middle management team, working for Cris Ingraham, the Plant Manager. Mac went to W4 to head up the Negative Program for Bill McCune and took that program to New Bedford as Plant Manager. He was elected Assistant Vice President and Assistant to the President in 1975; Vice President and Assistant to the President in 1976; Senior Vice President in 1977; Executive Vice President in 1980; Executive Vice President and Chief Operating Officer in 1982; President, Chief Operating Officer and Director in 1983, and President, Chief Executive Officer and Director in 1986. Booth was elected Chairman of the Board in 1991.

My former supervisor in the Battery Division, Bob Jacobs, hired Mac into the job in P60. Bob, many years later after Mac became CEO, would tease us by asking, "What do you think, can I pick 'em or what?"

When McCune decided to produce Polaroid's negative in support of the SX-70 film, Mac was put in charge of the team, initially in the research building W4 where both the chemistry and equipment development were conducted. Eventually a large

115

state-of-the-art plant was constructed in New Bedford, about 70 miles from Waltham. There have been many great achievements in the history of Polaroid. Most Polaroid followers would say the New Bedford plant was the gold standard. Mac recruited the best scientists and engineers in the company to work on the project.

As a coating engineer, I was tabbed to work at NB as a process engineer. I interviewed with Mac's number one assistant, Owen Gaffney, and Mac himself in 1971. I was excited to be part of the new team. Additionally, New Bedford is in close proximity to Cape Cod, one of my family's favorite locations. My wife, with our two young boys and newly born daughter, was not so favorable to the idea. Hal Page, the plant manager in W1 at the time, solved the problem. He asked me: "Milt, you've been here less than two years.. Why not finish what you agreed to do when I hired you?" Hal went on to VP level in the company. I stayed in W1; my wife was delighted. I have often wondered how different my Polaroid career would have been had I joined the team in New Bedford.

The chemistry, equipment and processes to produce a color negative are quite complex. The base material in Polaroid negatives is a special form of polyester (PET – polyethylene terephthalate). In order to capture the latent image on the silver halide structure, discreet amounts of color dyes (cyan, magenta, and yellow) have to be transferred from the negative to the positive. Between the layers of dyes there are spacing layers, timing layers and other chemicals. The machine to coat the chemicals was about five feet wide and processed with the PET, running at several yards per minute. The processing had to be done in a dark room so that light would not expose the silver halide. There are over 10,000 chemical interactions take place during the development of the color instant-film process. Polaroid designed and built the one-of-a-kind coating apparatus that extruded the chemicals in many layers simultaneously. The coating devices were remarkable and, in the 1960s, probably not available outside of Polaroid or possibly Kodak.

Mac's leadership in building and managing the New Bedford plant was exemplary. The team that worked under Mac to establish this plant provided a source of leaders at Polaroid for

116

the next two decades. Future managers such as Owen Gaffney, Jim Grunst and Paul Lambert went on to key roles in the company. Consistent with the employees' penchant for nicknames, the NB leaders were dubbed the New Bedford "Mafia." The New Bedford plant team had the reputation of being self-serving, elitist, and sometimes arrogant. They envisioned themselves a bit like the West Point of Polaroid, and indeed many managers and engineers were hired from the military during the Vietnam era. But they succeeded in producing a string of successful managers for the company. In the mid-70s Booth quickly went from NB plant manager, reporting to George Fernald, to becoming, in virtually one step, Fernald's boss, and then moved swiftly to the top job in the company.

Based on Booth's successful implementation of the New Bedford plant, Bill McCune assigned Mac the task of determining the longer range plan for plant film capacity. Now that Polaroid had its own negative manufacturing as well as internal battery sourcing, the company needed to ensure manufacturing capacity matched rapidly rising sales in the late 1970s. While the original SX-70 camera sales were somewhat disappointing due to the cost and complexity of Land's sophisticated camera, the new lower-cost versions were selling at a terrific rate. Starting in 1977, the OneStep Land Camera was the best-selling camera in the U.S. for more than four years. Mariette Hartley and James Garner starred in the very entertaining TV ads. This was a paradigm shift for the company: a move towards proactive, expensive marketing. In 1977, Polaroid sales exceeded $1-billion.

Over the years, the company had developed computer models to predict film sales rate based on the number of new instant cameras sold, along with cameras sold in previous years and still active. Film "burn" rates, based on individual camera types, were also important factors – actually the key assumption. Much of the prior history indicated the purchaser of an instant camera would buy about ten packs of film the first year of use, and then wind down over the next two years to about five packs per year; eventually, either ceasing to use the camera or replacing it with a newer Polaroid camera. A nice business, particularly at the high margin rates of film. In some camera systems which were sold at a loss, the first three packs of film purchased for that camera would bring the company to break-even. Each additional pack sold would create approximately $4 in margin. The margin would be even greater when films sales crossed certain fixed cost levels, reducing manufacturing and overhead costs.

So we have Mac's challenge: analyze the film sales potential over the next several years; establish existing film-manufacturing capacity; develop a scale-up plan for the sites with limited capacity. While the aforementioned computer model had considerable data, Mac also had to factor in possible new enthusiasm for instant film, based on very exciting marketing campaigns via the Garner-Hartley TV ads. The Integral Film sales in 1977-1980 were approximately 100 million packs per year. The film assembly machinery in Waltham and Enschede, the Netherlands, had a capacity of about 150 million packs using considerable weekend overtime. The single battery plant in Waltham had a capacity of 125 million packs using a seven-day work week. The New Bedford negative manufacturing and receiving-sheet coating plant in Waltham had capacity above 300 million packs using overtime potential and some minor machinery modifications.

There were estimates of over 15 million Polaroid Integral Film cameras in use in 1980. In 1978 over 9 million Integral cameras were sold. Although sales in 1980 dropped to about 4 million cameras per year, sales outside the USA were expanding and newer version cameras were expected to grow the 4 million figure. Kodak entered the Instant field in 1976; and, while they were taking about 25% of the market, it was felt their advertising helped expand the market. Additionally, Polaroid had filed a patent infringement immediately and was expected to prevail.

Mac proposed to McCune and the board that Polaroid should develop Integral Film manufacturing capability to produce 360 million packs per year by 1981, more than tripling current sales. While the analysis to reach this conclusion was not generally shared, using a burn rate of 10 packs per year for each camera in use suggests that 36 million Polaroid Instant cameras operating in any year could consume the 360 million packs. Polaroid sales had grown from $500 million in 1974 to $1-billion by 1976, so it was easy to see a possible doubling in the next five years. Additionally, once the plants were constructed and infrastructure established, Polaroid could add capacity, a few assembly machines at a time, matching capital expenditures and employee hiring to current sales forecasts. Mac's challenge was to start opening the faucet to increase capacity while managing expenditures. His initial actions were to expand the Integral Film assembly capacity with new plants in Andover, Massachusetts, about twenty miles northwest of Waltham, and in Newbridge, Kildare County, Ireland, thirty miles south of Dublin.

Chapter 2:
Integral Film Assembly – 360 Million Packs

The film assembly plant to produce SX-70 film was built on Winter Street in Waltham in the late 1960s. A three-building complex housed the old Roll Film product (R1), new SX-70 Integral Film (R2) and Film Division management and administrative functions (R3). The site was referred to as "the reservoir", as it sat above the water supply for the city of Cambridge. Money was not an issue at that time. I. M. Pei, one of the most popular architects of his time, created an expensive "Taj Mahal" with high ceilings and large windows. Peripheral aisles circled this multi-purpose building on all sides, creating some wasted space but providing a quite attractive, functional and pleasant workplace that served Polaroid well for over 35 years. A three-level open hole on one end of R2 contained an automated computer-controlled warehouse, supplying raw materials and finished goods storage for this 240,000-square-foot factory.

Similar to the Pack Film process in Waltham 3, the integral film assembly machines involved combining the negatives from New Bedford with the receiving sheets from W5 with the developer "pods" and packaging components produced in house. The batteries, produced in building (R5) were nearby. A plant in Enschede, the Netherlands, had been constructed in the late 1960s to produce, first, sunglasses and, later, peel-apart film as a second source to P60. The plant also produced the developer chemicals as well as pods. Over time, Enschede grew to over 1,000 employees, with the primary function to act as the second source of Integral Film capacity equal to the Waltham R2 plant and to be the primary supplier of the film needs of Europe, Asia, and Latin America. A major effort continued during the entire life of both plants to replicate exactly all film processes and quality results such that any film pack made in any plant would yield similar results transparent to customers worldwide. There was a combination of cooperation between the two plants with a healthy level of competition mixed in. The Dutch engineers and machine operators contributed greatly to improvements to the film-assembly process.

Both integral assembly plants included the pod machines, molding machines for the plastic cases and stamping machines to produce steel springs to assist the transport (exit) of the pictures from the packs. Other materials were purchased from suppliers. All told, the annual material cost to produce 100 million packs of Integral Film was about $400 million. R2 and Enschede factories were, needless to say, bustling enterprises and the major contributor to Polaroid sales and profits during the late 1970s. Max Lawrence, a seasoned Polaroid executive who had been a key leader in managing the P60 operations, as well as early battery machinery construction, was assigned as project manager for the Integral Film Expansion Program, reporting directly to Mac Booth. As Max relates his recollection of the projects:

We built new facilities in Ireland, Andover and modified R-1 to accept SX-70 Film Assembly machines. I walked the farmland on River Road in Andover with the farmer who owned the land, as well as owning a small produce stand along River Road. I selected a plot of land north of River Road and West of Rte. 93. It would be in back of where the current Chateau Restaurant is now located.

There were no buildings, no roads, and no activity of any type. Polaroid purchased the land and we deigned and built an elegant state-of-the-art manufacturing facility. We were desperate to increase our film output, so as the plant was under construction, we roofed over a section and commenced constructing

Film Assembly Machines around the clock. This was in the dead of winter, so we had a section of the plant looking like a cocoon to isolate it and provide heat for the troops. This was, as I remember in the year 1976. It was the beginning of what became the Andover Industrial Park.

In the 1977-'80 period, the R2 Waltham plant shifted to a 7-day/24-hour operation, creating an A,B,C,E,F shift arrangement when overtime had become a heavy burden. This period coincided with the ramp-up to the 360 MM pack expansion program which occurred on its heels. During the same time frame, the plant in Newbridge, County Kildare, Ireland, was constructed. Phil Scaringella was the Polaroid facilities project manager assigned to the project. As Phil relates, there were five buildings built on the site, including the utility plant. The camera building was a shell and never outfitted. The film building was laid out for twelve film machines, but only two were installed. The entire complex (camera, film, administration, warehousing and utility buildings) was approximately 300,000 square feet. Project cost was approximately $20 million.

Joe Oldfield, another former P60 leader, was assigned as plant manager to oversee the entire operation. During the next few years, many managers and Polaroid mechanics, electricians, and operators were assigned to help install and operate the assembly machines, training their Irish counterparts. At this time, manufacturing in Ireland was rather primitive; available workers were local farmers. This was to change dramatically over the next two decades with many U.S. companies setting up facilities in Ireland similar to the Polaroid operation in Newbridge. Larry Kivimaki was a technical manager at R2 and was tasked with assisting the establishment of the maintenance and installation support for Newbridge. He recalls:

Tim Dwyer, Tom Hutchinson, Mike Polito, Art Jordan, Vern Addie, Bob Cunningham, Tom Lynch, and others were assigned there for two years each with their families. My visit in 1981 was to monitor the

122

folks - mechanics – who were sent by my department for three months without families and to help with training needs and setting up the technical infrastructure such as spare parts. The expatriates were funded either to send for their wives or significant others at the six-week point for a visit, or they got the option to fly home for leave. Then it was back to work again. My remembrances were of more than one mechanic – many actually – who lived on the edge, especially those who were on the B shift (3-11 p.m.). They got off at 11 p.m. in the rain, tired, in the dark, driving on the "wrong" side of the road in a rental car with the wheel on the right – and went straight to the pub. Nothing good ever came of this scenario. The trip home from the pub often led to unpleasant incidents. One, I recall, was a near head-on collision of our mechanic with a very high-ranking Irish Army officer. We managed to ship him home quickly, ahead of his normal tour of duty, and thankful were nobody got killed.

All in all, the support from the U.S., and the shorter visits of technical people from Enschede was exemplary. Tim and Tom and their families embraced the culture. A few guys got in large with the horses that ran in the Irish Sweepstakes nearby. We heard about some money they made but never heard much of what they lost. A few invested in the ponies themselves. Frans Kiens, the Enschede technical manager, traveled weeks at a time from the Enschede film plant. Gerard Kienhuis, one of his electrical engineers, kept us in stitches telling the most hilarious, crazy stories about his family's trials and tribulations with the Irish plumbers, appliance people, and the landlord and his bizarre washing machine. In that regard, Tim recalls the appliance culture shock of the Americans. The washer/dryer was a single machine operating – slowly – to process each small load and it took some time to learn about these tiny creatures. Moreover, the Americans were determined to solve the food-buying experience by buying meat for the whole week and eliminating all those unnecessary trips to the butcher. Ignoring the puzzled looks from the Irish, the next problem that reared its head was discovered on arriving back home. The refrigerator was much too small to store all that meat, never mind the other food! And the Irish didn't need their beer at home to be kept cold either. Warm was fine and most of the drinking was down at the pub anyhow. But the Americans had to deal with the dual problems of refrigerator space for cold beer and meat storage. Both of these problems were eventually solved by buying a second refrigerator.

When I arrived for a week in Newbridge in 1981, Joe Oldfield (who was plant manager, site manager and country manager) and I talked about his job setting up the entire operation with the IDA (Irish Development Authority). There had been intense and important negotiations between Polaroid and the IDA to establish financial incentives and the labor and workplace rules to satisfy both parties. Tax breaks for this Polaroid operation were generous. I spent my time during the visit helping him set up the maintenance and spare parts system and the mechanic training program ahead of production operations. Companies like Digital Equipment had preceded us to the land of tax-break heaven and by 1980 there were local people with knowledge of computers and electrical controls, but we had the darndest time finding qualified mechanical people. In that part of Ireland the closest skill set came from the lads who fixed farm equipment. The IDA economic incentive program was too far ahead of the talent level and we had to search hard for the right people. I remember hiring – eventually – the future engineering/ maintenance manager and heard about his subsequent firing less than six months later.

Joe also told me about the problems of keeping the grass mowed. The lush green carpet kept growing from all the rain, and every day about four o'clock the local lads would show up with a mower or two stuffed in their car's bonnet but before they got too far in their mowing the rains came, so they quit and came back the next afternoon. The grass kept growing faster than their ability to cut it. Eventually, Joe fired the mowers and got sheep, and that did the trick.

The subsidies for the workers were attractive. The noon cafeteria meal became their main meal because of the low cost. I remember going in there each day for lunch and the lunch ladies insisted on loading up my plate with pork chops, veggies, three kinds of potatoes, and more. Refusal was not allowed. Bob Cunningham, among others, also made the inexpensive and prolific cafeteria meal his main one, pocketing much of the per diem 20£ he was allocated, to be used for other things. The workers arrived every day wearing the same clothes as the day before, just more or less – another shirt put on or taken off vs. the previous day depending on the weather. Many worked for six months or so and then abruptly quit. They had earned enough, or more than they ever had at any other job, so they just stopped showing up and chose to spend it down until they needed to work again. We had to educate a lot of people about work habits. For some, it sunk in, and for others, it never did.

The architect for the Newbridge plant provided the interesting comment related to an attempt to stop the project before completion:

"The industrial buildings were on extraordinarily tight programmes," recalls Kevin Kelly, who joined Sisk in 1960 and retired as managing director in 1999. "One morning, when a huge plant for Polaroid in Newbridge was nearing completion, Fred Browne and I went to meet the chief executive of Polaroid in London airport. We met him at Heathrow early in the morning. We shook hands and did the usual niceties and then he said, 'What will it cost me to abort?' I told him it would be the full contract price. It was absolutely devastating. Also, the whole town of Newbridge was expecting a huge employer. It later became a meat-packing plant and is now occupied by the pharmaceutical company Wyeth and is very successful."   (John Sisk and Son, History, 2007)

Max Lawrence received a call from Mac Booth in 1979 with instructions to stop every action related to the Expansion Program. Max relates:

The next day I met with Mac Booth and was given detailed instructions to stop all vendors, all facility work and all machinery work; negotiate termination of the contracts with all vendors; and start the procedure to reassign all Polaroid staff. We moved out of Andover like thieves in the night. Orders from Booth directed us to stop every activity the day the decision was made to pull the plug on the Expansion Program. We had a budget of $100,000,000 and he wanted it shut off immediately. We managed that without too many problems in the U.S.; however, we had a number of arrangements with the Irish Government: training, tax holidays, funding for the facility, etc. This took extra time to come to termination agreements.

The Irish plant produced saleable film during the last half of 1981 on two machines, running well with excellent quality and less cost than other sites. Three shifts ran for about six months starting in July, but ceased operations by Christmas 1981, with the U.S. expatriates getting notice on Thanksgiving to prepare to return home. The plant was sold a short time later to a meat packing firm. Presently the site is occupied by the pharmaceutical company Pfizer (formerly Wyeth). While the total experience was costly to Polaroid, the Polaroid employees who assisted the opening of the Newbridge plant had a wonderful cultural experience. Tim Dwyer reported that, on

December 21, as he and his family were packing to leave in two days, an unusual cold snap with snow hit that part of Ireland, freezing the pipes and cutting off the heat. Those two days for his family were the most miserable of the two-year period. After weathering the ordeal and arriving in the U.S. on the 23rd, Tim's wife turned to him and asked when they could go back again! As Larry Kivimaki reminded me, 1980 in Ireland was the beginning of one the greatest industrial western renaissances of the late 20th century, and made Ireland the envy of much of Europe –until Ireland's recent banking crisis reversed the trend. Polaroid, with its early foray at Newbridge, played a small part in establishing a manufacturing base in Ireland.

Integral Film sales stayed flat in the early 1980s at about 100 million packs per year, never approaching anywhere near 360 million packs. Top sales were 135 million packs in 1994, with about 25 million packs sold in Russia after the decline of Communism. Most of the U.S. film planning department never understood if the film sold in Russia ever actually resulted in many pictures taken, as the Russia sales dropped to near zero the next few years.

While Mac's 360 million pack plan was a bust, he would replace Bill McCune in 1986 as CEO. Joe Oldfield also returned to the U.S., taking on new responsibilities for Mac. He was first assigned to break up the large engineering facilities team who had built all the machines and plants in support of Mac's 360 million plan. Joe would soon become controller for the film assembly division, would later be elevated to vice president of Polaroid manufacturing and eventually executive vice president of photographic imaging. Executive management of Polaroid from 1986 to 1996 would be dominated by the team of Mac and Joe.

Chapter 3:
Mac Booth's Legacy

"I think instant film is going to be the dominant factor in electronic photography, and we know more about that than anyone in the world," says Booth. A color photograph contains an astonishing number of dots called pixels, much like the ones that make up a pointillist painting. A fine-quality 35mm image has about 18 million pixels. One big problem with electronic cameras is that the image sensors used on today's versions usually translate what they see into 400,000 or fewer pixels, nowhere near the quality of film. Even if they could match film, today's electronic cameras use peripheral computer printers that cannot reproduce enough pixels to match the quality of even a newspaper photo. In its new $30 million microelectronics lab, Polaroid is developing an image sensor that it hopes will close the gap. The sensor may be able to translate light into one million pixels, which Polaroid's engineers think may produce a good enough picture – about as good as today's Spectra prints – to please consumers. The company is also betting that instant film, not a computer printer, is the best way to get high-quality prints from electronic cameras. Its scientists have developed a gallium arsenide chip that can convert the electronic information back into light rays that expose Polaroid instant film. The electronic camera

128

is obviously a big gamble, but it probably is one Polaroid can't afford not to make. If the technology works, it could make cameras like the Spectra obsolete. If it doesn't, Booth believes, the champagne will continue to flow. Says he: "anyone who says instant photography is dying has his head in the sand." (Mac Booth, Feb 16, 1987, Fortune Magazine)

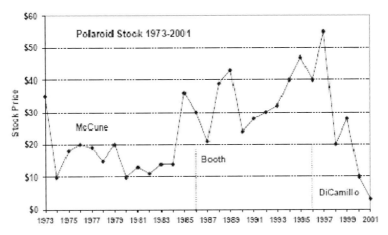

It would be unfair to measure Mac Booth's tenure as CEO based only on his miscalculation of digital imaging's impact on the viability of Polaroid instant film. Dr. Land and the majority of post-Land executives also strongly held the concept that instant film would continue to be the core driver for sales, both as a stand-alone product or as the hard-copy record of electronic devices. When Mac retired from Polaroid in 1995, sales were at $2.3 billion and Polaroid stock was about $46 per share. The chart above indicates Mac had the company trending in the right direction, with expectations the two programs, Captiva and Helios, would drive sales and earnings higher, increasing stock price. Mac had adopted the mantra "$95 by 1995." The expensive failure of Captiva and Helios, along with the $500 million, and growing, debt provided a formidable obstacle to further growth.

Beyond Mac's failure to lead Polaroid into the electronic age, Mac was viewed by most who knew him or, as in my case, observed him in action, as a dedicated, hard-working Polaroid executive who worked to drive Polaroid towards excellence. Unlike many CEOs of his era, Mac did not appear motivated to maximize his personal wealth at the expense of employees and stockholders. Mac's leadership in establishing the very successful New Bedford negative plant was a key milestone in the history of Polaroid. His effort to prevent the hostile takeover by Shamrock was also a major accomplishment.

One of my favorite stories about Mac Booth involved a program in 1993 to provide voter registration photos for Mexico. The program was initiated by the government of Mexican President Carlos Salinas de Gortari to promote equity and openness in its electoral process. Polaroid provided specially designed cards to eligible voters in Mexico over the next two years in preparation for the country's 1994 national election. Included in the ID system were cameras similar to the then popular U.S. driver license systems used in many states, special instant Polacolor film and voter registration photo cards with multiple security features to verify voter identification. The ID blank was made in Oklahoma by a company under contract to Polaroid. They required a major infusion of cash and technical help to ramp up to the quantities required. This ID blank was in the form of a butterfly. It had the voter information with space for the photo and fingerprint captured at the polling places; then the form was laminated and given to the voter. The lamination portion of the project was performed in Oklahoma City, Oklahoma, in a rented warehouse.

Several folks volunteered for the Oklahoma adventure. One employee in my department, John Rosa, a Polaroid supervisor and former Employees Committee representative, volunteered. As an experienced Polaroid supervisor, he would always arrive at work before his crew. So, on his first day in Oklahoma, John left the Motel 6 armed with a coffee and a local newspaper. In the plant at 6:45 a.m., he noted one guy sweeping the floor. John said, "Hey, Mac, you're holding the broom all wrong!"

It was CEO Mac Booth, out to visit the site and show support for the relocated team. John and Mac had sparred back in the early days when John was on the EC and Mac was a young

130

manager. I'm sure both John and Mac enjoyed the irony of the moment.

While Mac could be brutally direct at times, most Polaroid employees held him in high regard due to the sense he was a straight shooter, no hidden agenda. This characteristic was exemplified by the advice he provided a CEO, Marshall N. Carter, former chairman of the board of directors of the New York Stock Exchange. During a speech, August 13, 2010, "Making Sense of the Financial Mess," Carter said:

> You don't want any of your friends on the board. The first thing I would say is you don't want any of your friends on the board. I learned this the hard way. I was initially upset when I was appointed CEO. One of my board members, the CEO of Polaroid, Mac Booth, pulled me aside after the board meeting and in a very friendly way he said, "Marsh, just so you are clear, you do not have any authority to add anybody to this board. You may give me a few names if you want, and we will consider them, but you have no authority to offer a position on this board because they might have to be tough. That is why they are here."

Amen, Mac, all boards should heed your advice.

The next chapters will outline the two challenges that shaped the legacy of Mac Booth as CEO of Polaroid: the Kodak patent infringement and the Shamrock hostile takeover attempt. There are mixed reviews on how Mac spent the Kodak settlement and his actions during the Shamrock bid.

Chapter 4:
Kodak Law Suit

In 1976, Polaroid entered a costly and lengthy patent-infringement battle with the Eastman Kodak Company. Kodak had been producing the negative component of Polaroid's black-and-white film since 1944 and its color negative since 1957. With the introduction of the Polaroid SX-70, Kodak terminated its partnership with Polaroid and began its own instant-photography research. Kodak introduced the EK-4 and EK-6 instant cameras and PR-10 instant film in 1976. Polaroid filed suit within a week, charging twelve patent infringements in camera, film and design.

Legal preparations dragged on for five years, until the trial began in October of 1981. Ten of the twelve original counts were pressed. After 75 days of testimony and three years of deliberation, U.S. District Court Judge Rya Zobel ruled that seven of the ten Polaroid patents were valid and had been infringed upon. As a result, Kodak's line of instant-photography products was terminated in 1986. When settlement talks began, Polaroid claimed about $6.1 billion in damages, lost sales, and interest. The case was not settled until 1991 and resulted in a payment by Eastman Kodak of $925 million (portions extracted from Encyclopedia.com). During the trial, Polaroid members, from Dr. Land down to various managers in the planning and engineering departments, were either interviewed by Kodak lawyers or testified. Kodak centered its case on settlement payout on Polaroid's lack of capacity to market and manufacture instant film and cameras. The award was finally

132

decided by U.S. District Court, District of Massachusetts, on October 12, 1990. The presiding Judge A. David Mazzone concluded:

It would be ridiculous to conclude that Kodak's presence in the market did not influence how Polaroid conducted its instant business from 1976 to 1985. Other than losing the sales that Kodak made, however, Polaroid has not proven additional damage. It has not shown that it would have charged higher prices. It has not proven that it would have introduced the OneStep later. Even if I were to conclude that Polaroid would have waited to introduce the OneStep, it has failed to prove that would have resulted. Polaroid failed to prove, even in a rough way, what those consumers who historically purchased OneSteps and Handles would have done in a world without Kodak. Even giving Polaroid every benefit of the doubt, the Court is unable to conclude that the company would have reaped greater profits.

Liability does not extend to speculative damages. Polaroid has failed to prove that higher prices would have brought it greater profit or that Kodak caused price erosion. As a result, Polaroid has not proved that its damages extended beyond 1985; in its proposed scenario, the high prices and delayed introductions would have increased demand from 1985 to 1990. Polaroid's prices after 1985 were not affected by Kodak's infringement. Polaroid is only entitled to lost profits from the sales Kodak made minus those sales Polaroid would have been unable to make because of limits in its marketing capability.

The gap of Polaroid's claim of $6.1 billion dollars was diluted down to $925 million; the approximate amount of instant product sold by Kodak over the 9-year period, adjusted higher based on interest on the lost profits.

Eastman Kodak Co. paid $925 million to Polaroid Corp. yesterday as part of a surprise out-of-court settlement of their historic 15-year legal battle over Kodak's infringement of Polaroid's patents on instant camera technology. Kodak's payment included $873 million, the amount of damages awarded Cambridge-based Polaroid by federal Judge A. David Mazzone in January 1990. (That was a revision of his original $909.5 million judgment issued last October.) The balance represents $52 million in interest. Both companies had appealed Mazzone's ruling, the largest patent-infringement award ever. Polaroid said it deserved $12 billion; Kodak argued that it owed Polaroid $177 million. The companies said in separate statements that they were relieved to end their long court fight.   (The Boston Globe, July 16, 1991)

The settlement could have been tripled if Polaroid lawyers had proven Kodak willfully infringed on the seven patents at issue. Polaroid employees had heard bits and pieces that willful infringement was the case since an old Kodak memo had surfaced where the project leader at Kodak had written to the effect: "at this point, let's not worry about existing patents, let's just develop the best instant product we can." In reviewing the facts presented in the case, Judge Mazzone saw it differently and ruled:

According to Polaroid, no skilled attorney would have advised Kodak that the patents in suit were invalid or not infringed by Kodak's instant film and cameras. In its turn, Kodak states that, as it developed its integral instant photography system, it repeatedly obtained validity and infringement opinions from Francis T. Carr, a leading national expert in patent clearance and unabashedly praised by Polaroid's counsel throughout the damages portion of the trial. Since Mr. Carr's advice to Kodak

134

was so at odds with the advice Polaroid contends any skilled attorney would have rendered, Polaroid asks the Court to believe that Kodak somehow either manipulated Mr. Carr, or the information Carr received, in order to reach a result desired by Kodak, namely, various opinions of counsel that ratified and masked Kodak's willful infringement of Polaroid's patents. That dog will not hunt. Polaroid has failed to produce a single shred of evidence that supports this claim, as the following review of the record demonstrates.

Fortunately for Polaroid, no memos surfaced to indicate Polaroid lacked capacity in the various plants.

In 2001, a few years after leaving Polaroid, I spent a week working at Kodak's Rochester, New York, manufacturing facilities – Kodak Park. I had been hired by an International Standards Organization (ISO) Registrar to conduct an Environmental Management System audit of Kodak's manufacturing activities. Kodak had been required by the Environmental Protection Agency (EPA) to have a third party audit its site regarding a violation of certain EPA requirements.

At the opening meeting of the audit, I addressed the fifty or so Kodak managers in a large conference center, outlining the process my team would use during the audit. In describing my background and credentials that allowed me to conduct the audit, I mentioned my work experience at Polaroid, thanking them for the $925 million they provided Polaroid back in 1990. The comment did not receive much of a response, but before the plant tour, the VP in charge of the manufacturing operations asked if I had current connections with Polaroid. I said no, so I was allowed to see the film-coating equipment after I signed a "non-disclosure agreement." My tour guide had worked on Kodak's instant film project. We had a great chat. He made a point of showing me the portion of the facility that had produced the instant film. The area was now used to produce 35-mm silver movie film, a very sophisticated, high-tech process. Kodak's movie film business has been essentially eliminated by the current digital movie film.

Chapter 5:
Shamrock – Hostile Takeover

After five months of persistent rumors, Walt Disney's nephew, Roy E. Disney, announced yesterday that an investor group he heads holds 8 percent of the Polaroid Corporation and was prepared to buy the rest of the instant-photography giant for $40 a share, or $2.3 billion, in cash. His partner and close associate, Stanley P. Gold, added that their company, Shamrock Holdings Inc., would pay even more than $40 for the shares if Polaroid's directors agreed to negotiate. Mr. Gold added, however, that Shamrock had "not yet fully explored the financing arrangements and was, therefore, making the offer subject to its getting the money."

The lead paragraph from The New York Times published July 21, 1988, sent shock waves throughout Polaroid from Cambridge to New Bedford to Enschede, the Netherlands. Immediately, Polaroid employees assumed the scheme was being orchestrated by Walt Disney, which was untrue, although Roy Disney was Walt's nephew and probably used earnings from his earlier engagement with his uncle. Quickly, however, the battle lines were drawn: Mac Booth would be Polaroid's protector with Roy Disney's front man, Stanley Gold, assuming the perceived, evil carpetbagger role, plotting to take not only the anticipated multi-million dollar settlement from Kodak, but

137

also the overfunded employee Pension Fund. It was assumed Shamrock would sell off all the research and manufacturing divisions, forcing faithful Polaroid employees out on the street. Wall Street generally supported the hostile takeover bid, pushing up Polaroid's stock price $6, to $40. The shares were selling for about $30 in February, 1987, when rumors first began circulating that Mr. Disney was buying Polaroid stock.

Mac and the board of directors put together an Employee Stock Ownership Plan (ESOP). As employees, we had a crash course on ESOPs. We learned that since Polaroid was incorporated in Delaware, a hostile takeover would require 85% of shareholders to support the sale. With the ESOP, Polaroid employees would have control of 14-20% of the stock and the high majority of employees would disapprove of the takeover. To allow employees to "buy" the stock, our pay would be reduced 8.5%. Continuing with excerpts from the New York Times, July 1988, report:

Court records and letters from Mr. Disney and Mr. Gold to I. MacAllister Booth, president of Polaroid, show that Shamrock began accumulating Polaroid shares early this year. They used the code name Ice Capades to mask the buying. By last month, they held more than 4 percent. By June 16, Mr. Gold, who is chief executive of Shamrock, tried without success to arrange a meeting with Mr. Booth to discuss "Polaroid's future and Shamrock's ideas for generating additional value for Polaroid's shareholders." Shamrock, wholly owned by Roy Disney, has interests that include 3 television stations, 15 radio stations and 3 percent of the Walt Disney Company. Writing to the Polaroid chief executive on June 17, Mr. Disney said, "I was surprised when your secretary, in response to my call to you, said that you would not have any time to see Stanley Gold and myself during our visit to the East Coast next week or, as I understand from your secretary, at any other time." (Full Text in Appendix F)

Meanwhile, rather than meet with Gold, Mac set about meeting with employees to keep us informed of the situation. Mac did a great job in fending off the Shamrock hostile take-over. He teamed with the head of the Employees Committee, Nick Pasquarosa, to rally the troops behind the cause. There were rallies, complete with t-shirts, declaring, "Say No to Stanley." On the day Shamrock withdrew their bid, I encountered Mac on the stairwell of the Battery division; he was out visiting all the sites, thanking employees for their support. I thanked him for the great job and received a handshake and smile from the CEO – a nice moment in my Polaroid career. Shamrock challenged the ESOP as a hurriedly implemented tool to entrench management, approved in rubber stamp fashion by Polaroid's board. Reported the Boston Globe on October 22 and 25, 1988:

The fourth day of the ESOP trial opened yesterday with William J. McCune Jr., Polaroid's chairman, resuming his answers to Polaroid attorney Frederick A.O. Schwarz. On Friday, McCune testified to his longstanding support for an employee stock ownership plan and offered evidence that ESOPs had been investigated by Polaroid long before Shamrock Holdings' request in mid-June 1988 to meet with Polaroid's management. McCune flatly denied that the ESOP was adopted to "entrench management" as Shamrock charges. McCune, 73, testified that he has been an advocate of employee stock ownership plans since "before they were called ESOPs", and had discussed placing anywhere from 20 percent to 30 percent of Polaroid's stock in employee hands. McCune testified that he felt the 5 percent ESOP initially envisioned by Polaroid's board last March was "too small to do an effective job, but was a good start."

At that time in October of 1988, I wondered what evidence existed to support McCune's testimony of the prior support for an employee stock ownership plan as most employees did not

139

recall any discussions on employee stock ownership. In reviewing Polaroid Annual Reports, I noted that Polaroid had a "Paysop" (Payroll-based Stock Ownership Plan) in place since 1983. The plan provided compensation in company stock for all vested employees and officers based on income up to $7,500 per year, prorated on base salary. The 1986 Annual Report indicated a payout of $190. I vaguely recall the payout, but more importantly, the trial judge agreed Polaroid did have an employee ownership plan in place before Shamrock's takeover attempt. A Boston Globe article on January 7, 1989, explained the decision by the judge.

> In upholding Polaroid's ESOP, Berger found that "the evidence is un-contradicted that ESOPs promote productivity." After considering the mountain of evidence, including more than 3,000 pages of transcript generated by the trial, Berger was "satisfied that the Polaroid ESOP is fundamentally fair." The fact that the ESOP was "partly defensive," Berger wrote, "… does not make it unfair."

An article in the Boston Globe in 1998 suggested perhaps the Shamrock and Stanley Gold position was correct and Polaroid shareholders, suppliers and employees would have been better served with Shamrock running the company. The premise of the article was that Shamrock offered $3 billion in 1988 and now Polaroid was worth only $1-billion (Boston Globe: October 29, 1998, Steve Bailey and Steven Syre). The response to the article in 1998 by Paul Hegarty, a key collaborator on my book, summed up the position of most Polaroid employees.

> If Mr. Gold was successful in '89, I, along with some 5,000 to 7,000 of my coworkers, would have been summarily terminated. Mr. Gold's plan was to raid the Polaroid pension plan by as much as $300 million. He was also planning to "shop" Polaroid's camera business to anyone interested in a license and to "shop" the film business to Kodak and Fuji. The facts of Mr. Gold's strategy for the "disposal" of Polaroid

are irrefutable. The documents filed in the litigation phase of the takeover struggle spell out in chilling detail the ultimate outcome for Polaroid and its employees. The company is still struggling, but my view of the Stanley Gold plan is the company would be extinct if Stanley had won the day back in 1989.

(Paul Hegarty, Arlington, Massachusetts)

After reviewing the Shamrock saga with several former employees, I am left with mixed feelings on how Polaroid leadership addressed the take-over challenge. Some in finance felt Polaroid should have purchased more Polaroid stock a year before the take-over attempt. Remember that on Monday, October 19, 1987, the U.S. stock market had a major crash, over 20% –worse in Asia and Europe – called "Black Monday." The crash was caused by the early version of the automatic program trading using computers. Several members of Polaroid's finance department felt we should purchase a large share of Polaroid stock. It was at about $15 per share and was only down due to the crash. The company's finances were in good shape and Polaroid would be getting the Kodak settlement soon, maybe several billion dollars. The stock could be deposited in our matching donation fund for the employees' 401K plan. Polaroid did purchase 5% of its outstanding stock which was applied towards the employees' 401K matching awards. A major mistake in the opinion of many Polaroid retirees: not buying more stock at $15 or $20 per share, as it quickly went to $30, then as high as $42, with the Shamrock offer. We could have made enough to pay off most or all of the $300 million ESOP cost, placing Polaroid in a much better financial situation going into the 1990s.

Polaroid exited the Shamrock saga with $300 million in debt and paid Shamrock $40 million for their eight-month challenge. The executive staff was trimmed of vice presidents in Hal Page, Gerry Sudbury, and Cris Ingram. The loss of these experienced executives, along with the retirements of Dr. Richard Young and Dr. Derek Jarrett of the International Division in 1982, was a watershed moment in the eventual demise of Polaroid. Their replacements, who would lead Polaroid into the early 1990s, were mostly home grown, lacking in advanced business or technical skills. There was a somewhat singular strategy during this time: Make more instant film, cheaper and for new markets. Additionally, Booth and the board were criticized for not using part of the Kodak settlement to pay down this debt.

A $68 billion California pension fund planned to vote against Polaroid's board of directors at the company's annual shareholder meeting in May of 1992. In Boston Business Journal, April 13, 1992, Wendy Hower reported:

> The California Public Employees' Retirement System (CalPERS) wants fatter stockholder dividends and an end to "blank check" R&D spending on Polaroid's secret Joshua camera and Helios imaging machine, according to DeWitt Bowman, CalPERS' chief investment officer. If CalPERS has its way, Polaroid would set up a shareholder advisory board through which the poor performer would have to answer to investors. And CalPERS wants a say in how Polaroid spends the $925 million it won in a litigation settlement against Kodak last year.

Polaroid's ten largest shareholders didn't follow CalPERs' protest over Polaroid's poor performance between 1987 and 1991; Polaroid's board continued intact in 1992 and beyond; and Polaroid decided how to spend the Kodak settlement without the assistance of a shareholder advisory board. The CalPERs approach could have helped Polaroid, as will be evident in subsequent chapters.

I asked several Polaroid retirees whether they felt the company should have paid down the debt with the Kodak money; they universally agreed with Booth and the board. Polaroid needed a major boost to fight off the erosion of its flagship instant products, caused by the superior quality APS conventional film developed efficiently in one-hour developing kiosks. The selected platforms, Captiva and Helios, would be expensive. So, if the Kodak cash was used to pay off the debt, additional money would have to be borrowed in coming years. Hindsight is 20-20, I suppose, but Polaroid management

142

exhibited a troublesome trend during Mac Booth's time as CEO: they did not listen to shareholders – the California pension fund – and they ignored advice from employees – the financial managers. Later chapters will review Polaroid management's arrogance in not accepting input from analysts and employees related to the new programs, Captiva and Helios.

I received a sample of this close-minded leadership style when I made a presentation to Mac and his staff in 1986 covering the elimination of mercury from Polaroid's battery. The greatest accomplishment in my Polaroid career sure didn't feel so great during this meeting with Mac.

Chapter 6:
The Mercury Elimination Project and the Damn Battery!

Polaroid's battery in the film pack was based on Leclanché cell (carbon-zinc) chemistry, using a zinc anode and a manganese dioxide cathode. Similar to alkaline round cell batteries, the Polaroid flat battery contained a trace amount of mercury to control side reactions at the zinc anode and generation of hydrogen gas which, if not vented properly, reduced the performance of the battery. That is the good characteristic of mercury; mercury that is allowed to enter the food chain or water supply has a well-publicized, terrible history. In 1986, near Basel, Switzerland, a catastrophic fire in a building used for storing pesticides, mercury and other highly poisonous agricultural chemicals sent tons of toxic chemicals into the nearby Rhine River, turning it red. The Swiss government responded quickly, establishing restrictions on all products containing mercury. Fluorescent tubes and batteries were key targets because of the difficulty in keeping them from entering landfills.

As technical manager of the Battery Division, I was heading up the program to first reduce the amount of mercury in Polaroid's battery to meet the Swiss guidelines and then eliminate the mercury completely. A few months after the Swiss restrictions were published, a group from Polaroid's Film Assembly Division – Gary Levy, Plant Manager and my supervisor; Herb Ahrens, Film Division Director of

Manufacturing and Gary's supervisor; Art Hillier, Principal Battery Technologist – and I, were summoned to the boardroom to present to Mac Booth and his staff the status of our program to eliminate the use of mercury in the Polaroid battery.

Polaroid's boardroom at Technology Square in Cambridge in the '80s was the singular company location with trappings consistent with a two-billion-dollar company. It also provided linkage to the unique company that was Land's Polaroid. The photos lining the walls captured several generations of Polaroid executives and board members and, for a first-time visitor like me, were both inspiring and intimidating.

As the battery contingent entered the room, the other VPs chatted amongst themselves, mostly ignoring us. Shelly, Dr. Sheldon Buckler, Executive VP, did provide a brief hello. Shelly was one of the founders of the Battery Division; the closest connection to the Land Polaroid and often thought to be Land's successor until Mac prevailed. Even at my level, it was clear Mac and Shelly were not especially close and had different views on Polaroid's future: Mac, the engineer, bottom line; Shelly, the technocrat, science. They did share the "office of the presidency" for a few years; however, most observers considered that an image thing designed to mollify Wall Street.

"Tell me then, Milt, which federal agency or what country wants a mercury reduction of only 10%?" Mac posed the question in a way that indicated he already knew the answer. Before responding to Mac, I tried to collect myself to avoid getting into technical details that might be unfamiliar to Mac and the audience. Mac and most of the senior staff took pride in their product knowledge and would quickly pounce on a less-than-concise technical premise. I glanced at my colleagues, hoping for a few words that might allow me time to compose an acceptable answer. No luck – I was on my own.

The meeting had started badly. We had joined the staff following an executive session. I assumed the prior meeting was related to the recent poor financial quarter – actually several consecutive bad quarters. Although Polaroid was still a viable concern, pressure from Wall Street was intense and sales continued flat in the late '80s, with earnings declining and debt

145

growing. Harry Fatkin, Corporate Director of Environmental Management, opened the meeting by describing the situation in Switzerland, where a directive had been issued to prevent sale of batteries that contain mercury in that country. Although sale of Polaroid film in Switzerland was quite small, a similar restriction was being set throughout Europe; mercury in consumer batteries would soon not be acceptable. Several U.S. states, California, New Jersey, and Minnesota, were already initiating similar actions. This was obviously great cause for concern as integral film sales represented 75% of sales, and essentially all profits, during the prior several years. Polaroid was a small, relatively new player in batteries; my opinion was that we should follow the lead of the big battery guys who had considerable expertise in this field. My meetings with scientists at major battery companies indicated there were major concerns regarding possible replacements for mercury.

Prior to my technical presentation, Harry introduced the group and presented information about how waste batteries leached mercury into landfills. While the information about the way discarded batteries might contaminate water supplies in poorly designed landfills was interesting, the charts served to confuse the audience. The data was highly variable, making it incorrectly appear that we battery chemists did not know how much mercury was used in the batteries. Mac in particular appeared confused, almost offended, that the battery people were so primitive in what seemed like simple technology. He was one of the architects of Polaroid's negative plant, where every ingredient was controlled at extreme precision. What a segue for me and my PowerPoint slides! If I could present the data, I thought, the answer would be obvious. But Mac wanted a summary statement immediately. Gathering myself, I started:

Mac, we have some good early results using zero mercury; but, while the test packs with 10 per cent level of mercury perform about the same as the standard, full mercury packs, some of the data on battery decay won't be available for at least a year. After three months of testing, we are convinced we can get to 10% by year end, as the batteries are

146

performing identically to the standard mercury batteries. We are confident we can go to zero next year, beating the Swiss directive by one year. The next six months will allow us time to test the many possible interactions where mercury plays a role we are not completely aware of...

Before I could get into my discussion related to attacking a 100-year-old battery tradition and the role of mercury and my discussions with other battery companies, Mac interrupted: "Milt, tell me again what agency will be happy with us when we still use mercury at one-tenth? Will we be okay in Switzerland?"

Suppressing my need to attempt to educate Mac further on the subject, and responding to a nervous cough from Gary, "None, Mac, but..."

This time Shelly cut me off. "Mac, battery chemistry is more art than science; that's why Land loved his battery so much. As someone who spent a few years helping Land develop his battery, I understand the issues pretty well." I wondered whether Shelly was supporting me or reminding Mac of his lack of understanding of battery technology and Shelly's own Land connection.

Without responding to Shelly or even turning to face him, Mac proclaimed, "Why in the world would we make a change that no country requires of us? I want to meet every month or so until we get to zero mercury."

What was my take from the mercury vignette? Although I admired Mac Booth and respected him for the leadership in building the New Bedford negative operations, I was concerned with the management style he demonstrated during the mercury elimination session. Mac seemed to be still competing to be "top dog" at Polaroid, even though he had been CEO for several years now. Wanting to demonstrate his technical and product skills, he was often referred to, less than affectionately, as "Mac the Senior Engineer." Were Mac, Shelly and the other executives on the same page? When making important product decisions, did the somewhat combative, close-minded atmosphere I just witnessed prevail? I also wondered if the

147

managers who reported to the senior staff could express their ideas freely in this atmosphere. In this environment, it was natural for the next level of management to be politically sensitive and protective. Harry Fatkin, the Environmental Director, was under intense pressure on environmental issues on several fronts, and his career was probably on the line. Harry and I eventually teamed up to complete the mercury elimination project and worked well together on future issues. I believed the intense "win-lose" atmosphere that permeated Polaroid the last several years at the manager level, along with the declining profits, caused decisions to be made with less than open discussions.

What was the outcome of the mercury elimination program? The goal of zero mercury was achieved ahead of the Swiss requirement and before it was achieved at other battery companies. I presented this accomplishment in trade journals and at battery seminars around the world – everywhere, but never in the Polaroid boardroom again. The company suffered several million dollars in battery failures, and nearly interrupted the film supply on a few occasions because of bypassing the normal one-year shelf testing we had recommended. Batteries with zero mercury had to be aged 90 days before they could be released for testing and assembly into film packs; the mercury-containing batteries could be tested after 60 days. The transition plan could have achieved the same result without the loss. But, more importantly, the result could have been achieved in an atmosphere where conflicting voices could be heard.

How would Dr. Land have handled this situation? Ten years earlier, Land had patented a possible replacement for mercury, so he would have been leading the charge with one of his top aides, certainly not me. His impatience with getting products to market quickly, sometimes with high early failures, was well known in and out of Polaroid; but I don't believe he would have jumped as quickly as Mac did because he would have first wanted to understand the chemistry.

Upon returning to the battery plant after the meeting with Mac's staff, I replayed the meeting scenario to Frank Ceppi, the battery quality manager, describing my disappointment with the rejection of our plan to phase out mercury. Frank listened, and responded, quizzically:

Milt, I'm surprised at your reaction to Mac and the battery division. I recall you telling me that Mac has referred to the "damn" battery on a few occasions. We've been a necessary evil to most Polaroid executives ever since Dr. Land retired, and Shelly Buckler left the division. The catastrophic, multi-million battery failure and write-off that you and Bob Jacobs presented to Mac in 1983 dug us a credibility hole that the Battery Division will never climb out of.

I had to agree with him. While Frank did a good job establishing controls and test protocols to ensure material or process changes would not have a negative effect on the battery's performance, the Battery Division remained the "black sheep" of Polaroid right up to the end of production of Integral film.

I left the Battery Division in 1992 to take on a new assignment as Director of Materials for world-wide integral film, with responsibility for purchasing, logistics, supplier quality, finished goods packaging, and inventories. This job allowed me to get deep into the financial workings of Polaroid, the cost make-up of our products, and the pricing. The disappointment I had with Polaroid's leadership, demonstrated during the battery mercury-elimination project, continued as I attempted to direct the material and film inventory activities for Integral film.

Chapter 7:
Polaroid's 1980s Business Practices

"So class, you are about to board a DC6 on a flight from Boston to Hyannis," the instructor explained. "There are only six passengers on the flight: the president of Rice Barton Company with his wife and two young children; Bob Cousy, the star basketball player of the Boston Celtics; and you. The crew is the captain and co-pilot who served also as flight attendant."

The class was an evening course in "Value-Analysis-Value engineering"; the instructor, Professor Johnson, was from a local college, and the students were from area manufacturing companies in 1965 Worcester, Massachusetts.

.

"There is a one-inch-diameter bolt that, with four others, secures the propeller assembly to the cowling of the DC6. The quality department at Douglass classifies the bolts as 'quality critical', requiring 100% inspection to deal with the catastrophic potential of a housing failure. Your assignment is to define the value of each one- inch bolt. You have 15 minutes to present me with one answer," he instructed.

The students' inputs varied widely. Cousy had recently received some publicity as a $35,000-per-year athlete, considered unbelievable for the time period when engineers made about $7,000 per year. The president of Rice Barton, a 100-year-old Worcester company known to the students, might have been part of a family inheritance of near $1 million. The ten students, mostly young engineers from the area, provided their consensus answer: $25,000 for each bolt. Their notes included calculations of potential earning power, assumed insurance policies held on Cousy and the president, offset by probability of failure. Professor Johnson proceeded to the blackboard. Material cost, he wrote, high strength carbon steel: $0.02 each; director labor and overhead: $0.015 each; special inspection cost: $0.05 each; profit margin at 15% of costs: $0.013 each. "The total value of each one-inch bolt is $0.098, let's say 10 cents. You follow the math?" he asked.

Nearly jumping out of my seat, I exclaimed, "That's the sell price, not the value!"

"Why should your value, including fair profit, of an item you produce and the price your customer pays for it, not be the same? If we let potential consequences of a product or special market pressures dictate the cost or, God forbid, our profit margin, we are confusing value and reliability. At the manufacturing level, our responsibility is always to charge our customers with the value we add to items we produce, combined with a fair profit." Johnson responded.

Never one to give up easily, I started to understand his concept, but my youth caused me to continue, "But, sir, in the larger picture, the failure of that bolt had incredible cost implications should the plane crash."

"That is where reliability engineering and insurance companies play their role. Douglass Aircraft would pay upfront costs in studies to understand the potential failure issues; an engineering group or testing lab would be paid for their value added

151

activities. The insurance company derives their value add from premium paid on policies. Want to be an insurance actuary, Milt?"

Having been duly chastised, I responded, "No, thanks."

"I suggest you and your classmates remember this example as you advance your careers in manufacturing. We should all expect to be paid for the value we bring to the system. Attempting to take extreme profits because we have our customers in a bad position, as tempting as it may sound, will destroy the value system. Companies that understand this will prosper. They will have operating principles that will help maintain America as the industrial capital of the world", he concluded.

The value-add concept has stayed with me all these years. Imagine Professor Johnson's dismay at the current state of the business and finance world if he were alive today. I believe Land's business principles were consistent with my old mentor Johnson's. Instant film products were always sold at high margin, but the products were discretionary. No value, too expensive – don't buy. Consistent with his first aim: Our aim is to make products which are genuinely new and useful to the public, products of the highest quality at reasonable cost. In this way we assure the financial success of the company, and each of us has the satisfaction of helping to make a creative contribution to society. Land's pricing policy was to create wealth to provide for capital for expansion and new equipment and additional employees. Consistent with his second aim, profit dollars, after allowance for the capital spending, was shared with the employees: to share in the progress of the company as far as his capacities permit, to earn enough money so that the need for earning more will not always be the first thing on his mind – opportunity, in short, to make his work here a fully rewarding, important part of his life.

What a fantastic business model. I saw it work for my first several years at Polaroid, even though I was somewhat cynical, especially since Polaroid had a monopoly on instant film. If you had a unique product and wished to start a manufacturing company, wouldn't the first and second aims be a good basis for a business plan? But, also include Professor Johnson's "value" concepts. During Mac Booth's time as CEO, he installed a new set of values for the company, and Land's first and second aims essentially disappeared. Mac's goal was commendable in that his staff adopted worthy values: Excellence, Respect, Ownership, and Innovation. If you were in the presence of a senior executive in the 1980s, you very well might be asked to recite the four values. Not being good with memory of such stuff, I established the acronym Excellent Return on Investment, saved myself from certain embarrassment, and wished the company's business plan would have an EROI!

I was involved in two accounting practices which were rational in only publicly traded companies and were patently wrong to stakeholders – employees, stockholders and suppliers. Professor Johnson would have sniffed them out and exposed both in a heartbeat. These practices continue in the financial community and are almost an accepted part of doing business in today's global community, even though both have been routinely challenged by the economists.

Brian Milan, Planning Manager for film production, and I had a meeting with Carole Uhrich, Senior Vice President of Manufacturing, in October 1994 to review the end-of-year film manufacturing plan. The end-of-year film sales were extremely important to the company's financial results fourth-quarter sales could make or break the year; the holiday season had a positive impact. Brian had considerable experience in the planning and scheduling process. He reported to me; but, since most of my background was technical, I looked to Brian to take the lead for the planning strategy. Carole was an experienced Polaroid executive, having held management positions in technical, quality and manufacturing areas. She was well versed in the Polaroid product lines. Many Polaroid employees thought she might have the required background to succeed Mac Booth as CEO when he retired.

Polaroid had computer models going back several years that predicted film sales based on cameras sold in the current year, with consideration of obsolescence of older cameras. The key to the analysis of how much film would be sold was to estimate how many cameras were active and how much film each camera would use. The "burn" rate varied with the age and model type. Unfortunately, the sales group felt the computer model was outdated. They had their own plan, based on an undeclared algorithm. In manufacturing, we believed the sales forecast was mostly wishful thinking, influenced by the incentive bonuses of sales personnel.

For several years before this, the film manufacturing group had over-manufactured film in the last quarter in support of the consistently ambitious marketing forecast. This year, Brian and I decided to challenge the sales estimate, using the computer model which predicted fourth-quarter sales of about 75% of the current forecast. I felt we had an ally in Carole because she had a strong technical background. The numbers weren't that complicated; we would present our case, similar to an engineering challenge, complete with assumptions and options.

Carole listened and asked what our recovery plan was. We explained that, rather than use overtime to produce film in the fourth quarter – film which most likely would not be sold until the following year – the film plants would run the inventory down at year's end; if marketing came anywhere close to their plan, the plants would run very efficient overtime during the first quarter next year to make film that would be sold soon. Our plan would prevent the aging of the film, if the forecast was missed. Polaroid's film has a shelf life of about 12-18 months; so, if film sat in warehouses, there was the risk of outdated film or at least compromised picture quality. Carole was well aware of the film shelf-life concern vs. film quality.

A few days after the meeting with Carole, my supervisor, Ed Coughlan, Director of Worldwide Film Manufacturing, provided some feedback. Carole had relayed the proposal to her boss, Joe Oldfield. He asked Carole how I could know more about film sales than the marketing division and exclaimed, "Make the film!" Carole also suggested to Ed that I needed to work on "listening" skills, as I was overly confident in this plan.

154

We ended 1994 with approximately 18 million packs of film in inventory, 50% above the goal of 12 million. The film plant people had some nice overtime checks in the fourth quarter and scrambled for meaningful work in the next several months. My performance review suffered because I did not achieve my inventory goal.

Why did Oldfield allow the overproduction of film? Polaroid financial reporting procedures used "absorption based costing", which allows fixed overhead costs to be spread over manufactured product, even if the product was not sold in the same time period, providing the illusion of higher profits, even though the units were not actually sold in the same period. There are three consequences in using absorption costing for profit calculation, as opposed to variable costing, which connects manufacturing costs to sales during the same time frame:

- If beginning and ending inventory levels are equal, absorption costing profit equals variable costing profit.
- If inventory levels are run down over the period, variable costing profits will be higher than absorption costing profit.
- If inventory levels are increased over the period, absorption costing profit will be higher than variable costing profit.

So, by overrunning manufacturing volumes, Polaroid used the volume to absorb manufacturing costs, making the unit cost of film sold appear lower, increasing operating profits. Would a privately held company resort to such techniques? No. Cash flow for materials would be higher; cost of inventory and labor costs (overtime) would impact the company's balance sheet and income statement. Wall Street wanted profits, and Polaroid found a way to mollify the analysts, at least for a while.

The second technique, closely connected to absorption costing was "end of period loading" (EOP). This technique is common in many consumer products companies. Simply put, EOP is a process where the supplier conditions its customers over time to realize the supplier will lower the sell price at the end of a quarter or year. This technique causes sales volume to increase at the expense of profits. The reduced profits were somewhat disguised by the false operating profits generated by the absorption costing charade. In the department of worldwide film planning in 1992-96, the last few weeks of December were like a fire sale. If the Integral Film Division shipped approximately 2 million packs per week during most months, 5-10 million packs would ship the last two weeks in December to the larger customers: Walmart, Kmart, Costco and other retailers. Polaroid's sales representative with Walmart was said to have a higher salary than the Polaroid CEO Mac Booth during the late 1980s and early 1990s, based on a hefty bonus. Walmart would get the film for 10-20% less than the previous month and use the Polaroid Film as a promotional "loss-leader" attraction.

The financial world – in and out of Polaroid – knew of these techniques and mostly winked at them or factored the effect into estimated earnings. The tobacco industry was especially guilty of these practices; when they overproduced cigarettes at year end, they often had to recall product the next year due to "aging" regulations. In the mid-1980s, pressure was placed on the industry to start using Economic Value Added (EVA) and activity-based costing. EVA requires a company to measure its financial performance to include cost of capital or inventory. In EVA and activity-based accounting, products produced to build inventory could not reflect future profits without factoring in cost of inventories. Not too dissimilar from my old mentor's "value-added" principles of the early 1960s. Polaroid, along with many publicly-traded consumer companies, took a "pledge" in the '90s to stop the use of both practices, in order to have the income statements more reflective of the company's current results. Polaroid trained many of us in EVA and activity-based accounting and planned to initiate the new paradigm around 1990. A few terrible quarters later and Polaroid was back on the "bottle": EOP + Absorption=virtual profits.

During this time, recognizing the intense pressure Polaroid management was under from Wall Street to increase sales and profits, I could understand why the leaders of the manufacturing division would accept the bogus sales and marketing forecasts. Polaroid had their "silos": R&D designed the new products; marketing provided the programs; sales sold the film; and manufacturing made the film. If Oldfield accepted my plan, and subsequently there was not sufficient film to meet the demand, he would be in a terrible situation. The dysfunctional leadership scenario I described earlier during the elimination of the mercury battery program was systemic across the company.

Several years previously, a former supervisor of mine, Bob Jacobs, held the World Wide Material director's position, not just for Integral film, but for all Polaroid materials and finished products. Bob was a Polaroid legend for having worked in Land's laboratory, being corporate director of quality control in the mid-1960s, heading up the Copy Service Division, and holding the position of plant manager in the Battery Division. Jacobs knew as much about Polaroid as anyone and had great connections to most executives in the company, having hired several of them. He would go directly to the hands-on sales managers to sniff out the "real" sales forecast. When Bob ran the World Wide Materials Division, he kept two books, the one he shared with the executives and sales staff and the plan he used to establish schedules for the manufacturing plants. It worked well; Bob protected the senior staff from themselves, inventories were properly maintained, and the film produced was representative of actual operating profits.

Polaroid functioned much better when we had individuals like Bob Jacobs in key positions. While he never was a vice president, early in his career Bob had provided supervision to the two individuals who would lead Polaroid in the 1990s: Mac Booth and Joe Oldfield.

Chapter 8:
Joe Oldfield Runs Polaroid Operations

Joe Oldfield joined Polaroid in 1966, working as an engineer in the Pack-Film building Waltham W3, or P60 as described earlier. Joe worked his way up to P60 plant manager in 1973.

I first met Joe in 1970, when he was engineering manager for P60, and I was an engineer in the coating plant, Waltham W1. Type 108 color film products had a serious defect related to white specks in the finished print. As the "customer" or assembly machine representative, Oldfield would hold meetings with the component areas that could be contributing to the white specks; namely, the receiving sheet from W1, the reagent or developing chemicals and the group that produced the developer pods. For efficiency, Joe would convene the meetings during the lunch hour and about 10-15 engineers, managers and quality technicians would be present. Over the past several years, P60 had decided that meetings moved along more efficiently if the members had to stand; so the conference room had only a long table where quality samples could be displayed. At this particular meeting, one of the coating mangers was making a case that Oldfield's assembly machines were causing the specks, not the components, certainly not the receiving sheet.

A rather testy exchange ensued with several assembly quality technicians and coating engineers speaking loudly and at the same time. Oldfield, about five-foot, six-inches tall, had difficulty getting the attention of the attendees. He listened for about five minutes then jumped up on the table top. In the next few minutes, he laid out a plan, with assignments to each group, to obtain data to drive out the real cause of the problem. I was stunned, but impressed. It reminded me of Nikita Khrushchev's shoe-banging tirade in the United Nations in 1960.

Over the next twenty-five years, I would observe Oldfield using his organizational skills, coupled with feistiness and self-promotion, to rise to the number two executive position in Polaroid and potential successor to Mac Booth as CEO. He was appointed general manager of Polaroid Ireland in 1978, and group controller for worldwide manufacturing in 1983. In 1987, Oldfield was named vice president worldwide manufacturing and a few years later advanced to executive vice president for photographic imaging – next to the CEO, the most influential executive in the company. When Oldfield took charge of manufacturing, most of us in manufacturing were surprised for, although he had credentials as a plant manager in P60, his results there were spotty at best. As described in Phelps Tracey's "*P60 Express*" a history of the pack film plant, Joe didn't work effectively with his boss, George Fernald, Film division vice president, in the late 1960s. He would argue with Fernald's staff and the Employees Committee representatives. The approach he used in the 1970 white speck story didn't work as well with executives or employees.

Joe did a fine job in establishing the Irish film plant, but most visitors were surprised to see the size of the plant; the building was about 50% larger than the space needed to support the planned number of assembly machines. When Joe returned to the states, he regaled his followers with stories about how he stood up to the trade unions and received concessions on pay rates and schedules. The fact that Polaroid lost millions on the Irish adventure was irrelevant in his mind – style trumped results.

As mentioned previously, the Shamrock adventure had eliminated most of the seasoned manufacturing executives. Those who remained were near in age to Mac, so if Mac wanted to develop the next generation of executives, Joe was certainly a plausible choice. One of Joe's first moves when he headed up manufacturing was to visit all the plants and meet with each senior staff. We all presented slides to describe our education, work experience and important projects. Joe explained his overall strategy: no more short-term "band-aids" or quick fixes; the plants would be measured on a five-year horizon with specific goals and tracking. I was pleased to hear this approach, as over the past several years we had jumped from one program or quality initiative to another. Quality circles begot statistical process control which was replaced by Total Quality Management. ISO-9000 was quickly and poorly implemented when European hospitals would not purchase Polaroid film, unless they were produced in an ISO-certified facility. Self-directing work teams were sampled, as was re-engineering. Instead of using the best of these initiatives, the programs competed with each other – quite dysfunctional and confusing to the work force. Many called our strategy the "fad of the month" master plan.

Other than that one kickoff meeting with the manufacturing staffs, I don't recall Oldfield returning to review the five-year plan. He certainly reviewed all sorts of data, but his obvious concern was the bottom line and reducing costs not for next year, but for next quarter. While Oldfield and his staff brought a lot of energy and new ideas to the day-to-day operation of the manufacturing plants, Polaroid had always been driven by research under Land – the manufacturing groups just implemented the inventions. The major supplier to the film assembly plants, the expensive and complex color negative facility was under direction of the research and development groups. Mac Booth's mission was to keep driving Polaroid Instant film towards the quality and color rendition of conventional 35-mm film. Since the original introduction of both pack and SX-70 film, tremendous improvements had been achieved in instant picture quality. By the early 1990s, SX-70 film, when used in the proper environment of lighting and in close proximity (5-8 feet) to subject matter, did in fact approach 35-mm quality. Shooting the pictures at between 60 to 80 degrees Fahrenheit also worked best with the Polaroid Instant process.

Each new film development, either to improve picture sharpness, temperature latitude or color balance, was costly and ran the risk of creating a deleterious side effect; that is, if sharpness improved, then the red tones, under some photographic conditions, could create a situation in which the instant picture would be unacceptable. The assembly plants were continually at the mercy of the "new" film prototype. While the plant managers might have priorities to improve material yields or increase productivity to reduce costs, conflicting dynamics existed in the plants: support the latest negative development, nicknamed "Hybrid 4" or "P3"; and, if they don't work so well, find ways to absorb the costs and lost production time. It was truly a vicious cycle, which was a way of life for the film assembly plants in the 1990s. There were several occasions where millions of dollars worth of negative components or film were either scrapped or reworked or shipped to geographic locations where the unacceptable film would not be as obvious because of amelioration by lower or higher outdoor temperatures. The Battery Division also contributed several product quality issues.

A chance meeting with a long-time Polaroid manager, Tony Moreschi, at an airport in 2000, brought me up to date on Polaroid since 1996 when I had left. Tony had spent most of his Polaroid career in the SX-70 film assembly plant. He had been the plant manager and director of materials for worldwide film assembly and was probably the most knowledgeable executive in the company regarding SX-70 film history. I asked Tony, since all the key technical folks involved with managing changing film prototypes had left the Polaroid in 1996, how the company responded to major film problems. Tony's response was revealing, "Well, actually, one of new CEO Gary DiCamillo's first moves – and maybe his best – was to freeze the film prototypes. No more new Hybrid negatives. The SX-70 film plants are running well, no more product disasters."

In addition to the constantly changing film prototypes, Oldfield and his staff were at the mercy of the sales and marketing groups. Walmart and other large retailers dictated how the product would be packaged and displayed and even priced. Walmart, in fact, was essentially a "surrogate" member of Polaroid's product planning team. Walmart and its Sam's

Warehouse represented approximately $150 million dollars in sales for Polaroid in the early to mid-1990s. Starting about 1985, Walmart had decreed that, if Polaroid wanted to compete for the desirable "end cap'" display space with Kodak and Fuji, it would need to expand its offerings to include both conventional 35-mm film and VHS analog video recording cassette tapes. Polaroid partnered with 3M and Agfa to produce their 35-mm film inserted in a Polaroid film package. Polaroid did not invest in producing its own 35-mm film but had a different strategy for the VHS magnetic tapes. As in 35-mm film, the company would market and sell an established brand produced by JVC or Sony, but would also develop a prototype manufacturing capability to attempt to leverage Polaroid's considerable expertise in chemistry and coatings. The magnetic research never had any beneficial results; Mac shut it down soon after a few million dollars were spent on setting up second hand equipment in the coating area, W5.

While Joe Oldfield was effective in running the manufacturing plants during his time as Mac Booth's second in command, it was questionable whether the board of directors could select him to replace the retiring Booth in 1996 and lead Polaroid into the future. Polaroid faced many challenges after the recovery from the Shamrock hostile takeover attempt and in determining how best to use the payout from the Kodak patent suit.

What characteristics should Polaroid's board of directors look for in the next CEO? I discovered an interesting screening process developed by Dr. Modesto "Mitch" Maidique. Dr. Maidique holds a doctorate from the Massachusetts Institute of Technology; co-founded Analog Devices, Inc; and was president of Florida International University for many years. While a visiting professor at Harvard Business School, Dr. Maidique developed a concept to rate leaders by asking a central, most telling question: *Whom do you serve?*

Chapter 9:
Six Levels of Leadership

Dr. Modesto "Mitch" Maidique developed a topology of six levels of leadership, from sociopath to transcendent. Applied to society, business or politics, the screen opens the question of who you are serving: yourself, your group truly, or society at large? As I was completing my review of leadership at Polaroid from Land to DiCamillo, I thought this could be an interesting process by which to analyze the leadership styles of the various CEOs at Polaroid. Dr. Maidque's screen would be a useful tool in selection of executives by company boards.

Sociopath

At the base of Maidique's model – level one – is the person who serves literally no one: the sociopath. This type of leader has abnormally low empathy, making it difficult to create connections with followers, and destroys value for the organization, himself, and ultimately those who surround him. Example: Libyan strongman Moammar Gadhafi.

Opportunist

The opportunist serves only himself, often at the expense of others. Opportunists are obsessed with "What's in it for me?". Examples: Bernie Madoff, who developed the investment Ponzi scheme that primarily benefited him (until it sent him to prison); and Jeffrey Skilling, the ex-Enron CEO who also is behind bars.

Chameleon

Chameleons bend with the wind, trying to please as many people as possible by fitting in with everyone else's views. We know them in our companies and, of course, we also see them on the political stage. Professor Maidique says that in business they tend to be weeded out before they rise too high, but in politics many prominent individuals fall into this category. He cites two American examples: Massachusetts Senator John Kerry, who said of his stance on a bill to finance the war in Iraq, "I actually did vote for the [authorization bill] before I voted against it," and former Florida governor Charlie Christ, who repeatedly changed views on political issues and then jettisoned his Republican Party to run for the Senate as an independent.

Achiever

Achievers are probably the most common in executive rank – leaders who always achieve, or beat, their goals. Management guru Peter Drucker essentially described their attitude when he wrote about a "monomaniac with a mission." This individual is focused, energetic, and results-oriented. But the weakness is obvious: achievers can be narrow-minded as they drive to the goal without much consideration of the broader mission. Professor Maidique points to Mark Hurd, the ex-CEO of Hewlett-Packard, who doubled the company's stock price but "decimated the infrastructure and intellectual seed corn (R&D) of the company."

Builder

The builder goes beyond achieving a particular goal to building an institution. Builders manage for the long term without being seduced by the pressures for short-term profits and continual high stock market valuations. They have a grand vision for the future of their organizations, and they infect others with their energy, enthusiasm, and integrity. These are the leaders we write books about, study, try to understand, and lionize. Two legendary leaders: Tom Watson of IBM and Alfred P. Sloan of General Motors.

Transcendent

The level six leader type, transcendent, goes beyond his organization or group to benefit society as a whole. The Dalai Lama has said he starts every day by asking, "How can I make the world better today?" and Professor Maidique asks us to imagine what would happen if business and political leaders started their day similarly. Builders are scarce, and this approach is even rarer. Examples: Along with the Dalai Lama, Nelson Mandela and Martin Luther King Jr.

The screen starts to resonate with me when I attempt to classify Mac Booth and, even more so, Mac's staff. Mac and most of his team were classic Achievers without a hint of Builder. Mac's goal of stock value of $95 by 1995 without an articulated vision would make him the ultimate achiever. His staff members, notably Joe Oldfield and Carole Uhrich, were also driven to achieve results. Carole, during and after her Polaroid career, was frequently quoted as saying, "I make my numbers."

I asked Dr. Maidique to comment on where he believed Land would fall in his six-levels spectrum. His response: "Like all leaders, Dr. Land is a mixture of several levels. I would rate him as: 40% Builder and 40% Achiever with the remainder as Transcendent. He is difficult to categorize because he was multitalented and appears to have cared as much for his inventions as for his company. He also had a noticeable Transcendent streak."

A Builder, in my opinion, that the company lost was Carl Yankowski. He joined Polaroid in 1988 as a corporate vice president with initial responsibility for all business imaging, U.S. consumer and industrial marketing. He graduated from the Massachusetts Institute of Technology with simultaneous degrees from the Sloan School of Management and the Department of Electrical Engineering. In 1992, he was promoted to chairman of the Asia Pacific Division of Polaroid and helped establish the Asia Pacific headquarters. In 1993, Yankowski left Polaroid to become president and chief operating officer of Sony, Inc., a $6-billion, diverse electronics operation in the U.S.; a position he retained for five years.

Yankowski is a prime example of the way executives hired from outside of Polaroid rarely, actually never in my recollection, fit into the Polaroid culture. The chain of management just couldn't be broken – from Land to McCune to Booth to Buckler, Uhrich and Oldfield. When DiCamillo became CEO in 1995, he brought executives into the company, with less than stellar results. It was almost as if the reigning group of executives had passwords or secrets they wouldn't trust outsiders with. I recall an electronics whiz, a chemical expert from Bell Labs, and the inventor of fiber optics devices. They never stayed long enough to find the restrooms. Yankowski was different; he would have been a great successor to Mac Booth, in my opinion.

I worked with Carl on a few occasions. During his first week at Polaroid, I took him on a tour of the battery plant. Almost immediately, I felt comfortable with him, as we chitchatted during the tour. He asked names, shook hands and generally was at ease. He shared with me some bad news: The company he had turned down to join Polaroid was bought out; the stock options he would have received would have come due that week. "I lost a few million dollars," he recounted. "Bummer," I responded. "I hate when that happens." He laughed, "Nothing for nothing, there will be another day." There certainly would be other days, as Yankowski in the next years made millions with his various CEO assignments after Polaroid.

A year or so later, Carl came back to address the battery plant employees as part of Booth's commitment, after the Shamrock hostile takeover, to have executives communicate company status with the employees. He was very comfortable with everyone, answering questions openly and candidly even when he didn't know the answer. Again, I took him on a tour of the plant. When we entered a work area, he asked the name of an employee. "He's German," he commented. "Correct," I replied. "That's Kurt Krom." When Carl walked up to Kurt, called him by name and shook his hand, Yankowski had a new fan.

Over the next few years, I attended several meetings with Yankowski and a group from marketing and manufacturing, reviewing options to improve our packaging. We would meet in Carl's office, positioned around a circular table – no "power" position, as with a rectangular table. At the end of the discussion, Carl would ask each attendee if they agreed with the outcome of the meeting, and whether they could support the decisions made. That participative process was taught in various employee training sessions but seldom evident at any senior level meeting I had attended. He knew how to work with people at all levels. He was comfortable in his own skin, something lacking with many Polaroid executives, in my view.

Several months after Carl met with the battery employees, Mac came in for a similar meeting. At the start of the presentation, aforementioned Kurt addressed Mac with a compliment on how much he enjoyed the discussions with Yankowski. Commenting to plant manager Gary Levy, Mac responded: "What's the expression, Gary, all fluff and no stuff?" Mac quickly recanted, exclaiming he wished he could be more expressive like Yankowski. Too late; it was Mac's engineer style surfacing. But I guessed at that point Yankowski would probably not be a favorite of Mac who would be more comfortable with Joe Oldfield or Carole Uhrich, both somewhat uncomfortable around Polaroid workers. The three were Achievers, not Builders.

A shame really, as Yankowski would not have been subject to the "kool-aid," having to make products that use media. His career after Polaroid was dominated by electronic devices, so he could have led us into the digital age. After leaving Polaroid, he increased Sony America revenues from $6 billion to $10 billion; as president and CEO of Reebok International Ltd., he led the company through significant restructuring and global expansion. He had a hiccup during his days at Palm Computer but openly admitted his failures and moved on to new ventures. He would have been an effective CEO of Polaroid, I think. At the time, I had assumed Carl had left Polaroid because of the great opportunity to lead Sony America. I contacted him to see if he would provide some insight from his days at Polaroid. Carl did not disappoint me; my interview with him follows.

Interview with Carl Yankowski
February 6, 2012

I sent Carl an email, describing my writing to that point on the Polaroid history. He agreed to review the book and provide some insights on his time at Polaroid. Carl called, and we had a great discussion. Within a few minutes, it was clear to me that Carl still had the same infectious enthusiasm that I had found to be unique in a Polaroid executive twenty years previously. He recalled Mac Booth had told him how the Battery Division folks enjoyed his visit. He laughed when he read the "all fluff- no stuff" comment by Mac; he had not heard that version before.

Milt: "Carl, how did you get the great job as President and COO of Sony America? An American working for a major Japanese company must be difficult. I looked you up on Wikipedia. I never realized you had such hits: GE, 'We Bring Good Things to Light' and Memorex 'Is It Live or Is It Memorex?' The 'Pepsi Challenge' – good stuff."

Carl: "I was contacted by a search firm who was familiar with my background. I'd had some successes with the companies you described; that's how I got the Polaroid job. Let me go sideways for a minute. I interviewed Akio Morita, the founder and chairman of Sony. Morita had met with Dr. Land on a few occasions, probably about 1980. Akio called Land the most stubborn man he'd ever met. Morita described how he tried to convince Land that Polaroid needed to recognize their future should not be so dependent on the chemical processing version of imaging. By this time, Sony had some early electronic imaging devices – the Mavica was under development at that time. I think Sony wanted to partner with Polaroid to use Polaroid's Instant photography brand to market Mavica in the U.S."

Milt: "Paul Hegarty told me a similar story while on a Japan visit to Matsushita – Panasonic in 1981. He brought back a digital print they had produced, similar to the Mavica. Polaroid senior management joked about the poor quality of the image."

Carl: "Safe to say Polaroid missed the mark on electronic imaging. I'll tell you another story on a similar experience I had

168

in 1993 with Mac and electronics in a few minutes. Getting back to Sony; I hit it off with Morita, and he hired me. He had a sense Sony America was getting stodgy, passive in its leadership, so he took a chance on me.   Your question about how, or why I could work for a Japanese company, was also asked by former Polaroid CEO, Gary DiCamillo. We had both worked for Procter and Gamble early in our careers and had contact with the same search firm. Gary called to congratulate me on the Sony job but asked how I could be successful surrounded by Japanese managers. Easy, I said: Morita said if I had any difficulties, give him a call; he'd fix it. Somewhat the way I understand Land empowered his lieutenants to carry out his bidding. Anyhow I had a great five years; Sony America went from $6 billion in sales to $10 billion. I left when my father took ill."

Milt: "I think one of the reasons I wrote the Polaroid history was to try to understand how Polaroid's leadership after Land, could not get sales up from $2 billion to a profitable $2.5 billion in over 10 years. I really think it was the cultural thing, beyond the fixation with only selling chemical imaging media, as you described. A former executive like you could lead Sony from $6 billion to $10 billion, but you were not capable of leading Polaroid? Can you tell me why you left Polaroid? I always felt you were biding your time at Polaroid until a bigger company called."

Carl: "Well, sure, there are two parts to that story, but you were wrong about Polaroid being too small. I would have loved to lead Polaroid into the next generation of imaging or whatever. I learned a lot about Polaroid's business during my assignment as head of Business Imaging. We built some pretty successful platforms outside of consumer picture taking. Did you know that over 80% of Polaroid Instant film products were used in business applications, not consumer products? Business owners, body shops, insurance companies and the like would track film promotions at Walmart and pounce on discounted sales to buy film for their business use. We did extensive exit surveys at Walmart to understand how purchasers were using Polaroid film."

169

Milt: "I probably should have known that – still hard to conceive. You're telling me all those expensive packaging promotions geared to consumers were a waste of time and money?"

Carl: "Not completely, but certainly not as helpful to attract new business as thought by the folks who ran Consumer Products. Why do you think Captiva was such flop? In addition to the unacceptable cost per picture size, business owners had no use for the Captiva system. Getting back to my Polaroid experience – I liked Mac; he was a straight-shooter, loved running Polaroid, spent his whole professional life with the company. I made a mistake with him. I suggested he might drop back from the CEO position, continue as chairman of the board and find someone from outside Polaroid with electronic experience to become CEO. I said I was not campaigning for the job, but splitting the assignments would be a good idea."

Milt: "Wow, from my limited time in front of Mac, I can almost picture those steely eyes peering up from his glasses."

Carl: "It gets better. After pausing for a few seconds, Mac said: 'You really don't think I'm capable of both jobs? I don't know if I should punch you in the nose or fire you!' I left his office."

Milt: "In my view, Mac was always competing with other managers, particularly Shelly Buckler, who most insiders thought would have been a better CEO than Mac because of his scientific background and more outward personality. What happened next?"

Carl: "I never brought the subject up again, obviously. A while later, Mac was reorganizing the senior staff and wanted me to take a senior development assignment. I wanted the Asia-Pacific leadership position. Mac decided to take me with him on a worldwide tour of Polaroid's operations. He said he would observe me in action and either give me the Asia-Pacific job or fire me. The trip allowed me to get to know Mac – really a solid guy, grew up the son of an auto-industry executive; had two degrees from Cornell; was a track star."

Milt: "Never heard the track star part. The other background was known by Polaroid folks. I had a hard time finding a good picture of Mac – almost nothing on the Internet. I thought of trying to interview him for my book, but I never felt comfortable around Mac. In the dozen or so times I was with him he would often call me 'Marty'. We first met when I was a young engineer in W1 along with Marty Helsmortel, Marty Wirt, Marty Winn and Marty Kusmaul, so I must have been another Marty from W1. I did respect Mac and hope he'll enjoy my book, if he ever reads it."

Carl: "He probably will; you treated him with respect, from what I read in your book. So, on the trip Mac would watch me make a presentation, take copious notes on a yellow legal pad. At the end of the week, he said the Asia-Pacific job was mine. I stayed in Hong Kong about two years, when I was selected for the Sony job."

Milt: "So, obviously Sony was a great opportunity, but you said you would have been happy to run Polaroid if given the chance."

Carl: "I was considered for the Polaroid job later on. But, first, I knew I could never conquer the culture paradigms prevalent in Polaroid. During my time in Business Imaging, I was always on the lookout for alliances or companies Polaroid might make or buy to expand our offerings. I found what I thought was a great opportunity with a small start-up enterprise in Florida. They had developed some good technology around DSL and electronic imaging. DSL would have allowed Polaroid to push large image files over standard telephone lines digitally, in the early days of digital cameras, starting the transition away from film. I sent one of my guys, Dan Ting, out to explore the opportunity. Dan came back enthused, said we could have the company and technology for $500,000. When I made the proposal to Mac, the idea was quickly tossed aside. 'Carl,' he said, 'Polaroid doesn't sell what it didn't invent. You need to understand that concept; we've been burned in the past.' No discussion. I decided this closed-minded thinking was not a good fit for my future."

Milt: "Actually Polaroid sold a lot of conventional 35-mm film we didn't invent, also VHS magnetic tapes. As you know, Walmart pushed us into those products to compete for end cap space with Kodak and Fuji. Didn't have high margins, I'm sure;

so that might have been Mac's bias. I'm intrigued by your comment related to being offered the Polaroid CEO job."

Carl: "Not offered, considered. You recall Frank Jones, Polaroid board member from the Land era right up to the 1990s? I had attended some board meetings, got to know him a bit - we both had an MIT background. Anyway, in 1995, Jones called me and asked if I would like to be considered for the CEO opening, to replace Mac Booth. I was a few years into Sony, making some headway with PlayStation, so I had no interest in the Polaroid job. Besides, as I said, I knew the situation pretty well – they were still stuck in the silver-halide hard-copy-media syndrome."

Milt: "Great story. Believe me, most Polaroid members would have been pleased if you had become CEO. Last question, Carl, how did you get on with the other members of Polaroid management?"

Carl: "Bob Delahunt befriended me from the beginning; we would go to lunch and commiserate over how the company was stuck in the mud, spinning its wheels. Shelly Buckler is a classy guy. We had many wonderful discussions. I thought Bruce Henry was a strong member of the executive team. Most of the others were hardworking, well-intentioned, but quite inbred, without much vision other than making more film, faster, cheaper for new markets. It turned out to be a losing path to follow."

Milt: "Thanks for the time, Carl –really great copy for my book. You should write your own, would be quite interesting. I'll give you a title: 'Pringles to Pepsi to PlayStation to Palm – My Interesting Life, Carl Yankowski' – pretty good?"

Carl: "We'll see. Good luck with your Polaroid history, Milt. You might want to call it 'Insights – The History of the Polaroid Corporation as Viewed from Within.'"

*****

The next section describes the two major product failures at Polaroid in the 1990s that contributed greatly to Polaroid's debt and eventual bankruptcy. Polaroid leadership continued not listening to either outside analysts or its employees.

Section 4: Product Challenges

It's code-named Joshua and it's been three years in the making. Polaroid Corp. is clearly looking for big things from its new instant camera, expected to be in the stores by this fall.

"We are absolutely out to create resurgence in instant photography and bring out a family of products," said Bruce Henry, Polaroid's Vice President of Family Imaging Systems.

But those outside the company are placing their bets early. "Expectations for Joshua are very low," says Peter J. Enderlin, an analyst at Smith Barney, Harris Upham and Co. "A potential Edsel," shrugs B. Alex Henderson, an analyst at Prudential Bache Securities in New York. (*Boston Globe*, May 12, 1992.)

*****

"But Polaroid is struggling with a series of Helios missteps. Stalled for two years by engineering glitches, the system was finally shipped in March – just as hospitals were cutting back on equipment purchases. Helios should generate just $10 million in sales this year – well below the $25 million analysts originally expected." (Gary McWilliams, *Business Week*, December 27, 1993)

The decision to sell Helios by Polaroid's new president, Gary DiCamillo, marks the end of an unsuccessful attempt to use new technologies that will deliver rapid payoffs. Announced in 1991 by former chairman I. MacAllister Booth, Helios was not ready for sale until 1993. Since then, Polaroid has sold fewer than 1,000 Helios systems to hospitals and medical centers at a cost of $60,000 to $90,000. Polaroid did not have enough people selling it, and they really did not know the customer base of radiologists and hospitals. (*Boston Globe*, Ronald Rosenberg, October 31, 1996)

173

Chapter 1:
Captiva, The Last Chance Instant Winner

The sale of Polaroid Instant Integral film products leveled off in the 1980s at approximately 100 million packs a year as 35-mm photography improved and one-hour photo shops emerged. Coming off the settlement with Kodak and successful defense of the hostile takeover, Polaroid needed to boost sales, improve earnings, and satisfy Wall Street analysts. A team was established to explore options for developing the next family of film products. Hal Page, VP of quality, was assigned to lead the team. Hal was a veteran Polaroid executive who had served his time in various manufacturing and quality roles. I viewed him as one of the few executives with vision. Hal was a charismatic and often-demanding manager, but open to input. In his quality role, Hal established an internal statistical training program, requiring all engineers and production supervisors to attend eight hours per week, with homework and exams, for 20 weeks. The majority of managers in manufacturing groups attended. Interestingly, the research and development groups avoided the program, as their management did not see the connection to their role. Hal himself attended.

The previously described Frank Martin, Bud Ostberg and Tom McCole development/research links to Land represented the intuitive and scientific approach vs. the statistical control approach, required by large-scale manufacturing. During Statistical Process Control (SPC) sessions at "Hal Page University" we learned how the lack of robust process latitude and process capability in some features of film product design,

174

driven by Dr. Land's "line in the sand" on size constraints, created barriers to controlled manufacturing and made factory life difficult indeed. Greater process latitude within the film pack over the years could have helped drive down costs with higher yields. Hal had been sharing his view of a very simplistic strategy for Polaroid. Our share of the worldwide photographic market in the early '80s was about 8%. Hal suggested, if Polaroid could get to 12%, a modest increase of 4 percentage points, our sales would then increase by possibly 50% and the annual sales would reach $2.5 billion. Hal had obtained some external publicity related to his quality initiatives and would be asked to make speeches in various quality forums. Other executives dismissed Hal as a working-class manager, with minimal technical accomplishments. While Mac was nicknamed the "senior engineer", other executives were known to sarcastically deride Hal's passion for quality. "Wind Hal up, send him out, and he'll make his quality pitch anywhere" was the comment. Really unfair, in my opinion. Hal was open to input; much more than other executives I encountered.

Hal's team took on the code name "Joshua", derived from a children's cartoon, whereby the character felt trapped in a box, searching for escape. Polaroid's "box" was the inability to expand our photographic market share over the previous several years. To expand Polaroid's Instant product offerings, we needed to "think outside the box." In support of the concepts espoused in Hal's Statistical Training Program, diverse teams representing a cross-section of Polaroid employees were assembled to brainstorm concepts which would open up instant photography to an expanded market. Unfortunately, as I recall, the charter was limited to the instant photography field.

I was an enthusiastic member of one of the groups. Ideas, some quite old, flowed freely out of the exercises. Many correctly dealt with the simple fact that the then-current cost of Polaroid Instant film was about a dollar a picture to the user, about three to four times greater than conventional photography. Polaroid management seemed convinced that instant gratification was still worth the cost; we just needed to find new markets. Other concepts focused on the fact that Polaroid picture quality really worked best at distances of less than about six feet. This problem actually plagued Polaroid from the beginning. Instant film employed a full size negative; exposure of the negative required excellent management of light, much more difficult on a 3 x 4-inch negative than the conventional 35-mm negative when taking pictures other than within the five to eight foot range.

My brainchild had been to find ways to allow children to use their creativity with instant film. I had submitted several ideas to the company earlier that would provide a "toy" type camera that would allow instant birthday cards, baseball cards, etc., using overlays similar to Polaroid Instant driver's licenses. I was rejected, as Polaroid management informed me our culture was built on precision cameras, not low-cost toys. Many years later after I left Polaroid, I felt some measure of vindication, as Polaroid introduced the real "last instant winner", the i-Zone, sticker film, aimed at teenagers (later chapter).

While I appreciated Hal's process to involve many members of the company in the search for the next amateur photographic product that could carry on the success of the 600 and Spectra lines, when the conclusion was reached, I, along with several colleagues, wondered if the answer to the question "What is Polaroid's next innovative instant product?" had already been determined by our senior management and the R&D group prior to the organization of the Joshua teams. The product that resulted from the studies became Captiva, an elegant camera that produced an Instant picture that remained in the camera while developing. Captiva solved one customer criticism of previous Polaroid systems: what to do with picture #1 while shooting picture #2, etc. Rapid fire was a good thing, it burned film! Unfortunately, the Captiva film cost the consumer a dollar for a picture that was smaller than standard Polaroid film; the distance range was still five to eight feet, unless there was near perfect lighting conditions; the camera cost over $100 to produce (it was sold at a loss to Polaroid); the early product was loaded with failures in the customers' hands.

Captiva was a colossal failure, one of the two major expenditures (Helios instant X-rays being the other) in the '80s and '90s, costing the company over $1-billion each, which ignited the debt structure that eventually led to Polaroid's bankruptcy filing in 2001.

Trapped in Joshua's box? Easy to second guess now, but a history of some of the management decisions related to the management of the Joshua/Captiva program reveals that the lack of leadership allowed the program to advance with near reckless spending, even when signals (and employees) strongly suggested otherwise. The decision to move forward with Captiva was supposedly based on some of Polaroid's most extensive market research to date. In fact, during the midpoint of the project development phase, the program was halted for a time to reassess the product and the market. The decision was to move ahead again on the same track.

Chapter 2:
Captiva, Another Battery Problem

As described in earlier chapters, during development of the SX-70 film line back in the late 1960s, Dr. Land conceived the idea of providing a fresh battery with each pack of film to solve the unreliability of conventional round cells. Polaroid executives were vexed by the question of if and when Polaroid should remove the battery from the film pack and include it in the camera. The Polaroid flat battery had been a problem child from day one, with many product and quality issues. Additionally, the in-pack battery added 50 cents to the manufacturing cost of a pack of film.

By the early 1980s, battery technology was led by Japanese companies who were certainly equal to the task; Polaroid could have designed new camera/ film systems that used a battery in the camera.

I felt the time was right for Joshua (Captiva); the program team disagreed. The reasoning was that Fuji film would start selling film packs in the U.S. that would function in Polaroid Captiva cameras. Polaroid's battery patents would stop them cold or, they reasoned, the considerable capital investment would be a deterrent. At the time of the decision, about 1988, I was attending battery seminars with all the leading battery manufacturers, including the Japanese. If I learned anything at the meetings, it was that Japanese companies were not intimidated by battery technology – they led the field. If they saw a market, capital investment was a given, not a deterrent. Thirty years later, Fuji has not produced an instant integral film

178

product for sale in the U.S. (see note at end of chapter). I believed Fuji was focusing their film efforts on the 35-mm Advanced Photo Systems (APS), and would not pursue the instant film arena in the U.S. Perhaps Fuji saw the emergence of the one-hour photo shops and digital photography as the deterrent to growth of the instant film market.

As a member of the Joshua team, I was charged with researching alternate batteries that would work in the new camera and comparing them to the known Polaroid in-the-film-pack battery. At the onset of the study, I was biased towards the Polaroid case as our battery, because of the flat configuration, had tremendous high drain capability and more than sufficient energy to power the ten pictures in Polaroid film –actually a capability of at least three times the demand. Additionally, I had spent 12 years with Polaroid's battery, so my career and loyalties were certainly well-known by Polaroid's management.

The testing of alternate batteries resulted in my department's recommendation of lithium 6-volt cells, produced by either Duracell or Panasonic. To my surprise, both batteries, when included in the camera, not the film pack, allowed the user to rapid fire the ten film pictures equal to or better than the Polaroid battery. There was sufficient energy to allow 10-15 packs of film to be used before the battery needed replacement.

When I presented the recommendation to the program team, I recall the skepticism of many of the members. What was Milt's agenda? Why would he betray his team? Much discussion centered on the original $2-3 cost to include the battery in the camera, as well as the possible reluctance to purchase a replacement a year or so later (Polaroid film burn was by this time three to four packs per year; Captiva, it was hoped, would double that rate). I believed the best long-term plan was for the company was to start moving away from the battery-in-pack system. I felt the Lithium cell was a better fit for the Captiva system since the camera was prone to sudden surge in power requirements because of the requirement to turn the film 180 degrees as it exited the camera. My other issue was a manufacturing capacity problem in the Battery Division. The company had only one battery assembly machine that was running 24-hours, seven days. The addition of the 30 million

179

batteries anticipated for Captiva would further strain this equipment. The $15 million required to modify the equipment would place a drain on resources that should be spent on improving the efficiency and output of the assembly equipment. Talk about a box, I felt the battery division had its own "Joshua!"

I was unable to convince management to accept the proposal to go with the lithium battery. When I attempted to counter the $2 incremental camera cost (the cameras would sell for over $100) of the lithium cell with the 50-cent reduction in film price, I was reminded that Polaroid had marketing personnel who had worked that model. As to the assembly-equipment capacity concerns, the plant manager, not Milt, was responsible in that area.

Later I was informed that the overriding factor was that the battery in the film pack would prevent Fujifilm from producing a knock off film product. I was quite amused in April 2010 to learn the "new" Polaroid had announced a Polaroid-branded camera that prints out business-card-sized instant prints. The Polaroid 300 boasts four film settings, an automatic flash and is powered by four AA batteries.

"Instant is back!" declares Polaroid. But who will make the film? Fujifilm, of course. The 1980s "enemy" was now Polaroid's partner.

Chapter 3:
The Captiva Customer-Use Test

The Captiva product was truly a remarkable engineering achievement. The Instant film technology had advanced considerably in the prior several years whereby, with close-in shots, Instant pictures could often appear at near-35-mm quality. A team of highly skilled engineers had used state-of-the-art design and quality techniques to develop a precision camera. Customer feedback and focus groups had been used to state clearly the ideal requirements for the system. The film would develop in the camera – a most demanding challenge, as the multi-layer plastic film unit would need to "bend" a complete 180 degrees while being processed in the camera.

The Captiva team held periodic meetings to update team members from the various divisions on the status of the project. One meeting in particular remains vivid in my mind. The marketing group had set up a customer focus group using a cross-section of existing and future users. The focus of this group was to explore the acceptance of the new Captiva film size, about half the image size of the present Polaroid biggest seller, Type 600. The team presented the result – all very favorable – customers loved the sharpness of the pictures. When the display boards were passed around, I was also quite impressed. There were several scenic shots of trees and flowers that far exceeded any previous Instant pictures I'd seen. I asked how the pictures were processed, since I was not aware of a working model of the Captiva camera system. I was not impressed with the answer. "Well, since the objective of the test

181

was to check out acceptance of the picture size, we used cropped-down 35-mm pictures, cut to look like the future Captiva film," explained the meeting facilitator.

As I pushed for further clarification on why the results were not confounded by the sharpness attributed to the 35-mm system, I was reminded that I should stick to getting the new battery in better shape to deliver the energy needed and let the marketing team worry about how to conduct focus groups. Many Polaroid employees, at all levels, had been skeptical of Captiva success because of the picture size vs. cost. If the picture quality did not nearly match 35-mm pictures, it would not be a winner. At least two prior Polaroid ventures into smaller film size had been unsuccessful: Type 87/88 pack film and Type 20 B&W Swinger. To use cropped 35-mm pictures to replicate a future Instant picture was at best foolish; at worst, manipulation of data to reach a pre-determined answer.

Bob Ruckstuhl provided his summary of the Joshua program. Bob started at Polaroid in 1962 and retired in 2001. During his nearly 40-year Polaroid career, Bob held management assignments in corporate quality, negative development/ manufacturing and program management including Joshua. Having reported directly to both Hal Page and Roger Clapp, as well as working closely with Mac Booth, Bob has been invaluable to my research in several areas. His comments follow:

I was involved with the project from the time that Hal Page headed up the exploratory work to find the "next instant product" until the time that DiCamillo pulled the plug. From the very first days with Hal through the development of the product and the market research, I always felt that Captiva was the lesser of a bunch of evils. BUT, THERE WAS NOTHING ELSE! The brainstorming sessions that Hal conducted yielded nothing new (digital photography was too much of an unknown as a consumer product at that point) and the small-camera, small-picture concept won by default. My sense, from that point forward, was that we set about to do the best that we could with the default concept. There was no market pull; we tried to fit the product into the market. For the first time, we had a product that did not fit the model of "if you build it, they will come", although we tried to tell ourselves that it was the other way around.

I was intimately involved with the market research you cited. In fact, I was responsible for making the picture props that folks said were so sharp. We sincerely tried to make the market testing as objective as possible; but, in the back of my mind, I felt that we were approaching the research with the unwritten objective of confirming our preconceived vision of success. I distinctly remember a meeting with the program team and Mac one July. There had been enough skepticism expressed about the success of the product that Mac called a multi-month halt to the program while we assembled a mammoth market research program that would, once and for all, guide us in the decision to go or to stop. The test was as good as a test could be; but, from my perspective, the outcome was preordained. We did not have the guts to stop. There were no options other than Captiva. We had no place else to go, so we gave this one our best effort; we read the results of the market research in that light.

When it was all over, and the product was floundering in the market place, we gave Bruce Godfrey, a Brit working in marketing, the task of finding out why. If I remember correctly, one of his conclusions from interviewing many folks who had bought the product was they "didn't realize how small the picture really was."

This said to me we either didn't correctly represent the product in the research that we did, or we were sensitive to this shortcoming and played it down or spoke to it as a benefit that ultimately didn't resonate with the consumer.

Roger Clapp, I think, was driven in much the same way that Joe Oldfield was – that with the success of Captiva would come a big promotion. This was Roger's baby and he had strong opinions as to how it should proceed. If his marketing and customer thinking was flawed, his engineering vision and leadership were terrific. He would drive you into the ground and work you to the bone, but the engineering accomplishments of the Captiva product were state of the art. The "compact" size (for an instant camera), the folding concept, the storage chamber and the chute, the "wink" focusing system, among others, were significant engineering accomplishments. Not everyone enjoyed working for him, but he deserves a lot of credit in leading a team that brought a complex product and manufacturing process to market.

Another opinion, quoted from Glenn Rifkin, published June 11, 1991, in The New York Times, summed up the Captiva product succinctly; and this was prior to the official release of Captiva. "Analysts like Mr. Henderson are skeptical about the prospects for the new camera. He expects it to produce compact pictures the size of baseball cards. 'Personally, I don't know why anyone would want it,' he said." (B. Alex Henderson, an analyst at Prudential Securities)

While this early mistake was serious, later signals that could have lessened the eventual losses were also conveniently ignored. Why? The Captiva program was a well-managed program at the tactical level; each objective was stated, challenges were addressed and conquered. The project team had a license from Mac to charge ahead. The strategic program was the problem. There was no obvious leadership at the board of directors or executive level challenging whether the objectives being achieved were the correct ones! If Polaroid had been a privately-held company, immune from pressure of investors and Wall Street (Polaroid's own Joshua box), the executive team would not have glossed over the signals indicating so strongly that Joshua would be a clever product without a viable market. The Captiva sales estimates and capital

184

equipment spending was consistently based on incremental sales of 30 million packs in the fifth year after Captiva's inception. The sales never exceeded 5 million packs per year.

At a staff meeting of Executive Vice President Joe Oldfield I attended for my boss in 1995, a hot agenda item was preparations by Joe and his staff to request an additional $70 million to develop a low-cost Captiva camera. The initial camera was costing over $160 to produce and was selling poorly, even at $100. As a newcomer to the group, but as director of materials, I was quite knowledgeable of film sales and capacity. I questioned why the lower cost camera would help sell film when even folks who purchased the high cost version were only burning a few packs of film. The size was too small, in my opinion, the cost per picture too high. I was answered curtly by Joe, citing the marketing study.

At the break I was counseled by Dave O'Neil: "Milt, I would suggest you not challenge Joe on his Captiva plan." Dave O'Neil was Bruce Henry's Polaroid's vice president of family imaging systems controller. Henry had overall responsibility for Captiva, reporting to Mac Booth.

"Dave, we all know Captiva is a loser," I whispered.

"Maybe," he responded. "But if we don't push forward, we'll have to shut down the program and write off $100 million capital and program costs," he said.

"Well, best to do it and not waste another $70 million – the board will never go for that," I exclaimed a little too loudly.

"They probably will, but Milt, you don't understand Joe's predicament. There are no other alternatives. If Joe writes down all that unused capital, he has no chance at becoming the next CEO," concluded O'Neil. "The board could never appoint an 'insider' with a $100 million disaster in his portfolio."

The board approved the $70 million for the low-cost Captiva camera, later reducing the amount to $40 million. The product never received market acceptance. I purchased two packs of expired Captiva film in a drugstore in Florida for $2 each a year after Polaroid stopped production of Captiva. One worked; the other had a dead battery.

When Gary DiCamillo succeeded Mac as CEO in 1996, one of his first moves was to close out the Captiva program, writing down over $100 million in camera – and film - making equipment, some of which had never been removed from the packing crates. Joe Oldfield left Polaroid a few months later.

Chapter 4:
Electronic Imaging – Helios Meets Hillary

While many Polaroid veterans were not convinced Captiva would be successful, most of us were thrilled to hear about a move to diversify away from Instant film and cameras via entry into electronic imaging in the early 1990s. The program was related to medical imaging, a new X-ray product named "Helios," after the Greek sun god. I'm not sure who coined the name, but it was thought maybe Helios would brighten Polaroid's financial picture. Helios did have something in common with Instant film; both processes had a razor-razor blade approach: sell many cameras/ processors at low cost so users will buy high margin film or media. But with Helios there is a $50,000 processor, not a $25 camera – a pretty costly razor! An article in The New York Times by John Holusa, June 7, 1992, described the technology:

Polaroid's Helios, its new dry-process system, is based on carbon rather than silver-halide technology. Unlike photographic films that have to be protected from light and processed with wet chemicals, Helios film is insensitive to ordinary light and is developed through a dry, laser process. Helios film is a four-layer sandwich: a polyester base, a layer sensitive to laser light, the imaging layer with carbon particles in a polymeric matrix and a cover sheet. Helios can quickly create a

187

hard-copy record of images captured by highly sophisticated scanning equipment used for medical testing and diagnosis. Once captured, the images are sent to a laser inside a Polaroid machine that is about the size of a mid-sized office copier.

The laser – a high-powered, gallium arsenide model – then etches the image onto the Helios film. It works this way: the points the laser hits on the sensitive layer of the film are transformed chemically and lock onto the adjacent carbon particles. After the image is fully deposited, the top layer of the film is peeled away, taking with it all the carbon particles that have not been welded onto the light-sensitive layer. The retained particles comprise the image. Each 8-by-10-inch piece of film can record one to nine images; processing takes 90 seconds. The Helios laser machine can support up to four scanners simultaneously.

Polaroid executives say development of the system, which is still undergoing field testing, took almost a decade. "Back in 1983 we started to define the requirements of the market," said Leonard Aberbach, a vice president. "We'll do a full-scale introduction later this year." The system is expected to cost $40,000 to $50,000."

Polaroid went all out on this program, establishing a new division and building a plant in New Bedford, near the negative coating plant. All told the reported spending was $800 million; most insiders felt $1-billion was probably closer to the total when the non-recorded, development costs were included. Combined with the aforementioned $1-billion Captiva program, CEO Mac Booth and the BOD went "all-in" with $2 billion to re-invent Polaroid. This was a big gamble, quite a departure from the usual staid Polaroid leadership in the post-Land era.

The machinery to produce the Helios film was quite different from the equipment used to produce Instant film. By 1990, Polaroid's engineering and machine building had been reduced to essentially a management team. The large machine shops from the 1960s had been eliminated; much of Polaroid's engineering and machine building expertise were now outsourced. The Helios team researched various companies that could produce the machinery for Helios. One of Polaroid's major suppliers, Rexam Graphics, produced sophisticated coated materials for several of the film and battery components. In the late '80s, Rexam had built a plant in Runcorn, England, to support the growing demand for the photoresist market. Photoresist is a dry film material for advanced semiconductor packaging applications. The photoresist market had tanked by 1990 due to over estimates of the demand. Rexam eagerly volunteered to allow Polaroid to use the Runcorn plant to produce the Helios material. Bill Stimmel, Polaroid purchasing manager, responsible for materials from Rexam, arranged for the Helios team to visit the plant and see the proprietary machine. The team had no interest in using the Runcorn facility; they were on a research mission, taking away any technology they could from Rexam, including details on the machinery builder – Worldwide Converting Company of New Jersey.

Not long after the visit to England, Polaroid's Helios Division engaged Worldwide to construct the new coating line in New Bedford. The machine estimates were around $50 million as part of the $190 million complex. The due diligence on the financial strength of Worldwide was lacking. Additionally, Worldwide was heavy into outsourcing; that is, they were mostly a design company that used others to actually make the components. When it came time to start installing the machine in New Bedford, Worldwide had to admit they did not have all the components necessary to complete the machine; their cash flow had been stopped by bad bids on other projects. Polaroid had been making progress payments during the project that Worldwide had used to support other business. The engineers who visited the supplier in New Jersey conducted engineering reviews and project status charts but evidently did not visit the shops actually producing components for the machine. Polaroid had to provide $15 million above the original contract to get the machine completed. Worldwide eventually went into bankruptcy.

189

I tracked this situation, back then, as I worked closely with Rexam and received insider information from them. I felt it would be a "win-win-win" for Polaroid, Helios, and Rexam to partner on the Helios project. It would keep a major supplier to Polaroid viable using an under-utilized machine. Helios would avoid major expenditures while the process was being developed.

I believe it was unfortunate that the project leader let career advancement trump common sense. It was also a déjà vu for me from 1968. My first employer, Rice Barton, also a machinery builder, went into bankruptcy due to lack of cash flow for reasons similar to Worldwide. Rice Barton had been in business for 100 years building machines to produce paper. The last generation Barton had big plans and weak financial control. We would bid large $5 million contracts, at or near cost, and spend the progress payments on what we thought were high margin, small replacement projects. In my early 20s, I learned that if you are selling product at a loss, selling more will not result in profit due to higher volume! When Rice Barton went bankrupt, several large paper mills had to pay 50% more to get their machines completed. The smart customers would visit Rice Barton monthly and walk through the plant to be sure the equipment produced matched the progress payments. I couldn't believe Helios managers did not understand such a simple concept. The machine was eventually completed and, although there were many process problems, a saleable product was available in 1993. An excerpt from Gary McWilliams in Business Week, December 27, 1993, sums up the outcome:

> But Polaroid is struggling with a series of Helios missteps. Stalled for two years by engineering glitches, the system was finally shipped in March – just as hospitals were cutting back on equipment purchases. Helios should generate just $10 million in sales this year – well below the $25 million analysts originally expected. Meanwhile, Xerox Corp. has disclosed plans to team with 3M and Bayer's Agfa to deliver similar dry-process technology. Polaroid says its Helios problems are due mostly to weak

demand. "There can be no denying the negative impact of the current economic climate," says the company spokesman. But customer satisfaction is "extraordinarily high." And Booth has promised to bring Helios laser technology to the printing industry sometime next year.

Inside Polaroid, there was another spin on the failure of Helios: the "Hillary Effect." I was quite amused to hear the health-care initiative led by the president's wife, Hillary Clinton, was putting a roadblock on hospital capital spending until the plan was finalized. Wow, I thought at the time, Polaroid just can't catch a break.

In 1996, after it had invested about $1-billion, Polaroid largely abandoned its venture into medical imaging when it sold the bulk of its loss-making Helios unit to Sterling Diagnostic Imaging, Inc. This sale led in part to a $33 million charge recorded in 1996, a year in which the company reported a net loss of $41.1 million. The Helios coating plant was converted to a custom coating facility to provide specialty coatings to external customers. It never generated much interest. The external auditors had to remind Polaroid that the machine was written off the books in 1996, so how could it be used for saleable product?

In 1998, I was managing a custom coating plant (Division of Furon Corp.) in Worcester, Massachusetts. I received a call from Furon's president who was always interested in expansion opportunities. He forwarded a note from an equipment reseller, soliciting bids for the Helios machine. The note described the machine and volunteered that the machine was on Polaroid's books at $20 million. Seemed like the auctioneer volunteered too much; but the gang that couldn't buy a machine properly also didn't know how to sell it. I had toured the plant several years earlier, but decided to go to New Bedford again, to walk the plant and meet some old acquaintances. My contact at first enthusiastically told me to come on down; the next day I was told I needed to go through the auctioneer so as to not get special treatment. Since I knew the Helios machine was a poor fit for Furon business, I decided not to make the visit. The machine was too sophisticated, had too much material loss due to extensive web path and had only low temperature drying or curing. After my contact with the New Bedford folks, I did receive a pile of resumes from coating specialists looking to leave Polaroid.

The Helios story may have a happy ending for some of the former employees of Helios and Polaroid. The plant was sold to Konarka Technologies, Inc. in 2008 to produce sheets used as fabric for a cell-phone-charging window in a purse or briefcase or as an integrated window panel. In 2010, they started making extremely thin flexible solar panels to produce what it calls "power plastic."

The Helios failure essentially torpedoed Polaroid's entry into electronic imaging. The overspending, without any significant revenue, blocked Polaroid's development of other electronic program applications in emerging markets for advanced computer scanners and digital cameras, as well as the printing industry. Larry Gerhardt, CEO of Test Systems Strategies, Inc., an experienced electronics executive, was courted by Mac Booth and hired in 1993 to run that portion of the new business. He lasted a week.

> Conrad H. Biber, who in April retired as head of electronic-imaging research, says Helios "has taken more effort and funding than anticipated. Therefore, the other electronic-imaging thrust has been falling behind." Indeed, Biber and others say, the lack of financing was a critical reason behind Gerhardt's departure. Gerhardt denies that, but analysts say Polaroid will have to scrimp to meet its ambitious financial goals. As a result, "there's still a question long-term whether they can crank up these new businesses to cover the decline in instant-photography products," says Peter J. Enderlin of Smith Barney Shearson. (Business Week, December 27, 1993)

So the two-headed Hydra of Captiva and Helios combined to suck resources away from development of technologies that could have been the "new" Polaroid in the mid-1990s, moving away from total dependence on Instant film sales. Lester Thurow in an article published on Fastcompany.com, "Help Wanted: a Chief Knowledge Officer", Issue 78, January 2004, expressed the following opinion on the demise of Polaroid:

> Consider Polaroid. This icon of photographic innovation was toppled by the emergence of digital photography and one-hour developing. Polaroid saw it coming and made an all-out attempt to go digital. But it never stood a chance in this new digital world. All of its know-how was rooted in chemistry. Unfortunately, Polaroid made a mess of its own demise. The company's core business, instant photography, was declining only slowly. If it hadn't attempted to fight the inevitable, it could have steered itself to a very soft landing, providing a decent return to its shareholders and a lot more security to its employees. Polaroid needed a chief knowledge officer – someone who could ensure that its core asset had a profitable death.

Dr. Thurow, the well-respected professor of management and economics at the Massachusetts Institute of Technology (MIT), was making a point in his article on how technology based companies need a chief knowledge officer (CKO), to "cast a cold eye on the future, gather unbiased intelligence on emerging threats and opportunities, and make the tough recommendations to buy, hold, or sell." Thurow uses Bill Gates of Microsoft as an example of a CEO who moved into the CKO role, successfully hiring a talented CEO, Steve Ballmer, to manage the business. Polaroid was led by Edwin Land who functioned both as a CKO and CEO for over 50 years. He was never really replaced as CKO and the line of CEOs following Land tried to fill both roles; unfortunately, the BOD didn't understand Thurow's concept.

Chapter 5:
Electronic Arrogance

In solving quality problems, it is first necessary to understand what causes the problem and then provide actions not only to fix the problem, but also eliminate the cause. A common technique is referred to as the "Five Whys Root Cause Analysis" – question what caused the problem until you can no longer answer why something happened. Additionally, Kepner-Tregoe was a similar methodology introduced into Polaroid's training regimen which preached "questioning to the void"; i.e., peeling the onion layer by layer, using questioning to discover root cause. Many manufacturing teams attended Kepner-Tregoe training sessions. As an example: A car crashes into a store. Why? The gas pedal stuck. Why? Something got in the way. Why? The floor mat moved. Why? It wasn't properly secured. Why? The attachment design did not work. Why? It was either incorrectly installed or poorly designed. Why? I give up! Ask the car manufacturer. I have a colleague in the quality world who claims there are only two root causes to every defect in manufacturing: incompetent workers and arrogant management. Actually, he would say "and the workers are incompetent because management is arrogant!"

Polaroid's vision of electronics started with CEO Bill McCune's comment in the 1981 Annual Report:

Of course, electronic imaging has substantial, but perhaps longer term, implications for amateur photography as well. We recognize that the rapid development of this electronic technology presents both a threat to and an opportunity for photography. We are devoting increasing effort and resources to this field. While we are generally not known as an electronics company, electronics has for many years been a fundamental part of our technical base in both manufacturing technology and product design.

Over the next twenty years, Polaroid management displayed nothing short of arrogance and incompetence when insisting electronic imaging would never displace silver-halide photography; in fact, they insisted, instant photography would be an excellent partner with digital imaging, as the digital image, ink jet or laser printing would not match the superb quality of instant photography.

The company is also betting that instant film, not a computer printer, is the best way to get high-quality prints from electronic cameras. Its scientists have developed a gallium arsenide chip that can convert the electronic information back into light rays that expose Polaroid Instant film. Anyone who says instant photography is dying has his head in the sand.

(Mac Booth, Feb 16, 1987,Fortune Magazine)

Paul Hegarty, a member of the Polaroid Purchasing Department for many years and an oft-quoted collaborator on my Polaroid story, provided this early history of electronic imaging and Polaroid's management's denial on the subject:

One story involves a trip I made to Osaka, Japan, in 1981. I was in Purchasing and negotiating with Matsushita (Panasonic) on a contract involving solenoids for shutter assemblies. After we concluded our business, my host took me to the R&D center on the company campus. We went into a studio about 30,000 square feet. This was a display area for all their consumer products; and, in that studio, my host picked up a 35-mm-like camera only larger and took my

195

picture. He then plugged it into a TV monitor and my image came up on the screen. He pressed a button on a printer and in about 15 seconds he produced a 4x6 print. It was a digital image of mediocre quality. It was easy to see it was me, but my face and white shirt were a little washed out. The dynamic range was narrow. He then proceeded to tell me that his company had spent about $5 million on this project in the last several years. The company was not even in the photographic business at that time; they made televisions, and yet they were willing to explore this new technology with a substantial investment. When I returned to Cambridge, I shared that story and the picture with several top managers, including two officers of the company. The universal reaction was to criticize the quality of the picture and ignore the implications that a company not even in the business had solved all the technical issues of producing digital images in 1981!

At the same time, I was involved with Texas Instruments on Spectra Development, and a side activity among the leadership of both companies was a dialogue about a technology that TI had developed called DMD (Digital Micro-mirror Device). TI markets that technology today as a display, but in the old days it was thought it might be a low cost image-capture technology. The camera I saw in Osaka used a CCD (charge-coupled device) that was very expensive. One of the big cost breakthroughs in digital imaging was the development of CMOS (complementary metal oxide semiconductor) image-capture devices.

The thing that still strikes me today was the belief expressed by senior managers in 1981 that digital will never be as good as silver halide! That was an opinion expressed by Dr. Land when he was with the company. By the way, that demonstration I had in Osaka was in the fall of '81. Land left Polaroid in July of '81. You may recall that Sony introduced the first digital camera called the MAVICA. I think it cost about $3,000 and may have been less than one megapixel. I have a cell phone that is greater than three. We could have been part of that technology explosion if Land and other Polaroid executives listened to and partnered with Sony.

Polaroid did establish a microelectronics lab (MEL) and hired, or attempted to hire, several industry experts. Though Polaroid was one of the first companies to develop a professional digital camera, it took so long perfecting the device that, by the time Polaroid introduced it in March 1996, the market was full of cheap competitors. Eventually, under DiCamillo, Polaroid partnered with a Taiwan manufacturer to place the Polaroid name on a cheap digital camera. It was a top seller in the U.S. for a short time but contributed little in the way of profits.

The $1-billion wasted on the Helios X-ray process certainly blocked expenditures on consumer electronic imaging. But the overarching atmosphere was certainly that senior management, from Land to DiCamillo, felt that Instant film was the engine that would continue to drive Polaroid's profits. We were like the company that invented carburetors for automobiles and were in denial on the emergence of fuel injectors. Many of us certainly drank the "kool-aid" along with the executives; but employees, like Paul Hegarty, could have opened doors with major players that could have led Polaroid into a place in digital imaging and the 21st century as a viable concern, not a telemarketing broker of cheap imports.

The culture ingrained in several generations of Polaroid management always came back to the strategy that the engine that will drive Polaroid has to be hard-copy media, silver halide or other formats – but hard copy always. But, in addition to the cultural pedigree from Land to Booth, Polaroid senior managers were not very good listeners

Chapter 6:
Acquisitions, the "Beachhead" Strategy

As word of my Polaroid history book spread among Polaroid retirees, the list of collaborators grew. I received phone calls and emails from many former executives and managers eager to unload their stories and opinions related to missed opportunities; proposals and strategies that could have allowed Polaroid to prosper in the two decades after Land left the company.

In 1984, with Land gone, CEO Bill McCune established the plan to leverage the factories built to support the SX-70 film system. The lower cost Pronto!, OneStep, and Spectra cameras provided excellent integral film sales for several years. Land would not have been supportive of "cheapening" his exquisite SX-70 system. Likewise, Land would not have supported Polaroid looking to grow the company via purchase of other companies, especially if the business was not part of the photographic industry. Bill McCune recognized the need to look for new opportunities beyond instant photography.

Ed Bedrosian and Phil Ruddick were appointed by McCune to work with the investment banker Lehman Brothers to explore possible acquisitions. Ed was VP and Treasurer and Phil was director of treasury operations. Polaroid focused on two companies with potential.

The first proposal was the Shipley Company, a family-owned business in Marlboro, Massachusetts. Founded by the Shipley family in 1957, the company was a classic garage start-up; they made their mark with special chemicals for printed circuit

198

boards. It was a natural for Polaroid, quite compatible with Polaroid's chemical expertise with photographic materials. Shipley had developed a leadership position in the fledging electronics industry of the 1960s and was growing at a fast rate. Dick Shipley, the president, wanted to sell a portion of the business. Polaroid had a series of discussions and meetings to acquire them. Shipley had the potential to be a $500 million business. They were not willing to give Polaroid 100% of the company; but proposed 40% then, with the remaining portion to be acquired over several years. Unfortunately, Polaroid pressed on for full control. Several members in corporate management felt we should have moved for the partial ownership. Shipley had a value of about $125 million in 1980. Polaroid could have started with a $50 million ownership position and eventually owned the company. Rohm and Haas bought 30% in 1982 and took full control in 1992 when Shipley's sales were at $200 million per year. Rohm and Haas grew the Marlboro business and sold it in 2009 to Dow Chemical.

Shipley could have been a great fit for Polaroid; the high-margin semi-conductor chemicals, in a rapidly expanding industry, would have been an excellent offset for Polaroid's declining film sales and margins. Polaroid had the chemical expertise to support this emerging technology. Bob Marckini, a senior Polaroid executive in chemical manufacturing, left the company to run Shipley. Several Polaroid engineers and scientists went with Bob to help build the company into a $500 million company.

The second opportunity was a small company in Chelmsford, Massachusetts, ACT (Advanced Color Technology). ACT had developed unique ink-jet printing technology that had great potential in a market in its infant stages. With Bill McCune's approval, Polaroid purchased the company for about $3.5 million. We had significant technology in dispensing chemicals onto receiving sheets from our instant photography legacy. There was no significant competition in the early 1980s, so we had a chance to be one of the first players in this field and had the advantage of our global photographic distribution network and leading edge coating technology.

A cultural obstacle became a roadblock to success in this venture: our R&D team insisted ink-jet printing would never be as good as silver-halide imaging. As a result, research assigned low level engineers to work with ACT and never put significant resources behind the new company. What R&D didn't realize was that printing from digital sources, including computers, would not need silver-halide quality. Rather, ink-jet quality was very acceptable and would grow exponentially. Our technical team, working with ACT, did develop novel inks which improved ink-jet quality as well as the hardware used to deliver the ink to the receiving paper. Ultimately, ACT was underfunded as the R&D team focus continued to be silver-halide films. Hewlett-Packard and others would later develop ink-jet printing technology into a $2 billion business still growing in 2012. Polaroid had the technology not only to be one of the first to enter this market, but also had potential to be the leader.

In addition to these two sizable opportunities that were missed, Polaroid had adopted a "beachhead" strategy for McCune to make technical investments in emerging technologies: fiber optics, thin film solar coatings, laser technology, magnetic coatings and specialty pharmaceutical chemicals – the painkiller Motrin. The term "Beachhead" emanated from the concept that possibly small successes could lay the groundwork for achieving a larger acquisition and diversification plan for Polaroid. None ever developed into businesses. The two largest opportunities, ink-jet printing and the Shipley photoresist chemicals for the semi-conductor industry, collectively had the potential to generate more than $2 billion in revenue, nearly matching Polaroid's 1996 Instant photography business. If either or both had been pursued and developed, Polaroid in 2012 would still be a viable business.

To Bill McCune's credit, early in his tenure as CEO in 1981, he had the vision to recognize the rapid development of electronic technology and both the threat and opportunity it presented to Polaroid. He allocated resources towards acquisitions targeted at technology-based electronic materials such as the Shipley electronics chemicals and ACT's inkjet printing. Polaroid's R&D group did not share his vision; the finance guys could not drive the acquisitions without research's support and the programs died; and, eventually, so did Polaroid.

Polaroid, Kodak and Fujifilm were the dominant photographic companies for several decades. Polaroid is gone and Kodak declared bankruptcy in 2012. Fuji continues to thrive today. Presently, Fujifilm products can be found on LCD screens; it has applied its photographic knowledge of anti-oxidation for long print lifetimes to cosmetics, and it is producing medicine. Fuji had the vision and leadership in R&D lacking at Polaroid.

Section 5: Gary DiCamillo

"The vision is a very simple one: Polaroid will be to digital imaging what it was to optical imaging. We will provide simple, easy-to-use instant, picture-printing devices—and, specifically, the consumable media for instant digital printing." —Gary T. DiCamillo

The 2000 Polaroid Corporation Annual Report to shareholders outlined CEO Gary DiCamillo's bold vision for the company as released March 23, 2001. A few short months later on October 12, 2001, Polaroid Corporation and all of its U.S. subsidiaries voluntarily filed for Chapter 11 under the U.S. Bankruptcy Code.

Chapter 1:
Workbenches to Cameras

A chemical engineering graduate of Rensselaer Polytechnic Institute, Gary T. DiCamillo also holds an MBA from Harvard Business School. At the time of his hiring as CEO of Polaroid, DiCamillo was 44 years old. Prior to joining Polaroid in 1995, Gary served as president of Black and Decker Power Tools Corporation, where he earned a reputation for cost-cutting, improving productivity, and rapidly developing new products. One of the successful products developed under DiCamillo's leadership at Black and Decker was the portable workbench.

Polaroid's selection of DiCamillo was greeted with mixed reviews by Wall Street. The company's stock dropped $1.125 a share, to close at $40.875. Brenda Lee Landry was a consumer products analyst for Morgan Stanley and Co. Ms. Landry attributed the drop partly to the general decline in the market and to disappointment that Polaroid had not appointed someone better known than Mr. DiCamillo. "No one is jumping up and down about it because he's not a superstar," she said. (*Baltimore Sun,* October 24, 1995)

Polaroid employees were skeptical at best. While most realized the company probably needed a leader from the outside, they wondered how DiCamillo's success in selling power tools and workbenches would translate into moving Polaroid forward into electronic devices or expansion of its core imaging product offering.

I'm a big believer in shareholder value, shareholder return. I'm a big believer in customer satisfaction, in customer value, in giving an excellent value to the users of the product line. The introduction of new products will also be a focus. They (Polaroid) have some great, interesting technology.

The "new" Polaroid under Gary DiCamillo started with the above quotation in the 1995 Baltimore Sun and ended a short six years later with shareholders and employees not very satisfied.

I met DiCamillo just once. Gary attended a Film Division staff meeting of my boss, Ed Coughlan, in late 1995, just after he joined the company. After we introduced ourselves and described our positions, DiCamillo asked a question, a "loaded" question: "What's the plan for the excess Captiva film assembly machines?" A former supervisor of mine often asked me why I always felt compelled to speak when there was a pregnant silence. This moment was no exception. Since I was director of materials, essentially responsible for logistics, I decided it must be my question to field. "Well, we have asked the engineering group to review options of converting the Captiva format machines into the conventional Type 600 format which could use some added capacity."

DiCamillo's response told me a lot about the man. He responded, "Interesting." What he was really saying was good luck to you and the Red Sox. I'm sure he had already decided to scrap the machines, writing down $120 million in assets. It was heartbreaking to me, an engineer, to see all this state-of-the-art shiny machinery, still in the crates, simply destroyed. Realistically, the conversion to the larger size 600 film would have been expensive and probably not a viable plan. I should have said we were trying to smuggle them into Russia or South America at ten cents on the dollar. At least I might have gotten a laugh out of him.

An interesting anecdote regarding DiCamillo involved his first day on the job. Joe Oldfield, the highest ranking executive in the company after Mac Booth retired, rented a limousine to pick DiCamillo up at Logan Airport in Boston. During the ride back to Cambridge, Gary asked Oldfield another "loaded" question. "What do you think needs to be done to turn Polaroid around, Joe?"

Joe responded, "We certainly have some challenges."

"Challenges, Joe? Polaroid has some big damn problems!" exclaimed DiCamillo.

I heard about this because Polaroid was always a great family company; there were relatives working everywhere. One of my colleagues had a brother who worked part time for a limousine company and who was the transporter of Oldfield and DiCamillo on that day. He couldn't wait to spread the story of Gary and Joe's exchange all over the company. His version had a stronger expletive, as I recall.

Oldfield took a severance package in March of 1996, a month after many managers including my supervisor Ed Coughlan and I accepted a similar buyout. Would Oldfield have been a better choice for CEO than DiCamillo? Quick answer would be certainly, since Joe couldn't have done worse than leading Polaroid into bankruptcy. In fairness to the board of directors in 1995, it really seemed obvious Polaroid needed an outsider to bring new perspective to the company. Additionally, Polaroid, as a relatively small company (less than $2.5 billion sales), wouldn't attract a Jack Welch, a big-time operator. Gary's accomplishments at Black and Decker created a strong resume of achievements along with an excellent education. The Polaroid board assumed they had picked a winner. It is hard to imagine that, if Oldfield had been selected as CEO of Polaroid, he would have allowed the bankruptcy and subsequent sale of Polaroid at a greatly discounted price to occur as easily as it did. The Oldfield I knew was a fighter who would have taken the failure personally and would have resisted the move to bankruptcy. Both the financial community and bankruptcy lawyers were surprised.

> "It's possibly the worst case I've ever seen," says Lynn LoPucki, a law professor at the University of California at Los Angeles. The bankruptcy court's job "is to regulate the relationship between debtors

205

and creditors," he says; but, in recent years, debtors and the largest creditors, usually banks, "have taken control of the courts," and get from judges "whatever they want. Poorly supervised reorganization plans often result, and less-powerful parties are cowed into approving them – just to get some semblance of a return. The current system just destroys value," says LoPucki. (CFO Magazine, January 1, 2003)

DiCamillo was successful before Polaroid; his wealth grew during his Polaroid tenure; it continued to grow as he moved from various CEO positions in various companies, now in 2011 working for Eaglepoint Advisors, a turnaround, restructuring and crisis management firm. Gary for many years has served on several company Boards of Directors with handsome financial compensation. During an interview with the Wall Street Journal in February, 2010, after the latest Polaroid bankruptcy filing due to the Petters scam, DiCamillo was asked his thoughts on Polaroid nine years after his bankruptcy. "Polaroid was tough, I've got to admit," he said.

Yes, it was tough. While much of upper management and their select staff did pretty well financially for their six-year effort, hundreds of Polaroid employees and retirees lost their jobs, health coverage, stock value, and retirement benefits. Many stockholders and long-time suppliers also suffered severe losses during DiCamillo's tenure at Polaroid.

That was tough – damn tough!

Chapter 2:
Polaroid 1996-2000

When DiCamillo came on board, he put forth a strategy in his message to stockholders in the 1996 Polaroid Annual Report:

1. Revitalize Instant Photography sales through aggressive marketing.
2. Expand new markets in China and India similar to Russia success.
3. Improve service to commercial markets – government, insurance, real estate and similar.
4. New business segments: graphics, medical imaging, graphic arts.

This approach appeared to work pretty well for the first few years, with focus on expanded markets and new instant moneymakers and one potential moneymaker. I was still at Polaroid in 1994 when the Russian film sales went from zero to 25 million packs almost overnight. After the fall of the Soviet Union in 1992, markets for consumer products in Russia and Eastern Europe took off. The Russian currency, the ruble, did not hold a sovereign credit rating at that time, meaning U.S. companies were reluctant to accept rubles in exchange for products. Because inflation was rampant in Russia from 1992 to about 1998, the "bartering" system was used: vodka for Polaroid Instant film. By 1995, sales in Russia grew to $200 million; 1996 dropped in half; by 1997 Russia sales were minimal.

207

I called it the "Russian film mirage." What happened? Because the early film use in Russia greatly exceeded what could be expected based on cameras sold in Russia, it was generally believed that the film sold in Russia was not used in Russia, that it was part of the "grey market" whereby brokers bought Polaroid film in Russia at a low price and then resold the film outside Russia at a profit, sometimes amplified by a favorable exchange rate. During the mid-1990s Polaroid Instant film with Russian language packaging would show up on back alley photo shops in New York City. The net effect would be that what appeared to be huge gains in film sales resulting from demand in Russia would eventually reduce film sales in other parts of the world. The worldwide Integral Film sales dropped back to 100 million packs per year by 1998, due both to the minimal sales in Russia as well as the growth of competitively-priced, one-hour 35-mm conventional film. The China-India market never materialized because of both one-hour photo shops and, eventually, digital cameras.

The i-Zone camera was also a short-term success. The "i" refers to Generation I, for Internet, the exploding wave of the late '90s. The development of this product line, aimed at teenagers, started a few years previously in Japan. The toy-like, basic black camera had a distance range of up to four feet, produced mini-photos based on the silver-halide instant developing components. The prints were 24x35 mm, the size of conventional 35-mm slides. Upon launch in Japan, the camera was an instant blockbuster, selling out immediately.

In 1998, during a business trip to Tokyo, walking down the camera/electronics boulevard amid all the bright lights and neon atmosphere, I observed the several large advertisements related to the new Polaroid sensation –the sticker-style instant photos. It was surreal; I felt like I was walking through the maze of a pinball machine! Watching the enthusiasm of the Japanese teenage girls at the i-Zone kiosk, I thought, "Wow, Polaroid's future may rest on the whims of youngsters. How far we have wandered from the days of Dr. Land and Sir Laurence Olivier, even James Garner and Mariette Hartley."

Introduced in the third quarter of 1999, the camera became the number one selling camera in the U.S. Sales in 1999 exploded to $200 million; dropped to $100 million in 2000 and was discontinued in 2001. Several years later, expired i-Zone film could be purchased on the Internet. The eventual failure of the i-Zone products was probably the final blow to the company in maintaining sufficient revenue to offset increasing costs required to service the growing debt burden. As a colleague of mine, still employed at Polaroid, related to me: "In a Polaroid conference room in 2000, several over-50 Polaroid executives were attempting to guess what would be the next fad attractive to teenage girls." I guess the answer was probably tiny cell phones with digital camera technology.

The other major product development in DiCamillo's strategy that could have had an impact on Polaroid's future was the digital-imaging products Opal and Onyx. Opal generated color printouts; Onyx produced monochrome and black-and-white images. The systems utilize specially coated paper and a thermal process. Unlike traditional Polaroid instant photos, printouts created with Onyx and Opal required no drying time. They were intended to increase the quality and lower the cost of rapidly printed digital images. As planned, consumers would purchase home printers, capable of generating finished 4x6-inch images, in less than thirty seconds. Commercial printers would be able to create 50 to 60 images per minute. Other devices in the works included portable printers that would attach to mobile phones and handheld computers, cameras with built-in instant digital printers, and an assortment of teen-focused toys for printing stickers and temporary tattoos. The company also hoped to introduce Opal and Onyx to corporate and academic markets. As I tracked Polaroid announcements in 2001, Opal and Onyx sounded like a potential winner, although it also had a hint of the previous failure: Helios for medical imaging. The users would need to purchase the printing devices; completive systems, such as the digital Kodak kiosks, were planned to provide the processors to the users at no cost. Industry insiders had doubts as well. In an article in PC World, Stacy Cowley, IDG News, May 31, 2001, provided the following observations:

International Data Corporation analyst Chris Chute doubts that Opal and Onyx will spark the revolution among consumers that Polaroid envisions. The products would be sensational "if they existed in a vacuum," he says. "It's going to be kind of touch-and-go. They really haven't done much partnering before in this arena." Chute predicts that Opal in particular is several years away from maturity – and by the time it's a competitive system, "you're going to see so many products in that space that Polaroid entering the market is not going to be a new thing," he says. "The technology itself (behind Opal and Onyx) is great," Chute says. "Whether it can deliver is beyond the technology. It's up to Polaroid as a business."

Opal and Onyx never made it to market. Polaroid did not have the cash to support the program. At the 2001 annual meeting, May 8, 2001, Gary DiCamillo announced Polaroid would unveil the new printing platforms. On October 12, 2001, Polaroid voluntarily filed for Chapter 11 under the U.S. Bankruptcy Code.

DiCamillo's product strategy during his time at Polaroid was somewhat successful in the short-term. Reviewing the financial performance during his tenure would indicate Polaroid from 1995 on was "shoveling sand against the tide." As Russian sales peaked, other markets dropped; likewise, for the i-Zone and other teenage products.

Booth 1994-1995,   DiCamillo 1995-2000

($ in millions)	1994	1995	1996	1997	1998	1999	2000
Net Sales	$2,313	$2,237	$2,275	$2,146	$1,846	$1,979	$1,856
Restructuring	$0	$247	$110	$324	$50	$0	($6)
Operating Profits	$200	($158)	$52	($159)	($49)	$108	$109
Net Earnings	$117	($140)	($41)	($127)	($51)	$8.7	$38
# of Employees	12,104	11,662	10,046	10,011	9,274	8,784	8,865
Payroll + Benefits	$721	$709	$641	$609	$564	$545	$498
Pay as % of sales	31%	32%	28%	28%	31%	28%	27%
Average Pay	$59,567	$60,796	$63,806	$60,833	$60,815	$62,045	$56,176
LT Debt	$566	$527	$490	$497	$497	$573	$574
Short Term Debt	$117	$160	$125	$242	$332	$259	$364
Total Debt	$683	$687	$615	$739	$829	$832	$938

Since DiCamillo's first full year in 1996 through 2000, net losses totaled $172 million. Money was borrowed to cover the $27 million needed to cover the $.60 stock dividend. Head count dropped by 2,797 for payroll reductions of $211 million, but restructuring costs of $478 million resulted in a drain on earnings of $267 million. The above chart was extracted from Polaroid's 2000 Annual Report. Not a pretty picture for sure; but, as many Polaroid followers have noted, DiCamillo inherited a difficult financial baseline. In reviewing the data in retrospect, it is obvious Polaroid was in a tough financial position in 1995. That is why many long-time employees left the company when given a great severance package in 1995-96. I did not perform a detailed financial analysis of the company, but I had some strong "macro" level opinions as well as access to day-to-day sales numbers.

First, the debt structure had bothered me for several years. During the late 1980s to 1995, net operating profits had ranged from $50 million to $200 million per year. I estimated it was costing the company about $50-75 million to service the $500 million debt. So, some years up to 1995, almost all of the operating profits should have been used to pay down the loans. After 1995, when operating profits were negative, there was no money available to pay down the debt. Polaroid made bond offerings and other transactions which did not actually pay down the debt the way a private business would. Eventually the music stopped and the notes came due; it reminded me of my niece who paid her way through medical school by rotating charges against a dozen credit cards.

Second, I had lost confidence in the company's ability to spend money on major new programs – the Captiva and Helios $2 billion fiasco. From my position as director of materials for the Film Division, I knew the Russian film sales were mostly bogus.

As shown in the chart, DiCamillo inherited a large debt. Not as obvious to me at the time, he also inherited a payroll and benefits of 32% of sales with the average employee salary of $60,000. To compete in the world of consumer products, spending $.32 out of every sales dollar on payroll would not be a viable business model. In 1995, Polaroid paid an additional

$247 million in restructuring costs (mostly severance related), adding an additional $.11 in that year; $.43 out of each sales dollar went towards employees, either current or former.

In retrospect, what DiCamillo might have done was take the employee reduction all at one time; cut about 3,000 employees by July, 1996; and slash the severance program to where he had to take it in 1997 and beyond. Polaroid would have had about $200 million in payroll savings to put toward the debt and digital-printing platforms. Why didn't DiCamillo make the sweeping reduction in headcount and benefits in 1996? While the thought may have occurred to him, it was not part of Polaroid's culture to treat its employees with such disregard. Dr. Land had built his company differently. We had traditions, and DiCamillo must have decided to honor them – for a while. Part of Polaroid lore alleges that, when he first joined the company, DiCamillo told an executive, "You know one thing Polaroid does really well is to design and implement costly severance programs!"

Some analysts have now said Mac Booth and the Polaroid board of directors should have used the Kodak patent-case settlement of $925 million to pay down the debt in 1991. That move would have been less painful to the employees than a sweeping layoff in 1996; but the attitude at the time was that Polaroid needed the money to fund much needed new products. Most Polaroid retirees agreed we needed new products; leadership just picked the wrong ones, and we all managed them poorly.

The root cause as to why Polaroid failed was not digital imaging. It was not just a leadership void after Land. It was not only Mac Booth's or Gary DiCamillo's management decisions. While the board of directors certainly could have played a bigger role in controlling program spending and debt management, the BOD did not sink Polaroid. Polaroid's culture destroyed Land's once great company. There were certain concepts or principles ingrained in the Polaroid way of running the company that prevented the changes from occurring that could have allowed Polaroid to continue as a viable enterprise in spite of the digital challenge:

212

1. The business model always centered on "give-away" cameras to sell film; the profits are with the media.
2. Employees' welfare is paramount – no layoffs – many departments were grossly overstaffed at both the worker and manager levels. The lack of worker accountability started with the P60 experiment and was never really solved.
3. Executives hired from outside of Polaroid can't succeed because they won't understand or embrace concepts 1 or 2.

Additionally, as outlined in several of the previous chapters, Polaroid CEOs consistently ignored recommendations from internal and external analysts and employees; they resisted proposals from large shareholders – the California Public Employment Retirement on how to spend the Kodak patent suit settlement. There was a proposal to Polaroid's board in 1993 from another large shareholder that might have changed the way Polaroid was led, possibly changing the leadership culture: separate the CEO position from the chairmanship.

Chapter 3:
The Chairman and the CEO

In 1993 a group of stockholders from New York City Teachers Retirement System submitted a proposal to Polaroid's board to separate the position of chairman from that of chief executive officer/president. The group held 155,100 shares of Polaroid stock. Their premise was:

> The position of chairperson should be a nonexecutive role, whose basic responsibilities should include working with the directors to direct management operations and overseeing corporate strategy, compliance with laws, accounting principles and ethical standards applicable to our company. We believe that shareholders will best be served when the board includes a chairperson who is chosen from among the independent, outside directors. Such a person will bring objectivity and unique perspectives to issues facing our company.

Polaroid's board recommended against the proposal, citing the following justification:

> The Board of Directors believes that separating the position of Chairman of the Board from the positions of Chief Executive Officer and President is neither necessary nor desirable. The chief executive officer of the Company has been the Chairman of the Board since

the Company's founding in 1937. The arrangement has worked well. The combination of the position of Chairman and those of Chief Executive Officer and President does not create a conflict of interest, as suggested by the proponent. The Committee on Human Resources and the Board of Directors evaluate the performance and establish the compensation of the Chief Executive Officer and President. No officer or employee of the Company, including the Chief Executive Officer and President, serves or has served on the Human Resources Committee, and none participates or has participated in the Board's evaluation of the performance or establishment of the compensation of the Chief Executive Officer and President.

The Teachers Retirement proposal was defeated at the 1993 annual meeting; that same year Mac Booth was CEO and chairman. The board's comment that the arrangement had worked well, although somewhat self-serving, was mostly correct up to that time as related to conflicts regarding executive compensation. Remember, the 1982 board essentially had Dr. Land removed from the chairman position over disagreement on the Polavision product.

Many Polaroid insiders felt Polaroid's board was mostly a rubber stamp when supporting program spending post-Polavision. Perhaps a nonexecutive chairman with strong business acumen would have provided better governance on failed programs such as Helios and Captiva. In the years after Mac, the board approved some controversial payments to the CEO/chairman. Although the annual pay for the board members did not appear excessive for the time period, their special benefits also came under scrutiny.

The rejection of the proposal to separate the CEO position from the chairmanship was a seminal moment in Polaroid's history related to Polaroid's last CEO, last board, last employees and retirees and Polaroid shareholders. When Edwin Land was chairman, strong-minded, financially astute board members were able to stop Land's spending on Polavision as they believed Polavision was not in the best interest of

215

shareholders. The board under Gary DiCamillo apparently had minimal influence on the financial direction of the chairman/CEO, and Polaroid plummeted into bankruptcy.

Chapter 4:
Journey into Bankruptcy

The interaction between Polaroid's BOD and CEO Gary T. DiCamillo is outlined in the following chronology:

October 1995
Gary T. DiCamillo named chairman and chief executive officer of the Polaroid Corporation.
April 1998
Judith Boynton named chief financial officer at the Polaroid Corporation.
December 1999
Polaroid's board of directors extends DiCamillo's employment contract to the end of 2002. DiCamillo's original contract was due to expire October 2001.
March 2000
Judith Boynton promoted to executive vice president of Business Development.
January 2001
Judith Boynton resigns from Polaroid.
April 2001
DiCamillo granted $250,000 incentive bonus.
July 2001
DiCamillo granted $1.4 million payments plus $25,000 for legal expenses related to "protecting DiCamillo's interests in potential bankruptcy filings."
September 2001
Five Polaroid board members receive payments from their

"deferred compensation" plan ranging from $63,000 to $272,000.

October 12, 2001

Polaroid Corporation and all of its U.S. subsidiaries voluntarily file for Chapter 11 under the U.S. Bankruptcy Code.

December 2001

Polaroid seeks permission from bankruptcy judge to pay $29 million "retention bonuses" to 45 key executives. Judge reduces amount to $1.5 million.

June 28, 2002

U.S. Bankruptcy Court approved the proposed sale of Polaroid to an investor group led by One Equity Partners – the private equity arm of Bank One Corporation.

July 1, 2002

Gary DiCamillo, chairman and chief executive officer, resigns effective July 1, 2002, to become president and chief executive officer of TAC Worldwide Companies based in Dedham.

Many of the actions by the board came under questioning by stock analysts as well as Massachusetts elected officials.

The Judy Boynton hiring:

The Wall Street Journal provided an assessment of Ms. Boynton in a March 26, 2004, article by Laurie P. Cohen and James Bandler:

Ms. Boynton joined Amoco Corp. after graduating from the University of Chicago's Graduate School of Business in 1978. She served in a variety of finance positions, culminating as vice president and controller before she left to join Polaroid in 1998. Ms. Boynton's critics at Polaroid say they see parallels between her tenure at both companies. At Polaroid, these critics say, Ms. Boynton was more focused on pleasing her bosses than getting them to confront serious problems. They fault her for overly optimistic financial projections and for not having a better grasp on the details of Polaroid's business. "There were more background conversations in that company about Judy and Judy's inability to

218

handle the job than almost anything else that was being talked about," said Harvey Greenberg, the former head of human resources at Polaroid. William O'Neill Jr., Ms. Boynton's predecessor as finance chief at Polaroid and now dean of the Sawyer School of Management at Suffolk University in Boston, says Ms. Boynton shared responsibility for Polaroid's bankruptcy. "I give her a third of the blame, the CEO a third and the board a third," he says.

Polaroid's board of directors extends DiCamillo's employment contract:
During DiCamillo's first three full years, 1996-99, net losses totaled $210 million, total debt increased by $145 million and Polaroid stock dropped from $40 down to $20 per share. On the plus side, 1999 net earnings were $8.7 million. Hard to explain why the board needed to extend the contract.

Judith Boynton promoted to executive vice president of business development:
In "Out of Focus", an article in Forbes Magazine January 22, 2001, Michael K. Ozanian wrote:

A big problem has been defection. At least nine top sales or product development executives DiCamillo hired stayed only three years or less. Among them: Clifford Hall, who was key to developing the idea for the i-Zone Instant Pocket Camera, the bestselling camera in the world. People familiar with the situation say many of these folks left because DiCamillo named Judith Boynton executive vice president two years ago. The 46-year-old Boynton, who had been controller for Amoco for two decades, is a professional bean counter who had only been with Polaroid a year as chief financial officer before her promotion. "No one could figure it out," says one former top executive. "She never demonstrated any knowledge of the business." (Full Article in Appendix G)

It was difficult for most Polaroid employees and retirees to understand why the company needed a chief financial officer from outside the company. Polaroid's Finance Department had always been a strength of the company, along with the Patent Department, Polymer Chemistry Group and camera designers. A colleague of mine from the former Digital Equipment Corporation once told me his company used Polaroid as a benchmark for leveraging international exchange rates and other financial innovations. During the Shamrock hostile takeover, Polaroid executive Bruce Henry successfully led the company through the financial intricacies related to funding the ESOP. Certainly, the previous CFO, Bill O'Neil, or other experienced financial executives still at Polaroid could have filled the CFO role. Why DiCamillo felt she would also re-invigorate Polaroid's business is hard to comprehend.

The most troubling part of Boynton's three-year Polaroid career is the compensation package she received before, during and after she resigned several months prior to Polaroid's declaration of bankruptcy. Former CEO Mac Booth and Executive Vice President Dr. Sheldon Buckler, who had contributed much to Polaroid, saw their pension greatly reduced in 2002 after the Pension Benefit Guarantee Agency assumed control of the Polaroid pension. It doesn't seem fair, but as I'll describe in a later chapter, "in business, you don't get what you deserve, you get what you negotiate."

Polaroid board members receive payments from their "deferred compensation":
This action really caught my attention as I was a beneficiary of a deferred compensation plan (DC) after I left Polaroid. The primary benefit of most deferred compensation plans is the deferral of tax for a highly-compensated executive to a later date when the executive's major source of income is lower. While there are broad federal guidelines to these plans, most have the same general restrictions. The program I was in was with the Furon Custom Coating division. Per their plan, I was allowed to defer compensation above the Social Security withholding level. Since I was receiving my Polaroid pension at the time, and I was approaching retirement age, it was a great

way to enhance my future retirement using this tax deferral program. The money placed in my DC became an asset held by Furon in my name. I could invest the money in an assortment of funds similar to a 401K. The risk was that, if Furon were to go bankrupt, I would be treated as an unsecured creditor, possibly losing most or all of my money.

After three years at Furon, I decided to start a consulting business. My deferred compensation funds would come in handy while I established the business. There was one hitch, however; I left Furon in July and could not withdraw the money until February of the next year. The interest earned on deferred compensation funds is taxed at the company's tax rate, not the individual's rate, so Furon needed to close out their fiscal year before establishing how much tax to withhold on my money. I did receive my money the following February.

Compare my case to the Polaroid's board withdrawal of their deferred compensation in September of 2001. Why didn't the directors have to wait until after the close of the 2001 Polaroid fiscal year to determine the taxable portion? They probably did, but Polaroid decided to dissolve the program since they could no longer afford to administer the program. Jeffrey Krasner of the Boston Globe, on December 21, 2001, quoted Polaroid spokesman Skip Colcord:

> The deferred-compensation plan was terminated in August as part of the larger expense-cutting efforts going on at the firm. But, Polaroid's directors didn't know that a bankruptcy filing was imminent. They were certainly aware of the financial challenges the company was facing, but didn't have any prior knowledge of a bankruptcy when the deferred compensation plan was stopped.

So, returning to the previous chronology, in July 2001, as part of DiCamillo's retention payment, the directors also granted DiCamillo $25,000 for legal expenses related to "protecting DiCamillo's interests in potential bankruptcy filings." A few short months later, they extracted their funds. Legal, I'm sure, but it raises a question on how a board is required to receive shareholder approval to start a program like the deferred-compensation plan, but can simply dissolve a compensation plan at the company's discretion. The same Boston Globe article of December 21, 2001, included the following comment:

"I'm surprised by the payments simply because it just seems a bit odd that directors, knowing the company was on the doorstep of bankruptcy, enriched themselves at the expense of creditors and others who didn't get paid," said Jeffrey Jonas, a partner in the law firm of Brown, Rudnick, Freed and Gesmer. "I'm sure they were entitled to it technically, but usually directors, especially outside directors, are not serving at a company for the money," he said. "It strikes me as somewhat unusual that on the eve of bankruptcy they were cleaning up director payments."

In writing this book, I learned more about the way corporate boards function. When you think of it, many of the problems in today's financial world can be tied to the apparent erosion of the concept of fiduciary responsibility versus the current concept of making big bucks.

Chapter 5:
Whatever Happened to Fiduciary Responsibility?

A program I attended while at Polaroid was Effective Negotiating® conducted by Dr. Chester Karrass. More than 800,000 professionals (salespeople, buyers, corporate leaders, managers, engineers, financial officers, CEOs, and international business people) have attended this seminar. One of the basic tenets of the seminar is the concept that *in business, you don't get what you deserve, you get what you negotiate.* When I read about professional athletes and their exorbitant contracts, I recall this concept and assume the ballplayer had sufficient leverage to negotiate the deal. His counter negotiator, the team ownership, must have felt the contract would be a positive business transaction for the team, providing a return on the investment via ticket sales, TV payments, and possibly a Super Bowl or World Series championship.

In addition to chief executive officer, Gary DiCamillo also became chairman of the board of directors when he joined the company. Polaroid's board included a subcommittee, the Human Resource Committee, composed of non-Polaroid employee directors, to establish compensation for Polaroid's executives. The separation of the Polaroid employee board members from the nonemployee members was designed to avoid possible conflict of interest and protect the board's fiduciary responsibility. So, while Polaroid's board operated within established guidelines when hiring DiCamillo and dealing with his compensation, several questions surfaced when reviewing this period of 1995-2001. One of which was how Polaroid's board protected Polaroid's stakeholders when reviewing compensation for executives hired at the recommendation of DiCamillo, the chairman of the board. Did some executives hired by DiCamillo out-negotiate the BOD, using leverage they only held based on recommendation by the chairman? A more universal question, over the last twenty years or so, is whether the concept of boards of directors of publicly-traded U.S. firms has lost its bearings. Former CEOs and academics show up on multiple boards. They are paid well. If the company's CEO is also the chairman of the board, does that ensure conflict of interest won't occur? How well did Enron's board protect stakeholders? Whatever happened to fiduciary responsibility?

The fiduciary responsibilities of a corporation's board members include:

- Avoiding conflicts of interest
- Acting in the interest of the company, rather than the member's personal interest
- Providing oversight to assure that all company business is transacted legally
- Making decisions to protect the assets of the corporation

An article in USA Today on October 26, 2011, reported the pay to directors for U.S. companies continued to rise, up 9% in 2010. The median pay for a director on a board of a publicly-traded company was $234,000 per year. Their time spent on board matters averages less than five hours per week (National Association of Corporate Directors 2010). High-end directors are compensated almost $1,000 per hour, plus other perks. Many directors serve on several boards. Polaroid directors were compensated at the low end of the spectrum, related to payment for meeting attendance, but received some additional perks in stock options, pensions and deferred compensation. In researching the role of directors on boards, it occurred to me that part of the reason publicly traded companies have excessive compensation for CEOs and themselves is the weakness in the proxy voting system. If you do not vote your proxies or you

224

leave proxy items unmarked, your unmarked items are automatically cast with management's viewpoint. We, as shareholders, are approving CEO pay by default by not responding to requests for annual stock mailings. Unfortunately, only if you have the leverage of Warren Buffet or Carl Icahn can you affect BOD recommendations. If your stock is held by a broker, then you may not receive a proxy ballot.

What contribution do the directors make to deserve this compensation? Directors are tasked with overseeing management, executive pay and strategy. Most board members are either current CEOs of companies or retired executives, sometimes members of the academic world. Defenders of the director's high pay will highlight the litigation issues that have surfaced in the last decade (for example, Enron). The prestige brought by the esteemed CEOs could create confidence in the company's management, encouraging investors to purchase the company's stock. Polaroid's BOD, starting with Land, was made up of respected business leaders and members of academia. When Dr. Land was challenged with naming a president back in 1972, he consulted with board member Julius Silver before naming Bill McCune, causing a viable opponent, Tom Wyman, to leave Polaroid. The Polavision saga described in an earlier chapter ended when the Polaroid board went against Land not only to reduce spending on the failed program, but also to relieve Land of his CEO title.

The chart on the following page lists the board members during Mac Booth's last year as chairman and CEO alongside DiCamillo's board in 2001, during the bankruptcy. Board members Henry Necarsulmer, Frank S. Jones, Charles P. Slichter, Kenneth H. Olsen, and Yen-Tsai Feng had been on Polaroid's board back when Dr. Land was chairman, and, in fact, were part of the group that caused Land to give up the chairmanship in 1982. It's interesting to note that each of these members left the board during the first three years of DiCamillo's tenure. Other Polaroid veteran board members (Delbert C. Staley, Lester Pollack, and Ralph E. Gomory) who were appointed during McCune or Booth's leadership also left by 2001, before Polaroid's declaration of bankruptcy. By 2001,

225

four board members from the Mac Booth chairmanship remained, along with the five appointed after DiCamillo took control.

1995 Board (Last under Booth)	Joined	Left	2001 Board (Last under DiCamillo)	Joined
Henry Necarsulmer, Lehman Brothers Inc	1967	1997	Ralph Z. Sorenson, Sorenson Limited Partnership	1984
Frank S. Jones, Professor M.I.T	1973	1999	Alfred M. Zeien, Gillette Company	1985
Charles P. Slichter, Professor Univ. of Illinois.	1975	1997	John W. Loose, Corning, Inc	1994
Kenneth H. Olsen, Digital Equipment Corp.	1975	1998	Albin F. Moschner, OnePoint Services, LLC	1994
Yen- Tsai Feng, Librarian Harvard College	1981	1996	Bernee D. L. Strom, The Strom Group	1996
Ralph Z. Sorenson, Professor Univ. of Colorado	1984	Primary PDC	Stephen P. Kaufman, Arrow Electronics, Inc	1997
Alfred M. Zeien, Gillette Company	1985	Primary PDC	Carole E. St. Mark, Growth Management, LLC	1998
Delbert C. Staley, NYNEX Corp.	1989.	1999	Alfred Poe, Testamints, Inc.	2000
Lester Pollack, Corporate Advisors, L.P.	1989	1997	*Steven A. Bernazzani, Polaroid Corp.	2000
*James D, Mahoney, Polaroid Corp.	1993	1996		
Ralph E. Gomory, Alfred P. Sloan Foundation	1993	2001		
Albin F. Moschner, Zenith Electronics Corp.	1994	Primary PDC		
John W. Loose, Corning, Inc	1994	Primary PDC		

* Employee Representative

226

The board members noted as "employee representatives" were an artifact of the ESOP (Employee Stock Ownership Plan) during the hostile takeover. Starting in 1988, a non-officer member was elected to represent the employees' perspective. They were not allowed to engage in compensation discussions. The turnover of Polaroid's board can be attributed simply to the aging out of several members and replacement with a younger, more diverse group. The retention of Zeien and Loose, both experienced leaders, provided the board with some continuity with the Booth Polaroid. Several board members were retained as board members when Polaroid was sold during the bankruptcy as part of the "new" Polaroid, Primary PDC.

What is the legacy of the board of directors under Gary DiCamillo? While they apparently fulfilled their fiduciary responsibility avoiding conflicts of interest; acting in the interest of the company rather than the member's personal interest and providing oversight to assure that all company business was transacted legally, how well the Polaroid board made decisions to protect the assets of the corporation is not easily determined. The Polaroid Annual Report and proxy statement (issued March 2001) to shareholders does not describe the financial straits the company faced a few months later. The board's focus as recorded in the proxy statement was centered on compensation issues and stock option programs to ensure retention of key executives. If the chairman of the board was not also the CEO of Polaroid, would there have been more scrutiny of the company's financial viability during that critical time frame? Did the board assume DiCamillo was on top of the financial situation and, if his marketing strategy worked, all would be fine? We'll never really know what the board was thinking in early 2001, but perhaps the board members' quotes in the Boston Globe (May 9, 2002) upon DiCamillo's resignation from the company offer a glimpse of their support for the CEO.

Board member Alfred M. Zeien, retired chairman and chief executive officer of the Gillette Company, said: "We have been fortunate to have Gary remain to guide the company over this long, difficult period." Another member of the board, John W. Loose, former president and chief executive officer of Corning

227

Incorporated, said: "Gary has been steadfast in fulfilling the Board's wishes that he remain CEO. He has earned our gratitude, and we wish him only good things in the future."

Another accounting of DiCamillo's tenure at Polaroid was described in the Boston Globe on October 14, 2001, by Ross Kerber and Jeffrey Krasner.

As Polaroid Corp.'s chairman and chief executive, Gary T. DiCamillo has also been its biggest cheerleader, touting everything from its new instant-camera models to its stylish sunglasses. But in six years on the job, DiCamillo's emphasis on marketing failed to rejuvenate what had been a hidebound engineering company. New products were late or lost their way during development, even as consumers turned to digital cameras and away from Polaroid's traditional "wet film" printing technologies.

DiCamillo proved no more adept at managing the resulting financial problems, culminating in Polaroid's bankruptcy filing on Friday. One former executive, for instance, recalled an announcement DiCamillo authorized last fall that Polaroid would meet revenue expectations for the third quarter of 2000. The company didn't mention its earnings, however, and several weeks later disclosed that these had fallen short of Wall Street targets. For some who were frustrated with the company's leadership, the omission was the last straw. "Unfortunately, the frequent revenue and estimate misses undermine their credibility," said analyst Gibboney Huske of Credit Suisse First Boston at the time.

DiCamillo, who declined to be interviewed for this story, headed Black and Decker Corp.'s power tools division before he was hired to lead Polaroid in the fall of 1995, at the age of 44. His predecessor for a decade, I. MacAllister Booth, had invested millions in new imaging technologies for driver's licenses and

228

computerized X-ray machines. The efforts were expensive, however, contributing to a $158 million operating loss Polaroid reported in 1995.

Upon his arrival, DiCamillo was hailed as just the executive Polaroid needed, one who would capitalize on Polaroid's plethora of technologies and imaging patents to create products consumers would demand. "I don't think we have talked to the consumer in 10 to 12 years," DiCamillo said shortly after he was hired.

He also moved quickly to signal a new financial focus. He reduced research-and-development spending, cut 1,600 jobs, and took $265 million in charges. Many more cuts followed.

Some of the new products were hits. The i-Zone, a cheap camera that produced stamp-size instant photos, proved popular with teenagers in the United States and Japan. But other products took too long to develop, like Onyx, a hand-held digital printer for the wireless-data market. It wasn't scheduled to go on sale until next summer at the earliest.

Meanwhile, DiCamillo's efforts, and many of his senior executive appointments, ran up against Polaroid traditions stemming from days when the company could depend on its wet-film business for steady sales. Ongoing layoffs and the sale of properties like its longtime Kendall Square headquarters alienated many veterans. But DiCamillo's day-to-day manner and management style were generally upbeat and easygoing. "Literally, in the six years I've known him, I've never seen him angry," said one employee who spoke on the condition of anonymity. "Maybe that's part of the problem." Another former executive noted DiCamillo's frequent predictions of future growth and profits, and described him as "too much of a Pollyanna."

As digital cameras ate into Polaroid's core market, Carole Uhrich, a former Polaroid vice president, told the Wall Street Journal that she urged DiCamillo in

1998 to sell the company. The board didn't hire me to sell the company," she recalled him saying.

DiCamillo should have listened to Carole Uhrich; but in the Polaroid CEO tradition – from Land to McCune to Mac Booth to Gary DiCamillo – leadership didn't heed advice and the company went into bankruptcy in 2001, sixty-four years after Edwin Herbert Land founded Polaroid.

Chapter 6:
The Bankruptcy

Polaroid's declaration of bankruptcy protection in October of 2001 was a shocker. While many analysts following Polaroid were aware of the company's terrible debt burden and the precipitous drop in revenues the last quarter of 2000 as well as the second quarter of that current year, neither the company nor its auditor KPMG had triggered the alarm related to a firm on the edge of failure. KPMG evidently did not have cause to inform stockholders the company was on the brink of collapse by issuing a "going concern" warning on the 2000 financial statements. A going concern statement by an auditing firm indicates a company may not have the financial wherewithal to stay in business.

During a conference call on December 15, 2000, DiCamillo had warned analysts that fourth-quarter sales 2000 and earnings could be far worse than expected. He went on to say that 2001 wasn't looking very good, either. He was correct. In a few short months, on October 12, 2001, Polaroid Corporation and all of its U.S. subsidiaries voluntarily filed for Chapter 11 under the U.S. Bankruptcy Code. The company reported assets of $1.8 billion and liabilities of $948.4 million in a July 1, 2001, filing with the Securities and Exchange Commission. In the filing, Polaroid claimed revenue declines had stifled its ability to pay off or restructure maturing loans and bonds. It blamed the sales fall-off on a weak instant-film market, among other factors, while asserting that high manufacturing costs had penalized earnings.

231

While the sudden bankruptcy filing appeared premature in simple terms, $575 million in debt securities immediately matured when Polaroid defaulted on $26.3 million in bond payments in July and August 2001. The company could not secure loans to cover the payment. The music had stopped and Polaroid lacked a seat. It was bound to happen; it was only a matter of when. A possible savior was a buy-out, but that option was about two years too old. The debt burden was a problem, and the limited product options did not attract much attention from a potential buyer.

Ten months after filing, the company sold all of its assets to Bank One Corps One Equity Partners (OEP) venture-capital arm for an announced $255 million in cash and $200 million in assumed-trade liabilities. Some observers suggested that Polaroid didn't belong in Chapter 11 in the first place.

"OEP got the assets at a fire sale," says Ulysses Yannas, a Buckman, Buckman and Reid Inc. analyst who has followed Polaroid for 30 years. "It's a company that should never have died." In his opinion, "the judge should have forced the company to come up with a plan to run the entire company...properly." (*CFO Magazine*, January 1, 2003 – Full Text Annex H)

There were controversial issues both during and after the bankruptcy. Polaroid's overseas assets were not included in the filing. Most Polaroid employees assumed, since over half the instant film was assembled outside of the U.S., the assets should have been included, thus preventing the bankruptcy filing. In court, shareholder representatives and unsecured creditors also raised questions about the non-valuation of foreign assets. Asked by attorneys for a shareholder group why the foreign subsidiaries weren't valued, Polaroid's CFO Flaherty said they were part of Mother Polaroid and were essentially worthless if the parent ceased to be a going concern. "Any book value for the subsidiaries, art, patents, and trademarks," he added, "would be misleading." The bankruptcy judge concurred, ruling that the best way to value assets was in a "fair and open" bidding process.

On December 17, 2001, Polaroid filed its official Schedules of Assets and Liabilities, intended as a more-comprehensive summary than the preliminary "First Day" numbers used in seeking Chapter 11 protection. Suddenly, Polaroid claimed a far lower asset base: $714.8 million, compared with the $1.8 billion in the First Day report. Liabilities were listed as $1.1 billion, up from $948.4 million (*CFO Magazine*, January 1, 2003). So now Polaroid appeared more typical of a bankrupt company: assets $714.8 million; liabilities $1.1 billion, a deficit of $385.2 million. After the sale OEP, the "new" Polaroid continued to use the overseas plants, particularly Enschede, the Netherlands film-assembly site, for several years, producing the majority of OEP's revenue.

The retention payments to DiCamillo and staff members angered employees fired during the bankruptcy as well as retirees. Previous executives saw their pension plan reduced by as much as 85% once OEP took ownership of the company. Since OEP had no requirement or interest in funding Polaroid's pension fund, the Pension Benefit Guaranty Corp. assumed the responsibility. The PBGC was created in 1974 to protect workers in the steel mills, etc., so payment is limited to under $50,000 per year, far below the amount due highly paid executives. Polaroid's BOD had compounded the problem for previously retired executives by changing the Polaroid pension in 1998. Prior to 1998, a retiree would receive the pension as an annuity, providing monthly checks, proportionate to pay at termination and years of service. The lump-sum withdrawals of highly paid managers and executives who chose to leave the company post-1998 served to draw down the already deficient fund. The concern was amplified in 2001 after the Chapter 11 filing, when managers were eager to bail out. An article in the Boston Globe by Jeffrey Krasner, December 26, 2001, described the anger of former Polaroid executives.

A group of Polaroid's top retired executives - including two former CEOs - have appealed to the board of directors to stop making lump-sum pension payments to employees now leaving the company. "The lump-sum payments threaten to deplete Polaroid's already underfunded pension plan," the executives said. If the pension plan fails and is taken over by a government agency, the former senior officers would see their pensions limited to a government-mandated maximum of about $43,000 a year.

Ann Leibowitz, a former senior corporate attorney who advised Polaroid on labor matters, said the lump-sum payments the company is making are unfair, because those who retired prior to 1998 were not offered the option. They have to receive their pensions in monthly payments. She contended that by allowing the lump-sum payments to continue while the plan remains underfunded, the company is unfairly putting at risk the payments of those who left prior to 1998. "Polaroid's board of directors and the company have a fiduciary obligation to treat all participants with equal fairness," Leibowitz said. "A continuation of lump-sum payments when the plan is underfunded provides an unfair advantage to the people who are leaving now to our disadvantage."

The Globe article continued:
"We have no plans as of this moment of going to court, but that doesn't mean we won't tomorrow," said I. MacAllister Booth, a former Polaroid chairman and chief executive who retired in 1995. "While the $43,000 limit is significantly less than what I'm receiving today," Booth said, "ensuring the survival of the pension plan would protect the payments to many Polaroid retirees, not just senior officials and 'fat cats.' Hundreds of retirees could be affected."

William J. McCune Jr., a former chairman and chief executive who left in 1991, also signed a November 20 letter to Polaroid's board. "We think of ourselves as the people who created the value of the company in terms of innovation and products," said Sheldon Buckler, a former vice chairman who left in 1994. 'We helped make the Polaroid name. We earned our pensions as much as anybody did, and the extra pension was not munificent by anybody's standards. We lost a big chunk

234

of our pension." Buckler said that after taxes, the amount he got from Polaroid will support a monthly payment of only 15 percent of what he had received under the supplemental pension. "They pulled the rug out from under me," he said."

The fund's assets shrank from $900 million as of October 1, 2001, to $657 million by September 2002, in part because many people leaving the company in the past 18 months took their pension benefits in a lump-sum payment. Most Polaroid retirees sympathized with Mac Booth and Dr. Buckler. They had both worked to lead Polaroid for several decades and had earned their pensions. While their payout was greater than the average retiree, the payout was all part of a publicly-disclosed plan –we knew what we would get, and what the executives would get (or should have gotten). Several executives hired by DiCamillo, who spent less than six years in the company, extracted a disproportionate severance payment. Unfortunately, as explained earlier: You get what you negotiate, not what you deserve.

I was also disappointed in 1998 when I heard about the conversion to the lump-sum pension payout. I had been receiving the monthly annuity pension since 1996, but felt the lump sum, probably $500,000 to $600,000 for a mid-level manager, would have been a better deal. The cash-out was in your control, protected from potential reductions based on the elimination of the Polaroid pension and takeover by the PBGC. In reality, I'm grateful I have the monthly annuity; with the incredibly weak investment options since 2001, I can't imagine how I would have managed the cash.

While the bankruptcy was certainly a disappointment and financial loss for Polaroid retirees drawing an annual pension of greater than $50,000, it was a disaster for many Polaroid employees who worked at the company until the bankruptcy. The stock value in their ESOP fund had evaporated. Whereby an employee may have had a nest egg of Polaroid stock worth as much as $75,000 in 1998, it was now worth about $40! The company aggravated the issue by assuming the employees

235

would want to close the account when Polaroid declared bankruptcy. Many employees would have preferred to maintain the stock under the delusion they could use the 20% employee ownership of Polaroid stock to "fire" the BOD and executives who managed the company into ruin. In addition to the stock loss and job loss, employees current and retired lost their health benefits; employees leaving in 2001 were not granted a severance as offered in previous years, absolutely as devastating as could be imagined. Jeffrey Krasner of the Boston Globe reported on Jan 29, 2002:

> In a strongly worded letter, Massachusetts senators and congressmen have scolded Polaroid chairman and chief executive Gary T. DiCamillo for seeking bonuses for himself and other executives as the company cut benefits to retirees and laid-off workers. "Polaroid at one time stood proud as an example of corporate integrity," wrote the entire 12-member Massachusetts congressional delegation in a letter sent last week to DiCamillo. "It should continue to do so now." In the letter, the congressional delegation urged the Cambridge company to abandon plans to give bonuses to top executives and asked it to restore some of the benefits that have been stripped from retirees. "Polaroid's termination of life and health insurance benefits and reneging on severance payments for over 6,000 former employees and retirees is imposing a severe hardship on thousands of our constituents," wrote the 12 members of Congress.

In addition to the complaint by the Massachusetts elected officials, the committee representing unsecured creditors objected to the payments of the original bankruptcy bonus plan which called for forty-five key employees, including DiCamillo, to receive three different types of payments that could total as much as twice each individual's annual salary. The two sides reached a compromise under which $1.55 million was to be awarded in January and February, with $65,000 going to DiCamillo.

I knew some of those key employees targeted for the double-annual-salary payout. A few might have been worth the retention incentive; most were not. In fact, they should have been terminated along with the dismissed hourly group. The list of forty-five represented mostly the highly paid managers. In my opinion, company boards and bankruptcy judges probably don't understand which individuals need to be maintained during recovery from bankruptcy. There are two types of managers and executives in a manufacturing company: the strategic members and the tactical contributors. With Polaroid in bankruptcy, the majority of the strategic groups are essentially useless – they helped cause the company's failure. For Polaroid to emerge from Chapter 11 or viable sale, the money-producing products, film and cameras, have to be managed. The plant managers and most of their staff need to control the day-to-day activities to ensure shipment of products. The bosses of these folks, directors and vice presidents, don't produce today's revenue, so why would the company be concerned if they chose to leave voluntarily? In fact, most of them could not find a comparable job outside Polaroid, certainly not at the same pay. The managers who could find a job had already left the company with the lump-sum payout. I was director of worldwide materials when I left Polaroid in 1996; I was replaced easily. The CEO, DiCamillo and his staff were also quickly replaced, unfortunately quite a bit too late.

The mechanics and operators who kept the machines pumping out products; the purchasing agents who cajoled suppliers into providing materials with questionable payment options; the planners who insured shipments to the large retail stores; a few financial experts to arrange loans and provide cash flow; a few human resource specialists to carry out the personnel activities – these employees should have been the last to leave. When Polaroid was in bankruptcy, no one including DiCamillo should have been granted a retention bonus, in my opinion.

The great company built by Edwin Herbert Land, ceased to exist on October 12, 2001, with the declaration of bankruptcy. The company started to fail the day the board of directors relieved Land of his responsibilities in 1981. About 20 years later, the final board of directors would have embarrassed Dr.

Land with their actions. Imagine, Polaroid for over 50 years one of the best places to work in Massachusetts and the U.S.A.; Polaroid, a Wall Street darling, once a "nifty-fifty stock"; Polaroid, benefactor to numerous charitable activities – now, in 2001, a broken firm, its CEO publicly chastised by elected officials and its assets sold way below perceived value.

Section 6
Post- Bankruptcy

Petters's Polaroid files bankruptcy

By Emily Kaiser, Dec. 18, 2008

Polaroid Corp. is the latest entity to fall after its owner, Tom Petters, went to jail awaiting trial on an alleged $3 billion Ponzi scheme against investors. Polaroid filed for Chapter 11 bankruptcy Thursday, the Minnesota Star Tribune reports.

In a statement, the company said the filing will not impact day-to-day operations or introduction of unspecified new products in 2009.

Petters bought the Massachusetts-based company for $426 million in 2005. His business strategy was to use the Polaroid brand to sell more than cameras by placing the well-known name on plasma TVs, DVD players and memory cards.

When the investigation against Petters and his company Petters Group Worldwide became public, Polaroid assured customers their business was fine despite their owner's troubles.

The above headline in the *Minnesota Star Tribune* described the depths to which the iconic Polaroid name had fallen–a 2nd bankruptcy and the owner in jail.

239

Chapter 1:
Polaroid 2002-2011

In its last years, following the dissolution of Land's company in 2001, Polaroid continued, though it was less than successful.

April 2005: Petters Group Worldwide completed its acquisition of Polaroid for $426 million. Polaroid thus became a wholly-owned subsidiary of Petters. One of Petters' immediate goals was to begin introducing Polaroid-branded consumer electronics products in overseas markets.

2007: Polaroid stopped producing cameras.

2008: Polaroid stopped producing Instant film.

October 2008: The Impossible Project purchases the production machinery from Polaroid and leased building north of the former Enschede, the Netherlands, Polaroid plant. The Impossible Project saved the last Polaroid production plant for integral Instant film in Enschede and started to invent and produce totally new Instant film materials for traditional Polaroid cameras. In 2010, Impossible saved analog instant photography from extinction by releasing various brand new and unique instant films. To track the "old" Polaroid Instant film, visit the website www.impossibleproject.com.

December 18, 2008: Polaroid Corp. filed for Chapter 11 bankruptcy protection in U.S. Bankruptcy Court for the District of Minnesota. The bankruptcy filing came shortly after the criminal investigation of its parent company, Petters Group Worldwide, and the parent company founder, Tom Petters.

April 16, 2009: Federal Bankruptcy court for the district of Minnesota approved the sale of substantially all assets of Polaroid, including the Polaroid brand, intellectual property, inventory and other assets, to a joint venture led by Gordon Brothers Brands, LLC ("GBB"), and Hilco Consumer Capital, L.P. ("HCC"). Sale price was $88 million.

January 5, 2010: Polaroid partnered with Lady Gaga, appointing her as creative director for the company. A press release stated that she would be the "new face" of Polaroid.

April 29, 2010: Polaroid introduced the "new" Polaroid 300 camera. It uses a rebranded Fuji Instax film. The picture is business-card size and costs about $1.25 per silver-halide print.

As I close my history of Polaroid in April 2012, a company continues to use the name "Polaroid" and has its headquarters in Concord, Massachusetts, about ten miles north of the former Waltham campus. The Waltham site is presently under conversion to a shopping/office complex. Privately held, they employ fewer than 500. Manufacturing is outsourced.

In November 2011, Polaroid announced a new digital camera called the Z340 Instant Digital Camera that can print photos on the spot, much like classic Polaroid Spectra cameras of the 1980s. This new take on the retro form includes a 14-megapixel sensor as well as a 2.7-inch LCD image viewer among other new digital functions. It prints 3x4-inch photos on demand; and, since it is digital now, you can preview the images on the 2.7-inch LCD display before you print. The camera also comes with an SD card slot and can print up to 25 images and capture up to

75 images on a single charge. The Z340 is priced at $299.99, and the Zink (zero ink, thermal imaging) printing paper will cost $20 for a 30-sheet pack. The Z340 Instant Digital Camera is fairly bulky at one pound, seven ounces, due to its integrated Zink zero-ink printer.

The "newest" 2012 Polaroid is competing with the legacy Polaroid Instant film from Enschede. The new camera is heavier than you would think acceptable, but it does include digital imaging. A hard copy, non-silver-halide large print is produced instantly at $.67 per print, lower than the traditional $1 per instant print. Lady Gaga has replaced Sir Laurence Olivier and James Garner and Mariette Hartley as Polaroid spokesperson. The 2012 Polaroid is also selling a retro instant camera using film produced by former competitor Fujifilm of Japan. Some former Polaroid employees from the film plant in Enschede continue to make the iconic silver-halide film invented by Dr. Land.

I wish both the 2012 Polaroid and the Impossible Project the best of luck in their pursuits. As you may have guessed, the Impossible Project got the inspiration and company name from Polaroid's founder Edwin H. Land: "Don't undertake a project unless it is manifestly important and nearly impossible."

Chapter 2:
Lessons Learned

In compiling *Fall of an Icon* over these past several years, I became increasingly disturbed by the chaotic state of the world economy and the U.S. political system. When I started the book in 2007, the Dow Jones Industrial average was closing in on 14,000. As I completed my writing in early 2012, the DJIA was struggling to maintain 13,000. The stock market has essentially had zero gain in five years. The Tea Party group has hijacked congress; members of the U.S. Senate and House of Representatives either pledge not to raise taxes or face being cast from office. "Occupy Wall Street" captured the media's attention, but not much else. The top 1% continues to prosper at the expense of the 99%. The Eastman Kodak Company, another photographic company, is now in bankruptcy. In 2011, the U.S. finally ceased our long war in Iraq and is moving toward extracting our troops from Afghanistan after ten years.

We need to have the optimism of Dr. Land when he addressed Polaroid shareholders back in 1981, after the prolonged Iran hostage crisis, and the high inflation and interest rates of the late 1970s. America did recover from the malaise in the mid-'80s and experienced a wonderful twenty years of growth. It is hoped that the lessons learned during the recent great recession will shock our politicians and business leaders into more sane policies and America will again prosper. Land's early Polaroid was a microcosm of American industry. It came of age before World War II, prospered during the war, and showed resilience after the war in retooling to create the Instant film products.

When Land was essentially fired from his own company in 1981, he left the company with the warning: "There are men who organize ideas and men who organize people. It is the duty of the latter to protect the power of the former."

In 1980, a company CEO earned about 30 times the average worker. By the year 2010, CEO pay had risen to 300 times worker pay. In Land's model, organizers of people or CEOs had found a way to extract huge compensation without actually inventing or producing new ideas. CEOs such as Steve Jobs of Apple and Bill Gates of Microsoft are exceptions to this phenomenon. Polaroid lost it way after Dr. Land. The U.S. lost its industrial base over the last two decades and won't recover until company CEOs recognize they really haven't earned their exorbitant compensations and need to return to principled leadership.   Polaroid's board of directors in 2000 provides several examples of why boards need to consider overhauling and adding guidelines to increase transparency and protect stakeholders.

- Separate the position of chairman and CEO. Let the CEO manage the company and the chairman run the board. Polaroid had always combined the two positions. It may have worked when the board had strong minded business members such as Ken Olsen, former Digital CEO, but Polaroid's last board did not appear to be on top of the pending loan defaults prior to bankruptcy.
- Boards should limit how many other boards the CEO should sit on. Polaroid's last CEO/Chairman sat on four other boards in 2000. I would think the shareholders of a company drowning in debt and losing revenue would be better served with a CEO with only his company to occupy his attention.
- A BOD should not allow more than one member of its board to sit on the same board of another company. Polaroid's 2000 board had two members on the BOD of Pella Corporation. Too chummy; it amplifies the perception of fraternity-type recruitment.
- For several years, Polaroid's BOD had benefits of deferred compensation and a pension after five years. This should not

244

be necessary to maintain qualified members. Pay them competitively and grant them options, but limit the perks.

- Boards should limit the term of external auditors. The auditing firm should provide a new audit team every year to avoid potential complacency. KPMG's failure to recognize Polaroid's financial situation a few months prior to the declaration of bankruptcy was a concern to many. I've provided quality and environmental auditing to manufacturing companies for over ten years. I prefer to audit the same firm no more than three times as I feel we become too familiar with each other.

- Boards should more directly relate the stock options and stock grants for executives to overall company business results, with performance measured over a multi-year horizon.

While none of the above is new, the performance of Polaroid's board the years prior to declaration of bankruptcy was a disappointment to all stakeholders. Shareholders suffered terrible loss without sufficient notice; many employees and retirees saw their pensions and ESOP funds destroyed; and suppliers and many creditors also suffered great financial losses.

We shareholders need to do a better job managing our proxy votes. If you do not vote your proxies or you leave proxy items unmarked, your unmarked items are automatically cast with management's viewpoint. So, we as shareholders are approving BOD proposals by default by not responding to requests for annual stock mailings. Since most stockholders own their stock via a broker, many don't even receive proxy ballots. Unless you are a large stockholder fund, such as the California State Pension Fund or the New York City Teachers' Retirement System, you don't have much say. This system needs to change.

Epilogue

Edwin Herbert Land was truly an American icon, not just for his inventions, but in his wonderful sense of fairness, his eloquent prose and remarkable accomplishment in building a great company. Dr. Land would be saddened to see how his successors let the company fall apart, allowing a few short-term executives to extract financial rewards disproportionate to their contributions, while the dedicated, long-term executives and employees were stripped of their vested, just rewards.

All of our confidence has to come from making things... Let us not make more of something there is too much of. Let us find out what is desperately needed, although people may not know it. Let us find out what will beautify the world, although people may not know it. Then let's learn and learn and teach ourselves, and support each other in doing that until we lose ourselves in those tasks. (E. H. Land, February, 1960, Polaroid Annual Report)

Walter Isaacson's biography *Steve Jobs* included the following quote from Jobs of Apple: "Edwin Land of Polaroid talked about the intersection of the humanities and science. I liked that intersection. There's something magical about that place."

There certainly was something magical about Land's Polaroid in the 1960s and '70s, as witnessed by all of us fortunate to be part of the exciting introduction of first the pack-film type film/cameras and then the superb SX-70 Integral system. We all

246

had challenging, well-paid jobs – careers actually – thanks to the brilliant inventions and humanity of Dr. Land. Then Land was caused to leave his company in 1981 and the company was never the same. Continuing with the quote from *Steve Jobs*:

> I have my own theory about why decline happens at companies. The company does a great job, innovates and becomes a monopoly or close to it in some field, and then the quality of the product becomes less important. The company starts valuing the great salesmen, because they're the ones who can move the needle on revenues, not the product engineers and designers. So the salespeople end up running the company –when the sales guys run the company, the product guys don't matter so much and a lot of them run off.

Land's successor CEOs Bill McCune and Mac Booth put forth a sincere effort to grow the company. Unfortunately, under their leadership, Polaroid evolved away from innovation and became a sales-and-finance-focused company, managed by a group of marketers and MBAs who made key decisions based on Wall Street demands. For the next thirty years, after the introduction of Dr. Land's great SX-70 instant camera and film system in 1972, the Polaroid Corporation never had another invention that was a commercial success.

The last CEO of Polaroid, Gary DiCamillo, inherited a company in decline and helped orchestrate its death in 2001. He did not do a good job leading Polaroid in the opinion of most former Polaroid employees and analysts. I also believe the board of directors could have done a better job in directing Polaroid's last CEO and chairman.

*****

I asked several Polaroid colleagues to review my book both to verify the accuracy of my history and to provide some insights from their time at Polaroid.

Al Hyland, a former supervisor, read the book and met with me to pass on his thoughts. Al started at Polaroid in 1965, fresh out of the Harvard Business School. He worked in the Black-and-White lab alongside many of Land's scientists. Later he managed the Roll and 4X5 Film manufacturing plant in Waltham. When Polaroid needed to establish its own battery-manufacturing capability in support of the SX-70 program, Hyland was selected by Dr. Buckler to head up the division. The establishment of the in-house battery manufacturing was a seminal moment in Polaroid's history, as the battery being produced by the supplier Ray-O-Vac had little chance of success because of several design flaws. I worked for Al in the division. Since Al bridged the Land-McCune to Mac Booth eras, he was an excellent sounding board for me.

During our discussion, Al made an interesting observation:

When Dr. Land departed the company in 1982, Polaroid lost more than its visionary leader, the inventor-genius; Polaroid started to lose its "soul." In the next few years, several of the executives from Land's inner circle also left Polaroid. Drs. Richard Young and Derek Jarrett decided to seek opportunities elsewhere. Another top scientist, Dr. Stanley Bloom, passed away at Photokina, the annual photographic showcase in Germany.

The company started to reduce employee headcount, not by way of conventional lay-offs, but by very generous voluntary severance programs. Over the next two decades, up to 1997, Polaroid offered about a half dozen of these severance and early-retirement programs. Many of the top people, the ones who had skills that were attractive to companies outside of Polaroid, left. In my opinion, this steady erosion of talent created a scientific-leadership vacuum that was not adequately replaced by the MBAs and marketing people. Very few strong scientific types joined Polaroid post Land or, if they did, they didn't stay long.

Al's thoughts were very similar to Steve Job's premise described previously related to innovators being replaced by salesmen. Al suggested that in addition to the talent drain, two other issues emerged in post-Land Polaroid: lack of harmony at the manager level and fixation on various quality improvement or business models. Al and I agreed that the *soul* Land had shaped with his mantra of only working on near impossible projects, disdaining market research, was gone. While Land and Wall Street had an almost adversarial relationship (the Wall Street Journal always referred to Mr. Land, not Dr. Land), his successors allowed Wall Street to help manage Polaroid with their single-minded focus on Polaroid's stock price.

As I have related in this Polaroid history, the executives on Booth's staff were not consistently on the same page. There was the "team" from the New Bedford program (the "New Bedford Mafia") and Joe Oldfield's supporters (the "Irish Mafia"); each took a turn occupying, or trying to occupy, the leadership positions. Shelly Buckler was set in place as vice chair of the BOD with Mac Booth in 1990; but, to those who observed them, the two did not seem compatible. The managers at the lower levels were constantly competing for promotions. I was one of them. It was not a pleasant work environment.

Al also believed, and I agree, the company leaders had a need or mission to latch on to the latest innovation in the U.S. business-improvement model. Al described a few programs we both were involved in:

> While many of these programs had excellent applications in and out of Polaroid, the company would work on one for a while; when a "new" initiative emerged or a new officer was put in charge of quality or manufacturing, the previous program was discarded. When the Japanese "Quality Circles" became popular, we established circle teams in the battery division. The teams didn't work at Polaroid because, since only engineers and mechanics could change a process, the machine operators didn't stay involved. The company gave up the circles and replaced them with Total Quality Ownership (our version of Total Quality Management to match our ESOP). This program involved a lot of "brainstorming" –talking and training, but few actual

improvement actions. Thousands were spent on other programs such as "Re-Engineering", "Cycle Time Reduction", and "Self-directing Work-teams." We just didn't have focus, did we?

The two programs that did help improve Polaroid film quality were the Statistical Engineering Training Program, as described in the text, and the "Six Sigma" concepts. Ironically, several of the Polaroid employees who excelled at these techniques were hired away from the company into very well-compensated consulting jobs with the consultants who trained them!

The lack of focus was a bigger problem than I realized when I started my book. When Dr. Land decided to produce instant color film, develop the perfect Instant photographic process, the SX-70, make Polaroid negative or Polaroid batteries, employees at all levels jumped on board gladly. It was exciting to be part of; we had focus and got the job done.

The Polaroid Corporation was the embodiment of one person, Edwin Herbert Land; he was the founder, inventor and the protective father figure to his employees. When Land was pushed out of his company by the board of directors in 1982, his successors never found or maintained a viable focus again.

APPENDIX

A   Edwin Land Biography
B   Land's Philosophy
C   History of Polaroid-Marian Stanley
D   Polaroid Instant Camera History
E   Shamrock – NY Times
F   CalPERS – a Showdown at Polaroid
G   Out of Focus – Forbes Magazine
H   What's Wrong with This Picture?

Appendix A
Edwin H. Land Brief Biography
From *Wikipedia, the Free Encyclopedia*

Edwin Herbert Land

Edwin Herbert Land
Born
May 7, 1909
Bridgeport, Connecticut
Died
March 1, 1991 (Aged 81)
Cambridge, Massachusetts
Nationality
American
Known for
Polarizing Light
Notable awards
Perkin Medal 1974

Edwin Herbert Land (May 7, 1909– March 1, 1991) was an American scientist and inventor, best known as the co-founder of the Polaroid Corporation. Among other things, he invented inexpensive filters for polarizing light, a practical system of in-camera instant photography, and his retinex theory of color vision.

Early years
Edwin was born in Bridgeport, Connecticut, to Harry and Helen Land. His father owned a scrap-metal yard. He attended the Norwich Free Academy at Norwich, Connecticut, a semi-private high school, and graduated in the class of 1927. The library there was posthumously named for him, having been funded by grants from his family. He studied physics at Harvard. After his freshman year, he left Harvard for New York City.

In New York City, he invented the first inexpensive filters capable of polarizing light. Because he was not associated with an educational institution, he lacked the tools of a proper laboratory, making this a difficult endeavor. Instead, he would sneak into a laboratory at Columbia University late at night to use their equipment.[1] He also availed himself of the New York City public library to scour the scientific literature for prior work on polarizing substances. His breakthrough came when he realized that instead of attempting to grow a large single crystal of a polarizing substance, he could manufacture a film with millions of micrometer-sized polarizing crystals that were stretched into perfect alignment with each other.

After developing a polarizing film, Edwin Land returned to Harvard. However, he still did not finish his studies or receive a degree. Once Land could see the solution to a problem in his head, he lost all motivation to write it down or prove his vision to others.[2] Often his wife, at the prodding of his instructor, would extract from him the answers to homework problems. She would then write up the homework and hand it in so he could receive credit and not fail the course.

Land's company
In 1932 he established the Land-Wheelwright Laboratories together with his Harvard physics instructor to commercialize his polarizing technology. Wheelwright, his instructor, came from a family of financial means and agreed to fund the company. After a few early successes developing polarizing filters for sunglasses and photographic filters, Land obtained funding from a series of Wall Street investors for further

253

expansion. The company was renamed the Polaroid Corporation in 1937. Land further developed and produced the sheet polarizers under the Polaroid trademark. Although the initial major application was for sunglasses and scientific work, it quickly found many additional applications: for color animation in the Wurlitzer 850 Peacock jukebox of 1942, for glasses in full-color stereoscopic (3-D) movies, to control brightness of light through a window, a necessary component of all LCDs, and many more. During World War II, he worked on military tasks, which included developing dark-adaptation goggles, target finders, the first passively guided smart bombs, and a special stereoscopic viewing system called the Vectograph which revealed camouflaged enemy positions in aerial photography.

A little more than three years later, on February 21, 1947, Edwin Land demonstrated an instant camera and associated film. Called the Land Camera, it was in commercial sale less than two years later. Polaroid originally manufactured sixty units of this first camera. Fifty-seven were put up for sale at Boston's Jordan Marsh department store before the 1948 Christmas holiday. Polaroid marketers incorrectly guessed that the camera and film would remain in stock long enough to manufacture a second run based on customer demand. All fifty-seven cameras and all of the film were sold on the first day of demonstrations.

During his time at Polaroid, Land was notorious for his marathon research sessions. When Land conceived of an idea, he would experiment and brainstorm until the problem was solved with no breaks of any kind. He needed to have food brought to him and to be reminded to eat.[2] He once wore the same clothes for eighteen days straight while solving problems with the commercial production of polarizing film.[2] As the Polaroid Company grew, Land had teams of assistants working in shifts at his side. As one team wore out, the next team was brought in to continue the work.

Later years

In the 1950s, Edwin Land and his team helped design the optics of the revolutionary Lockheed U-2 spy plane. Also in this decade, Land first discovered a two-color system for projecting the entire spectrum of hues with only two colors of projecting light (he later found more specifically that one could achieve the same effect using very narrow bands of 500 nm and 557 nm light). Some of this work was later incorporated in his Retinex theory of color vision. In 1957, Harvard University awarded him an honorary doctorate, and Edwin H. Land Blvd., a street in Cambridge, Massachusetts, was later named in his memory. The street forms the beginning of Memorial Drive, where the Polaroid building was located.

In the early 1970s, Land attempted to explain the previously known phenomenon of color constancy with his Retinex theory. His popular demonstrations of color constancy raised much interest in the concept. He considered his leadership towards the development of integral instant color photography – the SX-70 film and camera – to be his crowning achievement.

Although he led the Polaroid Corporation as a chief executive, Land was a scientist first and foremost and as such made sure that he performed "an experiment each day." Despite the fact that he held no formal degree, employees, friends, and the press respected his scientific accomplishments by calling him Dr. Land. The only exception was the Wall Street Journal, which refused to use that honorific title throughout his lifetime.[2]

Land often made technical and management decisions based on what he felt was right as both a scientist and a humanist, much to the chagrin of Wall Street and his investors. From the beginning of his professional career, he hired women and trained them to be research scientists. Following the assassination of Martin Luther King, Jr., in 1968, he led Polaroid to the forefront of the affirmative action movement.

Despite the tremendous success of his instant cameras, Land's unsuccessful Polavision instant movie system was a financial disaster, and he resigned as Chairman of Polaroid on March 6, 1980. In his retirement years, he founded the Rowland Institute for Science.

Death

Land died on March 1, 1991, in Cambridge, Massachusetts, at the age of 81. Upon his death, his personal assistant shredded his personal papers and notes

Public service

Land was: [3]

- A member of the President's Science Advisory Committee (PSAC) 1957–59 and a Consultant-at-Large of PSAC from 1960–1973.
- A member of the President's Foreign Intelligence Advisory Board (PFIAB) 1961–77.
- A member of the National Commission on Technology, Automation and Economic Progress 1964–66.
- A member of the Carnegie Commission on Educational Television 1966–67.
- A Trustee of the Ford Foundation 1967–1975.
-

Honors

Although Land never received a formal degree, he received honorary degrees from Harvard, Yale, Columbia, Carnegie Institute of Technology, Williams College, Tufts College, Washington University, Polytechnic Institute of Brooklyn, University of Massachusetts, Brandeis University and many others. He was awarded the Presidential Medal of Freedom, the highest award given to a U.S. citizen, in 1963, for his work in optics. He held 535 patents, compared with Thomas Edison's 1,097 American patents.[2] In 1967 he was awarded the Frederic Ives Medal by the OSA. In 1977 he was inducted into the National Inventors Hall of Fame. In 1988 Land was awarded the National Medal of Technology for "the invention, development and marketing of instant photography."

Notes

1. World of Physics. ©2005-2006 Thomson Gale

2. Wensberg, Peter C. (1987-09). Land's Polaroid: A Company and the Man Who Invented It. Houghton Mifflin (T). pp. 258. ISBN 0395421144.
3. "EDWIN H. LAND: SCIENCE, AND PUBLIC POLICY", by Richard L. Garwin, The Irish Colleges of Physicians and Surgeons, 1993

Appendix B
Land's Philosophy
Time Magazine, June 26, 1972

Polaroid is anything but a conventional corporate giant. It has no long-term debt, because Land is convinced that he should be "financially conservative and technologically audacious." In Cambridge, the company seems to feed on the intellectual and technological ferment of neighboring Harvard and M.I.T.– where Land occasionally teaches courses in specialized sciences–and sometimes on social ferment as well. Soon after the Kent State killings in 1970, Polaroid employees were invited to send any message of their choosing to President Nixon at company expense; some 2,200 did so. Polaroid technicians have gone to extreme lengths to protect the environment, once even rigging a costly twist in pipes leading from a chemical plant in order to save several trees. One of Land's personal embarrassments–until the "garbage-free" SX-70 film was designed–was the amount of litter that his product created.

Land has built Polaroid very close to his own self-image–part scientist and part humanitarian philosopher. The latter side of the corporation's personality is most strongly expressed in its extraordinarily forward-looking community-relations program, which has served as a model for other big corporations. Polaroid now donates money or some other form of assistance to 143 community projects in the Boston area, including day-care centers and tutoring projects. Says Cambridge Mayor Barbara Ackerman, a Democrat and social activist: "Polaroid is the only industry in this city that you can go to for money, for land or for some other contribution to the community. Polaroid considers itself a neighbor and actually does neighborly things."

Polaroid is interested in the world far beyond its immediate neighborhood. The company's community relations director, Robert Palmer, recently spent ten days helping mediate a prisoner revolt at Massachusetts' Walpole state prison, and has condemned as dehumanizing a proposed ID card system for

Massachusetts welfare recipients–even though an ID system pioneered by Polaroid might well have been used. This year the company reached a longtime goal of employing one black in each ten jobs, about the same ratio as blacks in the total population.

As a socially conscious corporation, Polaroid is also, as Palmer puts it, "a choice target." In October 1970, a dozen black-militant employees tacked up posters on Polaroid bulletin boards accusing the company of supporting apartheid in South Africa by allowing its cameras and film to be used in internal passports and by paying much lower wages there to blacks than whites. The charges turned out to be embarrassingly accurate. Even though the Polaroid operation in South Africa is owned by an independent distributor rather than by the parent corporation, Land was deeply hurt by the employee protest. He decided on a novel solution: he asked a group of employees, including blacks, to visit South Africa and study the case. "Your decision will be implemented, whatever it is," he promised. The group eventually agreed unanimously to stop selling to the government but to continue other operations in South Africa, while ordering Polaroid's distributor to upgrade black wages.

Appendix C
Marian Stanley, Polaroid Corporation
Vice President of Emerging Markets
Renee Garrelick, Interviewer, *Concord Oral History Program,*
May 16, 1996

Marian Stanley has worked at Polaroid Corporation for thirty years and is currently one of two women officers of the company. She describes the distinctiveness of the corporate culture that Edwin Land influenced.

When I first joined Polaroid in 1967, it was very much still a start-up company. When it was originally incorporated in 1937, it was formed by Dr. Edwin Land, the founder of Polaroid, around his invention of polarized lenses. Those lenses were anti-glare devices which he had hoped would be put into automobile windshields to prevent accidents. Dr. Land was hoping that these polarized lenses would be put into car headlights and car windshields as a safety measure. Automobile companies at that time were not interested in the idea. He was very disappointed but moved on to other inventions.

He was on vacation with his family in New Mexico, while still having this very small polarizing business he was struggling to get off the ground, and he took a photograph in New Mexico and his daughter who was 7 or 8, innocently asked "Why can't I see the picture right away?" Being the type of person he was, a very creative person, he wondered himself why she couldn't see the picture right away. He immediately started to think about how one could see the picture right away. He came back to Cambridge and shifted his sights from polarizing lenses to instant photography. He introduced the first instant camera in 1947 to a really astonished public.

In 1967, the company had had a tremendous growth period. It was a very hot stock, but also it had an incredible reputation as a very unique environment. The unique environment was very much a product of Dr. Land and the type of person he was and the type of people that he attracted. When I joined, I was a young teacher teaching in a small Catholic grammar school and

I was halfway through my master's. I was teaching every subject to a group of 7th graders. There were 50 in the classroom at the time. I enjoyed it very much but for a young girl of 23, it was not an active social life with the children, the nuns and me. So I was eager to work with other adults who were not in a habit, although they were all lovely, lovely women. I happened to see an ad in the paper for a customer service representative, and I applied. It was not something that I thought about in terms of evaluating the company or the culture. I wanted a job where I could use some of my skills, but I honestly didn't think I would be working there very long. In those days, women who took jobs after college usually didn't think they would be working anywhere very long and I was really quite typical. So it was only an accident of fate that I stumbled upon this really intriguing company.

I was hired as a letter writer. In those days a letter writer responded to customers' complaints with these voluminous letters about how they could improve their photographs. We sat in small offices and spoke into Dictaphones. I was surrounded by other women letter writers who were all the wives of men at the Harvard Business School, Law School or Medical School, also thinking that they would only be in these jobs for a few years then they would be replaced by another young woman whose husband was in some professional school. As fate would have it, my husband to be, and I married him when I joined Polaroid, was also in graduate school, so I was one of the many women who were there.

As I learned more about the company, I discovered over the next few months what an extraordinary place this company was and that it had a very special environment. Dr. Land had surrounded himself with extraordinary people. They were people who were not always credentialed people, but who were always extraordinary. He believed in the mixture of science and art so that many of the people that surrounded him in the labs were not necessarily scientifically trained. Many of the people that made the fundamental inventions for Polaroid photography were not scientifically trained. He had women running his labs which was quite extraordinary at the time. My first supervisor there, who was a tremendous influence on me, was a woman

261

who had graduated some years ago from Smith. This had a tremendous impact on me as it was very unusual for the time.

His corporate philosophy was that the company existed for two reasons. One, to create useful and exciting products, and secondly, to bring the best out in people and give them useful, exciting work. This was called the dual aim or the two aims of the company. The first aim was exciting enough, but the second aim was very, very unusual in those times. We were constantly experimenting with different ways for people to contribute to the company, and it was important to create exciting jobs but to also create exciting products. As a result he was able to do both.

For example, the man that invented color instant photography, since the first instant cameras were black and white, was a man called Howard Rogers. Howard Rogers was an automobile mechanic that Dr. Land thought was particularly skilled. He gave Howard a lab and money and told him to go away and develop color photography. Dr. Rogers went away. (Later, he was an honorary doctor because he'd never even finished college.) He came back some years later with not much heard from in-between time, and said I think I've done it. And he had done it. Similarly the people that worked in the laboratories were not credentialed. The lab techs – I ran a film program seven or eight years ago and the best scientists, if you consider empirical scientists, were his old lab techs who came to him out of the Navy or other such places and never had college educations. When I worked on the film program with them, it was so interesting. A couple still had tattoos up and down their arms. They understood the chemistry after working with him and so they understood empirically how the chemistry would react. It is really quite amazing. He believed that every person had enormous potential. Because he treated everyone that way, people responded.

He also worked constantly and in order to work with and for Dr. Land, you had to be completely devoted to him. He would call people many, many times, and there were many nights when they never went home. There were cots in the labs. There were many vacations never taken with families. He demanded and people were just dying to give him complete

262

allegiance and complete control of their time. He was a very charismatic individual and enormously bright. The only other person with more patents to his name is Thomas Edison. The thing about him was not only his tremendous interest in science but his interest in all things; his ability to appreciate art and music. The way he expressed himself was really unique. I have a book of his essays in which he describes science and reading about the science, it is really quite beautiful. The writing is beautiful and his references are artistic references. He surrounded himself with a lot of beauty and a lot of color. He believed that each of our annual meetings was a marvelous adventure with lots of colors and showmanship.

He took care of his people in a very old-fashioned, paternalistic way but in a very nice way. I remember when I worked in customer service that we had a customer reception area where we were rotated when we were not writing letters. We had an old fellow called Dr. Cutler West, who apparently had worked in the lab previously and was always somewhat eccentric, but had clearly gone around the bend by the time I joined. He usually arrived at the customer service center on his bicycle looking as if he needed both a bath and a change of clothes. He would always be looking for more film or some such thing. We were just instructed to take care of Jerry West, so we like everyone else in the company took care of Jerry West by giving him film or cameras. We would talk to him for a very longtime. When you worked in Polaroid it just wasn't considered odd. As I look back now I can't think of very many companies that would have absorbed some of the kinds of eccentrics that Dr. Land did.

The product at the time was getting more and more sophisticated. The first films were very beautiful but tended to fade. We moved from black and white to color. The cameras became more and more sophisticated. The cameras then began to be used for scientific and industrial applications. Actually right now our business is one-third industrial-medical-scientific, one-third business and only one-third consumer. That really started in those years. Our films began to be used for microscope photography, for ultrasound tests and a variety of other applications. As a result, our work in customer service became really quite complicated because you could have someone taking a birthday picture on the end of the telephone or you could have a scientist. I found that very exciting. We were given a list of people to call with questions so that we could always be able to respond to a customer, if not immediately but to get the answer. We were very well connected with all the scientists and the technical centers, which is really interesting for us.

Probably one of my most interesting experiences was when I was assigned to answer Dr. Land's letters, and that was customers who had written directly to Dr. Land. I would write letters for his signature which was very exciting for a young woman. As time went on, it was obvious to me, because my father had run a factory, that although the letter writing may have been a very charming way to respond to customers, it wasn't what customers were interested in when they got in touch with us. It seemed that they were interested in fairly crisp instructions and another pack of film. As I saw it the work designed to do that was really quite different from having cubby holes of offices with people writing very long letters. We established a crisper way to get back to customers, mostly by telephone but sometimes by postcards and just a pack of film.

As time went on, I was promoted within that small department to head of letter writers, etc. During this time, of course as a young person, I never really thought I would be at Polaroid for very long and then I began to take through the next 15 years what was quite a series of leaves of absence – first to go back to school and finish my master's, and then I had four children and for each child I took a leave. It was really unusual for companies at that time to allow people to take these kinds of leaves. So Polaroid was really tremendously socially innovative. The first time I took leave I went back to school, but then I needed to pick up money because we were both in graduate school, so I would drop in and do some additional work. Then when my husband finished his doctorate, it seemed it would be a great time to drive across the country and I got another leave. All these things really were very, very unusual. In addition, it was a time of tremendous change in the country. That was reflected at Polaroid as well.

264

During this time we had civil rights riots. Our little building was on Windsor Street in Cambridge near the housing project in Cambridge. We were escorted to the bus by policemen and we were threatened a number of times. It was a very strange environment. The building in back of us was the Margaret Fuller Settlement House which at one time was taken over by the Black Panthers. It was a bit of an unreal situation. In addition we had the Vietnam War going on. I felt quite strongly about it, and my first supervisor who I said was from Smith – Dr. Land had quite a few women from Smith throughout the company – was very upset because the students had very aggressively interrupted Hubert Humphrey during his speech. I said "Well, really important events are happening and you can't proceed as normal just to be polite." Well, for this woman that was quite a unique thought. That began a series of very interesting conversations. During one of the marches against the Vietnam War I asked to take the day off to march, and she was distressed but let me do that. I said I would work on Saturday. I came in on Saturday and there was Lois who stayed with me the entire day working silently. As time went on, her perspective on politics changed quite a bit.

In addition we had a tremendous situation in South Africa. At that time we had a distributor in South Africa called Paul Hirschon. Apparently he was selling our film to the government for identification cards to identify people from townships traveling to other townships essentially to curtail their activities. So that our film was being used really to curtail the civil rights of people in a country very far from home. Two of our black employees protested that by picketing in front of our headquarters. Polaroid was stunned, number one. I would say we were quite an insular company. We were very U.S., if not to say very Cambridge, and Cambridge behind MIT based so that this was a stunning experience for us. By some act of fate I was asked to respond to customer letters on South Africa because they started coming in. That was a powerful experience for me. We eventually ended up, I believe to our credit during those troubling months when we were actually trying to figure out what was happening and how we could be associated with such a thing, by withdrawing from South

Africa. We have only just entered South Africa again last year. I just returned to South Africa this month as vice president of the company.

So it was a time of great growth in this company with tremendously interesting products, where you had the equivalent of a dark room and a small pod of chemicals with positive and negative, and you were completing all the steps in a dark room, in a color processing dark room, in 60 seconds. It is really an extraordinary invention. So you have this invention that the world just loved, you had this charismatic, extraordinary man who had created this culture that I don't think there was an equivalent in any companies that we knew of in the U.S. – much in terms of groundbreaking approaches – and thirdly, you had this dynamic experience of the '60s. So it was a very heady time for all of us.

As we moved on to the '70s, the products became more and more sophisticated and the marketing became more and more sophisticated. Previously it just sort of happened. We had sophisticated marketing campaigns such as a famous series of ads with James Garner and Mariette Hartley which for some reason were enormously satisfying to people and became kind of our trademark of advertisements. When we were at trade shows, we were always the hit of the trade shows, great showmanship. It was a high flying time. People stayed in very expensive hotels it seemed to me at the time. The money really flowed freely in the corporation.

When I first came to Polaroid in the late '60s the corporation was probably at about several hundred million dollars and we're at $2.4 billion this year. The number of staff at that time was probably in the single digit thousands, maybe under 5000, and we reached a peak about five or six years ago at 12-15,000 if you include international.

Even for that size of corporation in the early days it was extraordinary for people to feel that way about Dr. Land. If you didn't work for him directly, you felt it. Obviously, as the company grew and the people worked out in the factory which swells your population, people still felt intensely connected, but I think it was the Cambridge base which really had the deepest connection.

As we moved into the '70s, I started to have children so I took of course more leaves of absence. During that time again it was really quite unusual to have meaningful part time work in a major corporation. Polaroid being the company it was also allowed for unorthodox pockets of managerial styles. So what I did was essentially shop for managers who were a little unorthodox, and I got great part time work for all those years. During that time, Polaroid became much more professional in its marketing and the sales of its products. It went through some wonderful inventions. It built factories with incredible speed and was obviously a company with tremendous skill and tremendous cash reserves. We had a lot of connections with the universities in the area particularly MIT, and to a much lesser extent Harvard, though Dr. Land had gone to Harvard for two years. He graduated without a degree and only years later was given an honorary degree.

Polaroid started to level off in the late '70s and early '80s, the result of a lessening of the product cycle. There were fewer more significant products coming out. They tended to be variations on the same products. At that time, Dr. Land also had invested heart and soul very heavily in an instant movie system. He was absolutely right and terribly visionary in thinking about that, but he really hadn't taken into account the movie systems that were being created in terms of video photography, so that his instant movie system, which was really a marvelous system, had no sound and required a large player and other equipment and the customers were unwilling to invest in, at least to invest in a significant enough way to justify the investment.

At that time I was named Services Manager for this product to deal with all the customers that had had difficulty and eventually we phased the product out which was very painful and was a very big write-off. At that time Dr. Land was so crushed that he left the company in 1982, and I would say the character of the company essentially changed. If I had to think about a critical juncture that was really it. Number one the leader left and number two he had made a very bad call, so he

267

was human. The whole thing was quite a stunning experience for the population at the time.

I personally only met Dr. Land two or three times though I wrote his letters and interacted on all these things. I was really operating always on stories. I guess in many companies with charismatic people that there are so many stories, and there were so many Dr. Land stories.

When Dr. Land left we had people that were trained as engineers within the company essentially took over the leadership position. The first person was Bill McCune who took over for Dr. Land. Bill McCune was a marvelously energetic, talented guy that had worked with Dr. Land for a longtime. During the time of Bill McCune's tenure, once again I think probably one of the more extraordinary efforts was the building of the New Bedford plant which Mac Booth did. That plant went up in record time and was done so that we could stop depending on Kodak negatives. There were a lot of extraordinary engineering developments at that time, cameras that were really quite exciting for consumers. Again, iterations of the basic invention of instant photography but iterations that customers found very compelling.

At the time that we were using Kodak negatives, and this is not my highest skill in reaching back to technology, essentially our product was a sandwich of a positive and a negative with a pod of chemicals between it that broke open as you pulled it out of the camera. That negative was purchased from Kodak. They were vendors to us. We felt very uncomfortable having this volume of film dependent upon a supplier that was not always sympathetic to our need for a reasonable cost of materials and was not always sympathetic to our needs for certain kinds of supplies, so the decision was made to build our own negative plant. This was a very difficult effort for us. It was a very complex factory. That plant went up in record time and it is still one of our most productive plants. At the time it was considered revolutionary and quite an amazing achievement. As I said, I did have a responsibility for a major film program perhaps six or seven years ago so I spent quite a bit of time down there, many nights down there. It is essentially one large machine coating negative that the entire factory is built around.

268

It happens largely in darkness. When you see the machine first start up, you see the chemicals coming through and you often see these rainbow sheets of chemicals that are really quite beautiful. It is a very beautiful sight, highly automated and highly computerized.

I would say most of our achievements during this time were largely not basic science not fundamental science, but still largely exceptional, technical achievements. Within the marketplace, our marketing was probably at its highest level of achievement in the late '60s and early '70s. The company really moved from that type of high profile marketing, high profile advertising to more muted kinds of advertising and more muted kinds of marketing. Only now is it once again approaching the similar approach to marketing and advertising that it had in the '60s.

As the company moved into the '80s, we encountered the problems that a lot of companies did in that we were struggling in some parts of our business. During that time we had a lot of different approaches and attempts to reinvigorate the product line. Some were successful and some were not. Probably the most significant events of the '80s in my mind had to do with our discovery of ourselves as an international company. This is when we started to move overseas with our product and discovered it was very successful there. We started to build plants overseas in the '70s and '80s. We built a plant in Enschede, The Netherlands and in Ireland which we did not maintain for a variety of reasons. We later sold it actually to Digital. We built a plant in Vale of Leven, Scotland which is one of our major plants. We started to establish overseas subsidiaries in Japan, Germany, the UK and Korea. We have subsidiaries all over the world now, but this was really just the beginning I believe under the aegis of a fellow called Dr. Young who led the way for us in that regards.

Russia is a very exciting story. In the mid-'80s we not only decided to concentrate on what we would call mature developing markets as we were establishing our business in all of these countries, but we elected to focus on some of the new emerging markets. We chose three – Russia, China and India as markets that were problematic, but we felt were not

269

enormous and had great potential at some point in time. I think this decision shows great foresight, and it reminded me of Polaroid in the early days, of something very, very big that really can't be explained because of course, when we went into these markets, people thought we were crazed to be in Russia in 1986, China in 1986, India in 1986. In India the film tariffs were 200%, in China it was 80% on cameras and 50% on film, very problematic leadership; in Russia we could barely find a place to open an office. The system was so inefficient and there were no customers. In Russia and China we had to have a joint venture. In Russia the Svetesor plant was a joint venture with the atomic energy commission and in China it was with the Shanghai Motion Picture Limited company.

It was really Bill McCune through his technical contacts who had a vision of what Russia could be. As a result, we had a small team that worked on these three markets. Russia in 1986 actually gave us no profit or no sales to speak of. We started to see some sales in about 1993 of about $1.3 million, then currency convertibility hit, and we were probably the only company, because we had created a structure that was poised to take advantage of it, that leapt last year to well over $200 million, and this year Russia will be our largest worldwide subsidiary. We celebrated five years of opening our new office in Russia last year with a celebration called Picture America and 25,000 Russians took part. It was an extraordinary experience. In China our business doubles every year. We did over $40 million last year and we'll do in the high $70 or $80 million this year. We have five offices including in the interior. We have a large factory in China that makes a million cameras and two million circuit boards. We have significant business in China.

In India we just got our 100% owned subsidiary which was an achievement. We had the film tariffs reduced from 200% to 21%. We put our own senior manager in there, and we have a factory there that manufactures industrial hardware, and this year it will begin manufacturing our large volume consumer cameras. So the internationalization of Polaroid really happened I would say starting in the '80s. Today well over

50% of our volume comes from offshore. We also have factories in Mexico.

Each of these international markets is somewhat different. I would say Russia is the exception. Russia is largely a consumer market. There are no mini-labs in Russia so when people started taking all those rubles out from under their mattresses which we're convinced they were in little jars in every kitchen, they went out in groups and usually it would be an apartment building that would buy a Polaroid camera and then share it. Each family would buy a pack of film for special events. There were no real mini-labs that could process their pictures efficiently for them so instant pictures were absolutely the ticket. The extraordinary thing is that we have really only concentrated on St. Petersburg and Moscow. We haven't gone outside those two cities, and we have not gone into our industrial occupations at all, so that the potential in Russia is really staggering to us.

In most emerging and developing markets, our biggest business is in passport identification and government programs like driver's licenses and things like that. We also have what I consider is the beginning of consumer photography in street photography which is a very big market outside this country, and that is in markets where people cannot afford a camera but can afford a picture. So there are small entrepreneurs at temples, festivals that take pictures of a family for a fee. Every time a street photographer takes a picture like that, of course, he is doing a product demonstration for you, so that as time goes on and the economy improves, people can understand instant photography, they are familiar with it, and you've got your market development done. Street photographers often times form unions and organizations. I have a very large picture over my fireplace painted by the head of the Indonesian street photography union. They are very competent people who know how to take instant pictures very, very well and sometimes they are quite artistic, and so the pictures are quite nice.

During this time Polaroid also decided to concentrate on other developing markets and so we've entered markets like Vietnam, Indonesia, Peru. All of these markets are generating quite a significant amount of business for us, and they really changed

271

our lives a great deal so that Polaroid has come a long way in terms of how it views itself in the world. It views itself now not so much as a Cambridge company but as a world company. It's employees are not only U.S. citizens but from all over the world. The officers of the company are very different now.

When I first came to Polaroid the officers of the company were all white males who had been technically trained often at the same institution and they tended to live in the same towns. They were all wonderful men and amazingly expansive in their understanding of people as time went on and the world changed in their willingness and desire to give people of a different gender or a different race an opportunity. It was still very much a company of white males of goodwill. Today if you look around the officer ranks of the company, you will find two senior women, one of whom is me, the head of all of manufacturing is headed by a woman and that was always the most plum job in the company that makes it extraordinary for it to go to a woman within the company, the head of one of our business research units was born in Egypt, the head of our research and development group comes from Bombay, we have two black vice presidents and the head of Asia Pacific is black. So this is really quite an exceptional transition for the company that I think Dr. Land would have approved of. Our vision as a company is significantly more expansive than it was when I first joined. The product has changed significantly now into many more electronic imaging products. There are many ways to take a picture other than photography. We are into non-silver material. Photographic material is customarily made with silver and that is the basis of photography ever since photography was invented, but with new technologies, electronic technologies, you can have a non-silver material with a thermal material or ink jet material that makes a very beautiful image so that we are now selling those, and we have designed a really very fine medical system, a non-silver medical system.

The dry or non-silver process is interesting because ordinarily it is very difficult to get as beautiful a grain in an image in photography. It's very difficult to get that any other way than photography, however for medical imaging, a product that is dry is obviously much more useful for the hospital, and a product without all those chemicals to wash down the drain obviously is much more healthful for the environment. We see our future in products like this in contributing to both the cost needs of the hospital in not having to have big dark rooms but also to the environmental restrictions that all of us are placing on ourselves now.

We produce scanners now. We produce electronic digital cameras. We sell entire systems with databases and software linkages. We have a very big electronic imaging group with a very large software contingent. We're opening our first software development center outside Delhi, India, in a development park so we are as much connected now with computer companies as we were in the early years with camera companies.

With consumer products you tend to get obsolescence. For our industrial products, you'll often find camera backs that are refreshed, repaired, etc., but they've been around a very longtime. Consumer products tend to need refreshing after three or four years. You need to continue coming out with new lines in order to keep the franchise refreshed, and it has to be something that appears significant to the customer and different. That's a tremendous burden for consumer products companies but as they say, it really comes with the territory. For professionals and industrial users I would say it is not quite the same. They are really interested in functionality. As far as functionality is concerned, if you look at some of the old cameras made, they are very fine, beautiful cameras, Leica lenses, and the old black and white films took very beautiful grain, fine toned, nice soft contrast, very nice products, so for consumer franchise, you do have to refresh but for some of the other customers, functionality is more important.

I think the company is at a very important juncture. One of the other important elements of this has been the capacity for dramatic change that this company has had. When I was given an opportunity six or seven years ago to be on the Board of Directors, I was on that board by virtue of Mac Booth who followed Bill McCune as president, because Mac had agreed to have an employee or actual worker sit on the Board of Directors, which again was unusual. He really led tremendous

273

change for the better in terms of worker participation in the company, as well as the beginning of medical imaging products and some other big technical changes that took a great deal of courage. I can remember from the board seat seeing much as I do now that the vision of the company is at another stage of enormous change, technical change. We get closer and closer to more of a computer software kind of environment as we become far more international and our locus or our center of interest is no longer Cambridge, Massachusetts; it's in other world capitals. We now have a young CEO, Gary DiCamillo, who has succeeded Mac from outside the company with a business marketing background, tremendous energy, so I see another chapter with great change and I'm very, very hopeful about where we'll go next. Our new CEO came to us from Black and Decker. His family came from Niagara Falls, New York and they own a bakery there. It's highly successful and besides that makes a wonderful biscotti that's sold through Bloomingdales. He went to RPI, another engineer, but then he went to Harvard Business School and has really come up through marketing careers at Proctor and Gamble and Black and Decker. He maintains a tremendous energy, but I would say an old-fashioned view of what a good company, not exactly a bakery, but a good work ethic and a sense of the population as a community, which is very good.

Appendix D:
Camera Division History

Walter Byron joined Polaroid in 1968. He spent most of the next 33 years as a manager in the camera division, including several years in camera development. Walter kept notes during his time in the Camera Division, including a tally of all the various cameras produced over those years. His history of Polaroid's camera operations follows.

*****

Polaroid cameras were first introduced in 1948 with the Model 95 which took its name from its $95 starting price. For the next twenty years, Polaroid managed the manufacturing of their many models of roll film and pack film cameras primarily through contract manufacturing, using Bell and Howell in Chicago and U.S. Time (Timex) in Hot Springs, Arkansas, and Dundee, Scotland, as suppliers. During this time, the contract manufacturing management group evolved into the Camera Division, which was located at 640 Memorial Drive, Cambridge. That building, which was leased from MIT, had been the original Boston based Model T assembly plant built by Henry Ford. Dr. Land had used part of the building in earlier years to work on his approach to night headlight glare reduction by using Polarized sheet on windscreens and headlights, an unsuccessful venture as the automotive industry did not adopt his ideas. From 1948 to 1971, some thirty four and one half million cameras were made by those two contractors for Polaroid. These were cameras that used the peel-apart roll or pack-film types.

In the mid- 60s, management, recognizing that a decision had been made to internally manufacture the future SX-70 cameras, began to bring in-house the manufacturing of some of the pack camera sub-assemblies (non-rotating spread system, folding boot assembly, shutter, etc.) in order to grow the internal manufacturing expertise necessary for that future camera factory. Another reason for the move to in-house manufacturing was because there had been a shift of high volume camera production from Timex to Bell and Howell which brought a concern about their expertise on shutters and spread systems. Additionally, an evaluation of which of the four types of parts of the camera, optics, electronics, mechanical parts, and packaging / literature, to vertically integrate was made, resulting in a decision to establish an Optics Manufacturing unit, but continue to purchase the other parts types. The nascent Optics unit was housed at 640 Memorial Drive. The in-house manufacturing also offered the opportunity for closer coordination between the film and camera manufacturing organizations for better product performance as a system.

While Polaroid's primary marketing was to consumers, in an effort to expand the sale of pack film, there had been a determined effort to develop the Industrial and Commercial markets as well. Consequently, a small internal Industrial Hardware Manufacturing group was established in the early to mid-60s under Camera Division management. This was located at 640 Memorial Drive until space in the building became a premium due to Camera Division expansion and the group was moved next door to 620 Memorial Drive in the late 60s. Products included various types of film holders as well as ID Cameras which were sold into the Drivers License programs of the various US states. In the early 70s space became available in 640MD and the group returned to the 640 building.

The Camera Division in the late 60s was led by Mark Sewall, a veteran Polaroid manager, who oversaw both the Contract and Internal manufacturing parts of the division. When Sewall retired at the end of the 60s, a new leader was appointed, Christopher C. Ingraham, also a Polaroid veteran from the Film Manufacturing side of the business where he had successfully led the start up of pack film manufacturing at the W3 plant along route 128 in Waltham. Chris led the division for the decade of the 70s, through the startup of SX-70 camera manufacturing in Norwood and beyond into hard body integral camera manufacturing both in Norwood and at the Vale of Leven factory near Glasgow, Scotland. While there were many in division management who contributed to the successful growth of the division, other key leaders of the division in the decade of the 70s included, Hugh MacKenzie – Engineering,

Gerry Sudbey – Quality Assurance, Vince Gatto – Materials Management, Bob Wood – Optics Manufacturing, George Trumbour – SX-70 Factory Manager, Bill Lally – SX-70 Final Assembly Manager, Bob Eastman – SX-70 Shutter Manufacturing, and Marshall Snider – Industrial Hardware Manufacturing.

The SX-70 camera, a single-lens-reflex design which folded up, Polaroid's first integral-film-using device, was to be produced in a new building in Norwood where Polaroid had purchased the estate of William Cameron Forbes in order to create a new manufacturing campus, and where building N1 was constructed to be the camera factory. The task of delivering a new revolutionary product with all its technical complexity while simultaneously building a new assembly factory with all its administrative and manufacturing processes proved to be a daunting task which was accomplished, but with difficulty, at considerable cost, and after many process and material inventions. At that stage in its life, Polaroid had not absorbed the concept of manufacturability in its camera design process. The result was a most elegant and sophisticated SX-70 camera design which had some of the most complex, costly, difficult and time-consuming manufacturing processes, both for parts at suppliers factories and in-house on the assembly floor. It would have been difficult for a mature factory to produce, but was by necessity launched in a new factory. Polaroid learned, however, and the engineering design team led by Milt Dietz and John Pasieka, augmented by people from the Norwood factory with camera-manufacturing experience, produced a follow-on, non-folding hard body camera design (the Pronto!) that, in its many variations, was eminently cost effective, much easier to manufacture and in its many design variations, lasted 30-plus years. Not only was the camera design improved, but as the decade of the 70s proceeded, the factory operations matured as manufacturing and support personnel gained experience and proficiency.

Unlike film manufacturing where multiple large film assembly machines were used to assemble and package film packs by the hundreds of thousands per day, camera assembly was people intensive, used many jigs and fixtures and machine

277

assists, and required lots of inspection along the assembly flow to assure that the resulting cameras would meet their demanding performance and reliability requirements. A number of attempts were made to automate the assembly process. The initial effort involved machinery designs which were typical of the 1970s, rotary tables, pick and place mechanisms, all with rudimentary machinery controls. They proved to be difficult to maintain and not flexible in incorporating product design changes. The few that survived did prove that, along with labor savings, the quality of machine-produced assemblies was superior to that of manual assembly.

For the SX-70 camera, a continuous flow production system, similar to automobile assembly, was chosen as the camera production methodology. Personnel training was key and was emphasized by the many production line supervisors, assisted by a training department and complemented by an Industrial Engineering effort at individual job design and production line flow analysis. "People are our machines" was often heard in explanations to film manufacturing personnel about how the camera assembly factory worked. Hiring and training was a constant process with a great deal of personnel turnover at the hourly level. To compound the seasonal hiring and cutback demand, there was a constant drain of hourly talent to other divisions through the job posting and bidding system. The Personnel Department (Later called Human Resources) worked like Trojans to recruit, screen and hire people when the production demands came during the year and to backfill promotions to other divisions. The elected members of the Employees Committee worked with both the employees and with management to create a smooth working relationship and to deal with hourly personnel problems when they arose. Polaroid's personnel policies were fair and generous, stemming from Personnel Policy 101, which stated:

"We have two basic products at Polaroid: Products that are genuinely unique and useful, excellent in quality, made well and efficiently, so that they present an attractive value to the public and an attractive profit to the Company.

A worthwhile working life for each member of the company - a working life that calls out the member's best talents and skills - in which he or she shares in the responsibilities and rewards.
These Two Products are inseparable. The Company prospers most, and its members find their jobs most worthwhile, when its members are contributing their full talents and efforts to creating, producing and selling products of outstanding merit."
During the SX-70 startup, many teams of Polaroid manufacturing engineering personnel lived at suppliers' factories for months assisting in the development of supplier parts manufacturing processes. This happened on later cameras also, but to a much lesser degree and never to the extent experienced at multiple suppliers simultaneously during the SX-70 startup.
The SX-70 system was first sold to the public in October, 1972, in Miami, followed by a regional rollout across the U.S. and the rest of the world as production ramped up. About a half a million were delivered by the factory in 1973, about a million and a half in 1974 and another million in 1975. Over its entire life, six million of the various SX-70 camera models were produced. SX-70 camera production at N1 ran on two shifts during those years. In 1976 production of pack cameras was begun at the Polaroid facility at the Vale of Leven just outside Glasgow, Scotland, with half a million delivered.
As the SX-70 camera sales and manufacturing matured over a short few years it was followed up by the first hard body, integral film, camera the Pronto!. That product was introduced in 1976 with about two and a quarter million produced in N1 that year. In 1976 Kodak introduced their version of an integral film system. This challenge was met by Polaroid with an intense six week period of redesign and factory reconfiguration to adapt the Pronto! camera design into the OneStep which became the best selling Polaroid camera ever. Over two and a quarter million were delivered by the N1 factory in 1977, and fifteen million over its life. If you are of a certain age you will remember the entertaining Garner - Hartley TV ads which ran during the late 70s and into the 80s introducing the OneStep and later models to every household in the country.
Also in the year 1977 production of cameras using integral

film was begun in the Vale of Leven factory with four hundred thousand hard body cameras being produced, followed by two and one half million in 1978. With the subassemblies for cameras being produced in the US during that first year of the Vale integral camera factory start up, close coordination between the two factories was required. The year 1977 also saw the end of a long tail of contract manufactured pack film cameras at Timex with delivery of about a half million cameras. Polaroid cameras and film were so well received in the marketplace that 1978 saw a worldwide production of more than nine million cameras from the N1 and Vale factories and a half million from contract manufacturing, for a total of nine and one half million. The N1 facility was running around the clock on three shifts and the Vale factory was on two shifts at this time. Camera Division population peaked that year at over 4000 in the Norwood factories.

Sales of Polaroid cameras and film followed a seasonal pattern, very slow in the first quarter, a second quarter bump with the spring holidays and graduations, a big third quarter to stock the wholesale and retail chains for the Christmas season and a slower fourth quarter. Production tended to follow that pattern which meant hiring and training lots of people each year to build up production, usually increasing the number of assembly people by double or even triple, followed by cutbacks as the production schedule peaked and then dipped. This put a strain on factory personnel. Additionally, the Norwood N1 facility was bulging at the seams, as more camera production was called for. Chris Ingraham regretted that he had had to release a chunk of N1 space to the Sesame Division (instant movies and instant 35mm film) in the early 70s before camera volume had peaked. Now, when he needed the space back, he could not reclaim it. A second floor of building N2 had also been converted to subassembly manufacturing to ease the space crunch and Division headquarters had moved temporarily to a building a mile away in Westwood. It was then that a decision was made to build an additional factory on the Norwood site. This effort was led by George Trumbour and resulted in a 225,000 square-foot N4 building, constructed on Governor General Forbes' old polo field, which opened for business in

July, 1979.

The new space available led to movement of manufacturing units within the Division. SX-70 and hard body camera manufacturing moved from N1 to N4, Optics moved from 640MD to N1 while Industrial Hardware remained at 640MD, and Division headquarters moved back on site, occupying Forbes' old mansion.

Polaroid was known for its technology, and while camera assembly was a people intensive operation, there was considerable technology involved in the equipment used for manufacturing, assembly and testing of the parts, subassemblies and final cameras. In the Optics area over the years there developed an expertise in mold insert making and polishing, injection molding and vacuum coating of lenses. In spread systems that squeezed the developer out of the film pods and spread it uniformly across the film as it exited the camera, there developed expertise in roll grinding and, via electric discharge machining, roll texturing, the latter of which was done in house. Multi station rotary tables were used in assembling the SX-70 Fresnel lens (part of the viewfinder) and moving mirror assembly. Design of Polaroid owned molds and stamping tools for mechanical piece part manufacturing at suppliers became a critical skill. Expertise in manufacturing transducers used in ranging systems was gained. In addition the mechanical and electrical support personnel became experts at quick reconfigurations of production lines and conveyor systems on the factory floors as new products phased in and old ones moved out, and as multiple lines were required to ramp up production volume. In the early days, there was a world-class incoming inspection operation to qualify piece part lots before they were allowed to be released to the floor. Later, the responsibility for part quality was moved upstream to the suppliers who, when they became "certified vendors", were allowed to ship part lots directly to Polaroid which were issued to the production lines without incoming inspection.

Building on the SX-70 inception experience, the division developed a cadre of people who had the assignment of incepting new products into the factories. Usually, the production of all new cameras was launched first in Norwood.

281

For many of these years that group was known as the Program Office and was housed in a building at Technology Square in Cambridge, adjacent to the building where the Product Engineering group lived. For the inception of each new camera, additional personnel from the Norwood factory would augment the start up team. Both the camera design and the manufacturing processes were wrung out prior to reaching the final signatures on the "approval for sale" document and turning the product over to the factory for production ramp up.

In 1980 Chris Ingraham moved to a new position and Gerry Sudbey assumed the leadership as Vice President of Camera Division. Camera manufacturing had peaked in 1978 and in the first half of the 80s steadily declined to a worldwide low of two million eight hundred thousand in 1984. During that time the Sun camera version of the hard body camera design was introduced. This product incorporated a strobe to replace the flash bars that sat on top of the cameras and had previously been used to provide illumination during each photo taken. The next year, 1985 saw a rebound to three million six hundred thousand cameras delivered by the division's factories. Polaroid developed a larger format integral film, named Spectra, and set out to offer a new Spectra camera system to the marketplace in 1985. Difficulty in painting the outside camera body parts at a supplier in Canada using an electrostatic application method delayed the introduction for many months and the product was launched in 1986 when the N4 factory delivered six hundred thousand of that new product. The Spectra introduction gave a boost to Polaroid camera sales that year and the factories delivered five million cameras in total in 1986.

In 1984, Gerry Sudbey was promoted to lead all of Polaroid's worldwide manufacturing operations and a new leader of the Division was appointed, Paul Lambert. Paul came to the Division from the Negative Manufacturing operation in New Bedford, and was a longtime Polaroid veteran. He led the Division for about four years before Gary Hamann, one of the technical people from within the Division, who had been the Program Office leader, assumed the Division leadership role in 1988.

In 1985 and 1986, a movement began within the Division to think through how to upgrade the processes used within the Division. After much discussion, approval was given and a budget created for a small group known as the CIM (Competing In Manufacturing) Project to lead an effort at improving Camera Assembly, Materials Management, Human Resources Management, and Information Technology. The CIM Project was led by Tom Tait, a former manager of the Vale of Leven Camera and Film factory. It was through this project that both just in time manual assembly techniques and assembly automation (using SONY robotics technology) were introduced into the N4 factory. The scheduling, planning, purchasing and materials storage and handling were improved as all the units of the domestic division reached certification as Class A MPR-II operations. Improvements were also made in IT and personnel management. This project lasted about three years and made significant progress in improving the competitiveness of the Division when benchmarked against world class assembly factories. Robotic assembly of hard body camera sub-assemblies (shutters, drive trains) was completed using those robots developed by SONY, some of which subsequently also ended up at the Vale facility.

In 1986, the Division abandoned the 640MD building in Cambridge and the Industrial Hardware Manufacturing operation moved to Norwood into building N4. During the mid-80s this unit of the Division had organizationally been grouped with other pack film parts of Polaroid's business into a new Division known as Tech Photo. In the early 90s the Industrial Hardware unit in N4 was closed down and that manufacturing was transferred to the Vale facility

The years 1987 and 1988 saw factory production decline to four million two hundred thousand and three million two hundred thousand respectively. As in past and future years, many new models of cameras were produced each year. Most were minor variations on the basic design, with outside body shell changes, a new feature of two, new packaging and literature and a new name, while a few were more dramatic design changes such as with the Impulse version of the Sun hard body cameras.

In 1988, Polaroid devoted considerable energy, resources and money in deflecting a take-over attempt by Roy Disney. Among other things, that year saw the first company-wide severance program, designed to slim down Polaroid's costs, where longtime employees were offered attractive financial packages to leave the company. The Division, like all in Polaroid, suffered a loss of talent as a result. After the take-over attempt and its aftermath was behind the company, a concerted effort was made by the CEO, Mac Booth to rethink the company's future. At least two major bets were doubled down, a new medical imaging transparency system, internal code name Helios, and the development of a third, smaller, integral film format, internal code name Joshua. Both were projects that had been initiated before 1988. The former was established as a separate business unit within the company, but the camera for the new Joshua film would be supplied by the Camera Division. The Joshua film and camera development program had been led by Hal Page, but after he left in the 1988 severance, that position was assumed by Roger Clapp. Both were longtime Polaroid employees.

Another effort to address the company's future, under the leadership of the Chairman, Bill McCune, was to prepare for digital imaging for consumer products. A decision was made to have Polaroid develop its own "receivers" and "emitters"; i.e., the electronic sensor onto which the light would fall after coming through the camera's lens, and the electronic device that would be the light output onto the film (it was still proposed to have a film output option). A large electronic development facility was built and staffed in Cambridge for the purpose of designing and incepting those devices. Once these electronic devices had been developed, it was the plan to have an outside contractor manufacture them. Polaroid did produce and sell one of the first electronic consumer cameras in the marketplace. The PDC 2000, Polaroid's first digital camera, was unveiled in 1996 and met with high praise. This was produced in Cambridge in low volume, but follow on cameras were not produced and the electronic imaging future for Polaroid consumer cameras started and stopped that year. Over the course of a four year period, thirteen thousand PDC 2000 digital consumer cameras and another five thousand digital microscope cameras were produced through this effort. (One business unit of Polaroid did successfully make the transition to digital imaging, that being the ID Division, where digital ID camera systems were sold into state drivers license programs.)

Design of the Joshua camera proceeded in Cambridge while the factories produced current camera designs, delivering during 1989 three million, three hundred thousand, in 1990 three million, and in 1991 four million, one hundred thousand. During the CIM Project, enough had been learned and confidence gained about robotic assembly so that agreement was reached that the Joshua camera subassemblies would start up using robots from day one, instead utilizing the past practice of manual assembly first. The process of "design for automation" started at that point, which proved to also have benefits for ease of assembly in the manual mode. During those years while the Joshua camera was being designed, the design personnel from the Product Design group and the inception personnel from the Camera Division Program Office were moved to and co-located in Norwood, building N4, to facilitate conversations among and between them as well as factory personnel. As a consequence, the scale up of the Joshua camera was one of the better stories in the history of Camera Division. This Design / Manufacturing interface proved so successful that it was used on the follow on Joshua hard body camera as well, and was to be the model for all future design and inception efforts.

In 1992, the factories produced another four million, three hundred thousand cameras, including a few tens of thousands of the new Joshua cameras at the end of the year. The Joshua system was launched in 1993 under the name Captiva in the US, Vision in Europe and JoyCam in Japan, with the smaller integral film and a folding, single lens reflex camera with a chamber on the back into which the picture was moved as it exited the spread rolls. This allowed the user to shoot multiple shots without the worry of where to put the pictures coming out of the camera, as was the case with earlier designs of Polaroid integral film cameras. Significant market research had been done to confirm that the smaller film format would be accepted by users. However, after a couple of years in the marketplace, it became apparent that the number of packs of film being used per camera did not come close to other typical Polaroid cameras or to the program's planning numbers, and production of this camera ceased in early 1997. Also cancelled was the follow on hard body camera version using the same smaller film which had been planned to be the first camera whose complete assembly would be done robotically using the SONY robotic technology.

In 1993 a new Polaroid camera production factory was opened in Shanghai, continuing into the 2000s. From 1993 through 2000, the Shanghai factory produced nine million, six hundred thousand cameras. Also in that year, a small Polaroid camera plant was opened in Moscow where the final assembly of cameras was done using subassemblies made at the Vale. The Moscow operation was open for five years and produced about six hundred thousand cameras over that period. Camera production volume from the factories in 1993 was four million, seven hundred thousand. The next year increased to six million, nine hundred thousand, and 1995 was five million, nine hundred thousand.

In 1993, Gary Hamann relinquished the leadership of the Division and John Jenkins assumed that responsibility. The Vale and China factories, along with the other small overseas facilities, produced five million, two hundred thousand cameras in 1996, five million, three hundred thousand in 1997 and four million, eight hundred thousand in 1998. In 1996 a small factory was established in India which produced three hundred thousand cameras over its four-year life. The year 1996 saw the beginning of a series of annual severance programs as Polaroid shed costs to attempt to gain profitability. The Norwood camera assembly factory was severely downsized in 1996 and stopped all camera production. There were, however, about one hundred thousand cameras made there in 1998, but other than those, all production was at the Vale, China or via contract manufacturing, from 1997 on. Thus it was that the end of Norwood as a domestic camera inception factory and camera producer also marked the demise of the traditional Camera Division.

A new camera and film system, which produced postage stamp sized pictures, was developed and introduced in 1999 under the iZone name. Over the next few years, there were many variations of this camera design and there was also a version of the film offered with a sticky back, useful for placing the photos on various surfaces. Three million of these iZone cameras were delivered in 1999 from a Japanese contractor. Additionally, a small hard body Joshua film using camera was designed in both single use and reloadable formats. Three million, nine hundred thousand of these were delivered in 1999 from a contractor in China. Between what Polaroid's Vale, Shanghai and smaller offshore factories contributed at a volume of three million, nine hundred thousand, and the two contractors above, in 1999, ten million, eight hundred thousand Polaroid film using cameras were delivered. With the Norwood part of Camera Division essentially gone, management of the contract manufacturing of these Japanese and Chinese contractors fell to another group in Cambridge led by Norm Perrault. Norm had the additional responsibility to get the in house iZone film manufacturing up and running. He and his group were very busy that year. Additionally, Polaroid had begun to market contract manufactured non film using digital cameras and one half million were procured from contract manufacturers in 1999.

The year 2000 saw the Vale and the China factories deliver eight million, two hundred thousand cameras, of which over half were of the iZone family. Additionally, the Chinese and Japanese contractors produced eight million, two hundred thousand of the small Joshua Film cameras and variations of the iZone cameras, for a whopping total of sixteen million, four hundred thousand for the year. Most of these cameras were low price point items at retail with small profit margins.

In October, 2001, Polaroid declared bankruptcy, and most of the few remaining camera manufacturing people left the US operations, but the Vale and China factories and the contract manufacturers continued to produce cameras through the ownership by Equity One partners who purchased the assets out of bankruptcy court. When the Petters group purchased the company in 2005 there were still some cameras being produced.

Contract manufacturing of cameras continues to this day by the successors to the Petters ownership when they purchased the assets of the company out of the second bankruptcy. Many of these are digital, non-film using cameras, but with the start-up of The Impossible Project™ a Polaroid-type integral film is now on the market and "Polaroid" recently announced an agreement to work with them to offer Integral cameras and film to the marketplace in 2012.

The epitaph for the camera Division really reflects that of Polaroid in general. The story of the Division was one of increasing manufacturing competence, product quality and reliability, scale up ability, organizational growth, use of technology, etc., that was on a par with the best in the U.S. The philosophy that the company and the Division adopted of "make it where you sell it" unfortunately, toward the end, became "you make it so it can be sold to us." As with all parts of the company that achieved excellence in performance over the years, the Camera Division ceased to exist when the company failed.

Polaroid Camera Production
1972-2000

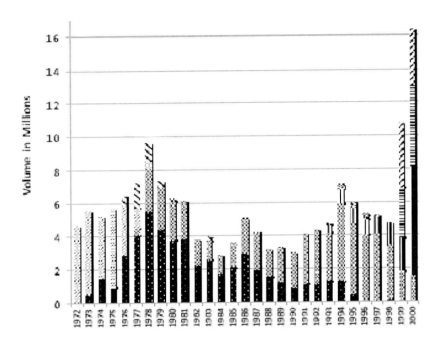

Appendix E
Shamrock Seeks to Buy Polaroid
Robert J. Cole *New York Times*, , July 21, 1988

After five months of persistent rumors, Walt Disney's nephew, Roy E. Disney, announced yesterday that an investor group he heads holds 8 percent of the Polaroid Corporation and was prepared to buy the rest of the instant-photography giant for $40 a share, or $2.3 billion, in cash. His partner and close associate, Stanley P. Gold, added that their company, Shamrock Holdings Inc., would pay even more than $40 for the shares if Polaroid's directors agreed to negotiate. Mr. Gold added, however, that Shamrock had "not yet fully explored the financing arrangements" and was, therefore, making the offer subject to its getting the money.

Cooperation Sought

"With Polaroid's cooperation," he said, "we are confident that we will be able to consummate the proposed transaction." Polaroid is widely expected to resist vigorously, but Harry Johnson, a spokesman, said only that directors would study the proposal with the company's legal and financial advisers and "not reply to the specifics until we get their response." Wall Street generally liked the hostile takeover bid, pushing up Polaroid's stock price $6, to $40. The shares were selling for about $30 each last February when rumors first began circulating that Mr. Disney was buying Polaroid stock.

With Polaroid now trading at Mr. Disney's opening bid, Wall Street professionals were speculating heavily that much higher bids could develop before long. Just a week ago, in what it called "a comprehensive plan of action," Polaroid announced that it would enter the highly competitive film business, eliminate up to 800 jobs and spend $300 million to buy back stock "from time to time." Among analysts the moves were widely regarded as anti-takeover tactics.

Polaroid also announced that it had created an employee stock ownership plan that holds about 10 million newly issued shares, representing 14 percent of the total stock outstanding. Four months ago, when Polaroid first announced its employee stock plan, it said the plan would own less than 5 percent of the company.

In his offer to Polaroid yesterday, Mr. Disney said his proposal was based on the 61.92 million shares outstanding before the additional 10 million were created for employees. Mr. Disney said he filed suit yesterday in Delaware Chancery Court to prevent the use of the employee shares to "frustrate a change of control." He also said he filed suit in Federal District Court in Boston, Polaroid's base, challenging the constitutionality of state anti-takeover legislation.

Polaroid has long been regarded as a prime takeover target, even more so in the last three years, after it won a patent-infringement suit against the Eastman Kodak Company over instant cameras. A trial to determine the damages to be paid was scheduled for next January, to be presided over by Federal District Judge Rya W. Zobel, who ruled on the infringement.

Judge Steps Aside
But Judge Zobel stepped aside last month after she inherited some Kodak stock, and she has been replaced by Judge David Mazzone. The situation is now somewhat clouded, but Polaroid is expected to collect damages eventually of at least $1-billion. Taking the lawsuit into account in making its offer, the Disney group said that instead of $40, it was willing to pay each stockholder less cash plus a pro rata share of any damage award. Court records and letters from Mr. Disney and Mr. Gold to I. MacAllister Booth, president of Polaroid, show that Shamrock began accumulating Polaroid shares early this year. They used the code name Ice Capades to mask the buying. By last month, they held more than 4 percent. By June 16, Mr. Gold, who is chief executive of Shamrock, tried without success to arrange a meeting with Mr. Booth to discuss "Polaroid's future and Shamrock's ideas for generating additional value for Polaroid's shareholders." Shamrock, wholly owned by Roy Disney, has interests that include 3 television stations, 15 radio stations and 3 percent of the Walt Disney Company.

Writing to the Polaroid chief executive on June 17, Mr. Disney said, "I was surprised when your secretary, in response to my call to you, said that you would not have any time to see

Stanley Gold and myself during our visit to the East Coast next week or, as I understand from your secretary, at any other time."

Conditions Set for Meeting

Shamrock's representatives, thought to be its adviser, Wertheim Schroder Inc., subsequently approached Polaroid directors, some of whom recommended that a meeting be held. Polaroid's advisers, believed to be Shearson, Lehman, Hutton, then set up "conditions." These conditions, the public documents added, were that Shamrock not exceed the 5 percent ownership level before the meeting or even shortly afterward and not make any proposals that Polaroid would have to announce. Securities regulations require public disclosure once an investor's holdings in a company reach or exceed 5 percent. Shamrock sought assurances that Polaroid would do nothing to affect Shamrock and was told that the meeting, arranged for July 13 in New York, was not "a stalling tactic" to give the company time to make major changes. Apparently close to the 5 percent level, Shamrock said it refrained from buying any more stock, even though the price at times was below $30. It said that, to prevent exceeding the 5 percent level, it also bought back "at considerable expense" some put options it had sold. On July 12, a day before the meeting, Polaroid announced its "comprehensive plan of action," including selling 14 percent of the company to employees.

Appendix F

CalPERS may force a showdown at Polaroid.
(California Public Employment Retirement System)
Wendy Hower, *Boston Business Journal*, April 13, 1992

A $68 billion California pension fund plans to vote against Polaroid's board of directors at the company's annual shareholder meeting in May if the camera maker does not meet its demands at a special meeting Friday.

The California Public Employees' Retirement System (CalPERS) wants fatter stockholder dividends and an end to "blank check" R&D spending on Polaroid's secret Joshua camera and Helios imaging machine, according to DeWitt Bowman, CalPERS' chief investment officer. If CalPERS has its way, Polaroid would set up a shareholder advisory board through which the poor performer would have to answer to investors. And CalPERS wants a say in how Polaroid spends the $925 million it won in a litigation settlement against Kodak last year.

"The company is facing a real watershed here, and how they choose to use that money . . . is a question I think needs to be addressed," Bowman said. The meeting between Polaroid CEO I. MacAllister Booth and CalPERS general manager Dale Hanson will take place five months after CalPERS criticized Polaroid's board of directors in a letter. CalPERS went public with its complaints in the March 30 issue of Business Week, where it named 12 companies –Polaroid among them –that it planned to target for special action during the spring annual meeting season. Polaroid's 10 biggest shareholders won't say whether they will follow CalPERS' protest over Polaroid's total return, which eroded 12.4 percent between 1987 and 1991. By itself, CalPERS could not oust Polaroid's 15 incumbent board members; it has holdings of about 0.6 percent of the company's 49 million shares of common stock outstanding.

Polaroid's nominees for its 15-member board include such heavyweights as company CEO Booth; Kenneth H. Olsen, CEO of Digital; Alfred M. Zeien, CEO of Gillette; and A. Michael

Spence, dean of Stanford University Business School. All of Polaroid's board members are elected to one-year terms.

Appendix G
Out of Focus-
Michael K. Ozanian, *Forbes Magazine*, January, 2001

On the morning of Dec. 15, 2000, analysts were given a shockingly cold shower by Polaroid Chief Executive Gary DiCamillo. During a 20-minute conference call DiCamillo warned analysts that fourth-quarter sales and earnings would be far worse than expected. He went on to say that 2001 wasn't looking very good, either.

Those words were hardly out of DiCamillo's mouth when analysts went into revision mode. Gibboney Huske of Credit Suisse First Boston, a veteran Polaroid analyst, cut her 2000 earnings-per-share estimate to 41 cents from $1.22 and her 2001 estimate from $1.40 to five cents. A few days later Moody's put $925 million of Polaroid's debt on credit watch for possible downgrade. The bad news has kicked Polaroid shares down 20% since the conference call. But falling short of expectations is nothing new for the company. Since coming over from Black and Decker in November 1995, where he was running the company's power tool division, DiCamillo, now 50, has started each year by talking about how Polaroid is poised for growth. But time and time again he has come up short.

With DiCamillo at the helm, net losses have totaled $166 million. Debt has climbed to 60% of capital, from 42%, in five years. Over the past two years the imaging company has had to rely on debt to maintain its annual dividend payments of $27 million and capital expenditures that totaled $360 million. On DiCamillo's watch Polaroid's stock has plummeted below $6 from the high 40s.

How did things get so bad? No question, these are tough times for the entire industry as digital imaging takes over from film. Huge capital expenses are required to make the switch, and digital products have much lower net margins than film.

But Polaroid is far worse off than its rival and the buck has to stop somewhere near DiCamillo's desk. A big problem has been defection. At least nine top sales or product development executives DiCamillo hired stayed only three years or less. Among them: Clifford Hall, who was key to developing the

295

idea for the i-Zone Instant Pocket Camera, the bestselling camera in the world. People familiar with the situation say many of these folks left because DiCamillo named Judith Boynton executive vice president two years ago. The 46-year-old Boynton, who had been controller for Amoco for two decades, is a professional bean counter who had only been with Polaroid a year as chief financial officer before her promotion. "No one could figure it out," says one former top executive. "She never demonstrated any knowledge of the business."

DiCamillo, who agreed to speak to Forbes only by email, pointedly evaded the Boynton issue. But he had this to say: "Of course I am not pleased by the stock performance. Nonetheless, we have made significant progress in turning Polaroid around." Boynton was not available for comment.

DiCamillo has taken little responsibility for the company's downward spiral. Skewered during the analysts' conference call, he actually chuckled at one point. A money manager was not amused. "You guys are laughing, but my shareholders are losing money," he told DiCamillo.

So far none of this seems to bother Polaroid's board. In December 1999–ten months before DiCamillo's employment contract was set to expire–Polaroid's board handed him an extension to the end of 2002. That same year DiCamillo received a $795,000 bonus, $10,000 more than he earned in salary–never mind that Polaroid grossly underperformed the S&P500.

.

Appendix H
What's Wrong with This Picture?
Kris Frieswick, *CFO Magazine*, January 01, 2003

Polaroid's passage through Chapter 11 exposes how bankruptcy can give debtors too much power. Ever since Polaroid Corp. slipped ignominiously under Chapter 11 bankruptcy protection in October 2001, it has been portrayed as a textbook case of how bankruptcy proceedings can help a failing company emerge with a promising future.

True, the Cambridge, Massachusetts, company, which introduced instant-imaging photography in 1947, still needs to find a way to recover from management errors that caused it to miss most of the digital-photo revolution – while making bad investments and bad recapitalization moves. But just 10 months after filing, the company had sold all of its assets to Bank One Corp.'s One Equity Partners (OEP) venture-capital arm for an announced $255 million in cash and $200 million in assumed trade liabilities. Secured creditors have been paid off nearly in full, while unsecured creditors are to receive a healthy 35 percent of a new, privately held Polaroid. Former Ford Motor Co. CEO Jacques Nasser has been named Polaroid's nonexecutive chairman, with responsibility for filling the vacant chief executive spot. (CFO William Flaherty and general counsel Neal Goldman have run the company since CEO Gary DiCamillo resigned last July.)

Officers of the debtor, the original Polaroid, have congratulated themselves for getting the escape from bankruptcy on track so quickly. In the waning days of 2002, Polaroid was close to a final reorganization that would end its case, if approved by the court. Not everyone has fared so well, of course, including Polaroid shareholders, employees, and retirees. The company has had sweeping layoffs and has discontinued some severance payments. And three days before its filing, it terminated retiree health benefits. Still, both OEP and Judge Peter Walsh, who presided over the case in U.S. Bankruptcy Court for the District of Delaware, have praised the results of the process, which Walsh calls "in the best interest of the estate."

297

But some critics are pointing to the Polaroid case as a demonstration of what's wrong with corporate-bankruptcy reorganization. They say the system is so weighted toward debtors that it fails to encourage the active bidding that could produce fairer, more-lucrative resolutions for creditors and other stakeholders. There are complaints, too, that the courts fail to scrutinize the financial and operational steps that debtors take before their bankruptcy filings.

Ultimately, these critics say, Polaroid provides a look at a system failing miserably even at its stated goal of maximizing returns to creditors and parties in interest. Among the questions emerging from this bankruptcy: Did Polaroid unfairly favor OEP over other bidders? Did it wield too much power over the sale process? In the end, was the price paid too cheap? By some accounts, OEP paid a net amount of less than $80 million, plus assumed trade liabilities, to gain a company with more than 1,000 patents and $1.5 billion plus in worldwide asset value.

"It's possibly the worst case I've ever seen," says Lynn LoPucki, a law professor at the University of California at Los Angeles. The bankruptcy court's job "is to regulate the relationship between debtors and creditors," he says, but in recent years, debtors and the largest creditors, usually banks, "have taken control of the courts," and get from judges "whatever they want." Poorly supervised reorganization plans often result, and less-powerful parties are cowed into approving them – just to get some semblance of a return. "The current system just destroys value," says LoPucki.

Was It a Fire Sale? Compared with the explosive wide-screen, Technicolor collapses of Enron and WorldCom, Polaroid's bankruptcy has been more of a long, slow fade. Yet because of the way it used the bankruptcy courts, Polaroid seems worthy of the same kind of scrutiny that accompanied those other collapses. In theory, of course, Chapter 11 is designed to provide financially troubled corporations with protection from secured and unsecured creditors while a plan is formulated for paying off debts. A court-approved plan gives creditors first crack – often in the form of equity in a new company – with common shareholders typically receiving little or nothing.

298

Along with the court, creditors themselves serve as watchdogs, making sure the company plays by the book and preserves value.

But in reality, according to LoPucki, the competition for business by bankruptcy courts – especially in Delaware and its closest rival district, New York State – creates "a race to the bottom" that invites venue-shopping by companies. The jurisdictions gain reputations for letting debtors call more of their own shots, he says. And this may contribute to a rate of repeat bankruptcy filings in the Delaware bankruptcy court that is 10 times higher than the average elsewhere, except New York.

Some observers suggest that Polaroid didn't belong in Chapter 11 in the first place. "OEP got the assets at a fire sale," says Ulysses Yannas, a Buckman, Buckman and Reid Inc. analyst who has followed Polaroid for 30 years. "It's a company that should never have died." In his opinion, "the judge should have forced the company to come up with a plan to run the entire company...properly." Polaroid's initial bankruptcy petition, citing a July 1, 2001, filing with the Securities and Exchange Commission, actually listed worldwide assets of $1.8 billion and liabilities of $948.4 million – although Polaroid claimed revenue declines had stifled its ability to pay off or restructure maturing loans and bonds. It blamed the sales fall-off on a weak instant-film market, among other factors, while asserting that high manufacturing costs had penalized earnings.

There are no strict standards for what companies qualify for protection, which experts claim may be a good thing. "The bankruptcy code is designed to be very flexible," says Harvard Business School professor Stuart Gilson. "When you base the reorganization on rigid rules and regulations, you can make costly errors. You can get a lot of gaming by management in that case." Still, of course, there's no guarantee that companies won't game today's system, either.

Current Polaroid executives, and most other principals, generally won't discuss the case, citing the continuing court proceedings. In his June 28, 2002, sale order to OEP, though, Walsh praised the participants and said unsecured creditors, particularly, had "achieved a significant result in producing value." Still, steps by the debtor, which unsecured creditors fought until the 11th hour, seem to have led ultimately to sharply lower valuations than might otherwise have been possible.

Anatomy of a Bankruptcy Early in 2001, Polaroid retained business advisory firm Zolfo Cooper and investment bankers Dresdner Kleinwort Wasserstein to help it restructure debt or complete a non-bankruptcy reorganization – efforts Polaroid abandoned when it defaulted in July and August on $26.3 million in bond payments. That caused the immediate maturity of $575 million in debt securities, magnifying its financial pressure. It then ramped up its efforts to find a buyer. But former Polaroid CFO William O'Neill, a 30-year veteran who left the company in 1999 and now serves on the board of Polaroid unsecured creditor Concord Camera, says chances were slim that then-managers could create a workable reorganization plan. "Where was the credibility of the old management?" asks O'Neill, by way of explaining Polaroid's financial plight at the time. "The company needed financing, and who was going to loan them money under the old management? The answer was nobody."

Dire financial straits notwithstanding, Polaroid paid senior executives and directors a total of $6.3 million in bonuses, consulting fees, and lump-sum pension payouts in the months before the filing. Payments included $1.7 million in incentive comp to former CEO DiCamillo, while former CFO Judy Boynton got $300,000 in severance, a $510,000 stock award, and a $638,000 lump-sum pension payout. (Boynton, now the CFO of Royal Dutch/Shell Group, is listed as an unsecured creditor, for an additional severance of $600,000 she is still owed.)

Even after its filing, the company continued trying to enrich senior executives, while lowering asset values. In November, it sought the court's permission to pay top executives who had stayed through the filing – including Flaherty, Boynton's replacement – up to $19 million in so-called key-employee retention programs (KERPs), including some proceeds from any future sale of the company. While KERPs are common, Judge

300

Walsh balked at the amount. He eventually capped a total package at $6 million, saying that "to swallow the...program that the debtors put forth, quite frankly, is too much for me." The following month, when the company asked him to approve the $32 million sale of one profitable Polaroid business, Polaroid ID Systems Inc., to a divisional president, Walsh instead ordered that it be put out for bids.

E.K. Ranjit, CFO of Digimarc Corp., which won the division with a bid of $55 million, says Digimarc expressed interest in the Polaroid ID Systems business before the bankruptcy filing, but "couldn't work out good economic terms." When Digimarc heard that a sale to a manager was being arranged, Ranjit says, "we approached them again, but they said, 'Sorry, we're selling to management.'" Only after the order for a bidding contest was Digimarc able to compete, he says.

Assets without Value? When Polaroid made startling changes in the financial picture it presented to the court, though, Judge Walsh went along. On December 17, 2001, Polaroid filed its official Schedules of Assets and Liabilities, intended as a more-comprehensive summary than the preliminary "First Day" numbers used in seeking Chapter 11 protection. Suddenly, Polaroid claimed a far lower asset base: $714.8 million, compared with the $1.8 billion in the First Day report. (Liabilities were listed as $1.1 billion, up from $948.4 million.)

Most of the $1.1 billion asset change reflected exclusion of cash, real estate, equipment, inventories, and accounts receivable belonging to Polaroid's foreign subsidiaries, which the company had chosen not to place under court protection. After its bankruptcy filing, Polaroid stopped submitting financial statements for the subsidiaries, which the 2000 annual report listed as generating up to 80 percent of Polaroid's net income (due in part to the concentration of marketing and R&D costs in the United States). Even though the foreign subsidiaries were not in bankruptcy, the company was required to list the value of its stock in them. Polaroid, however, called that value "undetermined," meaning that the subsidiaries were recorded at an effective value of zero in the asset schedule.

In court, shareholder representatives and others raised questions about this valuation of foreign assets and other items for which Polaroid listed the value as undetermined – including trademarks, patents, and a 24,000-piece art collection. Said Walsh at one point: "I'm not sure the revenue produced by the patents and copyrights are all that important in evaluating the company's affairs." It was a comment some in the courtroom considered strange, since Polaroid's entire revenue stream is generated by patented product lines. (Future revenues will also rely heavily on brand licensing deals, according to a Polaroid spokesman.)

Asked by attorneys for Stephen Morgan, leader of a shareholder group, why the foreign subsidiaries weren't valued, CFO Flaherty said they were part of "Mother Polaroid," and were essentially worthless if the parent ceased to be a going concern. Any book value for the subsidiaries, art, patents, and trademarks, he added, would be misleading. The judge concurred, ruling that the best way to value assets was in a "fair and open" bidding process.

A Creditors' Plan Last April, the company drew up a "placeholder" reorganization plan premised on the sale of all of the company's assets foreign and domestic to OEP, part of a so-called stalking-horse bid. This bid is a lead offer against which other offers are supposed to compete. (Polaroid's choice of OEP as the stalking horse reflected a search since "early 2001," according to testimony from Dresdner Kleinwort Wasserstein, Polaroid's investment bank.) The April plan allowed for competing bids to be received at a June auction, along with OEP's initial bid of $265 million, plus $200 million in assumed trade liabilities. But the bidding procedures, allowing the debtor to determine which prospective bidders got access to proprietary data, among other debtor privileges, drew numerous complaints from the U.S. Trustee counsel, Mark Kenney, engaged in the proceedings as an observer. The procedures, according to a written objection filed by Kenney, "vest the debtors with excessive and inappropriate authority to control the bidding process" and "to chill the bidding to ensure that the subject assets are sold to their handpicked buyer." He also noted that the committee of unsecured creditors had vehemently opposed the sale, and said he believed that Polaroid's plan was "to liquidate in a transaction that is primarily for the benefit of the secured creditors."

Indeed, the unsecured creditors and shareholder Stephen Morgan, along with the Polaroid Retirees Association, had opposed the bidding on numerous grounds, saying that Polaroid had dramatically undervalued its assets and should instead be reorganized. At a May hearing on the bidding procedures, a month before the auction, the judge overruled all objections, but changed some bid procedures and extended the auction date several weeks to allow the unsecured creditors to present a reorganization plan as a competing bid to the OEP deal. (Kenney indicated, without explanation, that these changes satisfied his concerns.)

Backed by financing from Congress Financial and Deutsche Bank, the unsecured creditors prepared their plan. It didn't contain a dollar value, since it was in the form of a reorganization. But it gave unsecured creditors 100 percent of the new company, after paying off the secured creditors, and raised the possibility of retaining the pension plan – which wasn't included in the OEP bid.

The June 26 auction, to determine who would eventually run Polaroid, presents one of the best examples of how Polaroid and its secured creditors seemed to control the bankruptcy process. Both OEP and the unsecured creditors' committee presented their offers, the only two in the auction. Polaroid attorney Gregg M. Galardi, however, disagreed with financial projections made by the committee, and said it lacked sufficient "exit financing" to get the company out of bankruptcy protection. The auction was recessed. The committee returned with an oral commitment for exit financing, but said it needed three days to get a written term sheet. Polaroid and secured creditors, however, were unwilling to delay the proceedings. Further, Galardi said they still preferred a sale to reorganization, suggesting that unsecured creditors would be out of the running in any event.

Seeing the writing on the wall, the unsecured creditors dropped out, agreeing instead to participate with OEP. For its part, OEP increased the participation for unsecured creditors from the original 6 percent to 35 percent, while lowering the total of the offer to $255 million, plus trade-debt assumption.

Getting Cash Back Walsh approved Polaroid's sale to OEP on June 28, after hearing testimony from Dresdner Kleinwort Wasserstein that the bidding had been open and fair. Because the unsecured creditors had withdrawn their bid, the judge didn't analyze the proceeding transcripts before making his ruling. "There is absolutely no testimony to support the conclusion that anything was withheld from the market in [this transaction]," he ruled. On July 31, Primary PDC Inc., as the "old Polaroid" shell is known, received a check from OEP for $186.7 million, along with 35 percent of the stock of the new company, to be distributed to unsecured creditors. OEP received all of Polaroid's assets, including all of its non-bankrupt foreign subsidiaries.

Of the $255 million total to be paid, $50 million went directly to prepetition lenders. Other terms of the deal, however, allowed OEP to reduce its price by $18 million. OEP got all of Polaroid's cash except for $45 million that Primary PDC kept for administrative claims and other costs. Neither OEP nor Polaroid has revealed how much cash was transferred in the deal (the judge allowed a filing of many sale disclosures under seal), but unsecured-creditor estimates show the company having at least $200 million in cash at closing. If the estimates are accurate, the $237 million in OEP payments would have returned it $164 million in cash (plus about $1.5 billion in other assets), for a net cost of $73 million.

Polaroid retirees had feared the results of a sale to OEP, and that fear was justified. After June 28, the company's cash balance plan was terminated and handed over to the federal Pension Benefit Guarantee Corp., meaning many retirees had their pension payments slashed. Employees on long-term disability received letters informing them that they would not be hired by the new company and that their benefits were being terminated. Indeed, the Massachusetts attorney general's office had difficulty convincing OEP, as owner of the new Polaroid, to sponsor the retirees' supplemental Medicare plan, even though that sponsorship costs nothing except time spent keeping the books.

An appeal has been filed in the U.S. District Court in Delaware by shareholder representative Morgan. (Shareholders never received official status in court, because the judge ruled Polaroid's assets were insufficient to pay them anything.) Several retirees and shareholders have requested that the judge appoint an independent examiner to investigate their claims that Polaroid engineered the bankruptcy filing in bad faith.

Retirees retain the right to sue the company's directors' and officers' insurance policy to cover claims. But Derek Jarrett, a former Polaroid corporate vice president of international operations and now a member of the 2,600-member Polaroid Retirees Association, says retirees are resigned to ending up with nothing, even though the fight continues. "The attitude of the retirees is simple," he says. "We've lost our ESOP shares, health benefits, life insurance, but we are going to get these people that robbed us of the respect for the company that we felt part of."

While most issues still in the appeals process relate to pro-debtor rulings in the bankruptcy court, a number of questions about the bankruptcy process itself will go unanswered. They include: How can a debtor's sealed financial documents and valuations be verified when contested? What checks can prevent the debtor – sometimes more interested in controlling the process than in winning top dollar – from abusing its authority to decide who gets access to proprietary information? Should judges place so much faith in asset sales as a way to maximize estate value? In short, how can the process, while granting corporate debtors protection from creditors, still hold those debtors to a high degree of public scrutiny and accountability?

As a private company now, Polaroid is no longer required to file financial reports with the government. But Jarrett and others from the once-great camera concern see liquidation ahead. "OEP knows that it's worth so much more as a break-apart for them," he says. "People on the inside that I've talked to say the situation is very bad."

Former CFO O'Neill, while more optimistic, is hedging his bets. "They've got great assets and opportunities," he says. "They will either run it well and succeed or run it poorly and fail."

Bibliography

Armour, Stephanie. "Polaroid Retirees Lose Benefits." *USA TODAY*, 17 Jan. 2002.

Bailey, Steve and Steven Syre. "Feedback on Polaroid was Instant." *Boston Globe,* 29 Oct. 1998.

Carter, Marshall: "Making Sense of the Financial Mess." *School of Business and Economics at Seattle Pacific University*, 13 Aug. 2010.

Cohen, Laurie P. and James Bandler. "Shell Finance Chief Has Faced Scrutiny Before." *Wall Street Journal*, March 26, 2004.

Cole, Robert J. "Shamrock Seeks to Buy Polaroid." *New York Times*, 21 Jul. 1988.

Dumaine, Brian. "*HOW POLAROID FLASHED BACK.*" *Fortune Magazine*, 16 Feb. 1987.

Edelman, Lawrence. "Kodak Pays Polaroid $925M." *Boston Globe,* 16 Jul. 1991.

"Eyecatchers: Polaroid's New Picture." *Time Magazine.* 3 Feb. 1975.

Feintzeig, Rachel. "Bankruptcy Beat Snapshot: Gary DiCamillo." *Wall Street Journal*, 5 Feb. 2010.

Fitz Simon, Jane. "Polaroid Case Heads Back to Courtroom." *Boston Globe*, 3 Nov. 1988.

Fitz Simon, Jane. "Shamrock Withdraws Polaroid Bid." *Boston Globe*, 28 Mar. 1989.

Frieswick, Kris. "What's Wrong with This Picture." CFO Magazine; 1 Jan. 2003.

Garrelick, Renee (interviewer). "Marian Stanley." Concord Oral History Program, 1996.

Garrelick, Renee (interviewer). "William McCune." Concord Oral History Program, 1996.

Greenberg, Harvey. Federal Reserve Bank of Boston Regional Review, 1996.

Hower, Wendy. "CalPERS May Force a Showdown at Polaroid." *Boston Business Journal*, 13 Apr. 1992.

Isaacson, Walter. *Steve Jobs*. Simon and Schuster; 2011.

Krasner, Jeffrey. "Polaroid Paid Directors as Bankruptcy Neared." *Boston Globe*, 21 Dec. 2001.

Land, Edwin. *Generation of Greatness* (speech) Massachusetts Institute of Technology; 1957.

Ozanian, Michael K. "Out of Focus." *Forbes Magazine*, 22 Jan. 2001.

"Polaroid's Big Gamble on Small Cameras." *Time Magazine*, 26 Jun. 1972.

Rifkin, Glenn. "At Polaroid, More Than Snapshots." *New York Times*, 11 June 1991.

Rosenberg, Ronald. "Heeeeeere's Joshua." *Boston Globe*, 17 Sep. 1992.

Rosenberg, Ronald. "Polaroid to Sell Flagging Helios Laser Unit." *Boston Globe*, 31 Oct. 1996.

"Steve Jobs" (interview). *Playboy Magazine*, 1985.

Strauss, Gary. "Board Of Directors Rake In Perks, Too." *USA TODAY*; 13 Apr. 2011.

Syre, Steven. "A Magical Meeting." *Boston Globe*, 7 Oct. 2011.

Tracy, Phelps. *P60 Express*; Polaroid Corporation, 1977.

Wensberg, Peter. *Land's Polaroid*; Houghton Mifflin, Boston, 1987.